Poems Containing History

Poems Containing History

Twentieth-Century American Poetry's Engagement with the Past

Gary Grieve-Carlson

LEXINGTON BOOKS
Lanham • Boulder • New York • Toronto • Plymouth, UK

Published by Lexington Books
A wholly owned subsidary of Rowman & Littlefield
4501 Forbes Boulevard, Suite 200, Lanham, Maryland 20706
www.rowman.com

10 Thornbury Road, Plymouth PL6 7PP, United Kingdom

British Library Cataloguing in Publication Information Available

Library of Congress Cataloging-in-Publication Data
Grieve-Carlson, Gary.
  Poems containing history : twentieth-century American poetry's engagement with the past / by Gary Grieve-Carlson.
      pages cm
  Includes bibliographical references and index.
  ISBN 978-0-7391-6755-7 (cloth) -- ISBN 978-0-7391-6756-4 (electronic)
1. American poetry--20th century--History and criticism. 2. Literature and history--United States--History--20th century. 3. History in literature. I. Title.
  PS310.H57G84 2013
  811'.509358--dc23
  ISBN 978-1-4985-5045-1 (pbk)   2013024260

For Bridget, Timothy, Jessye, and Grace

Contents

Preface

Ezra Pound's glib definition of an epic as "a poem containing history"[1] raises more questions than it answers, for surely a poem that simply "contains" a passing reference to an incident or person from the past does not "contain" history in any particularly significant way; moreover, it would seem that a poem that "contains" history in a serious way need not necessarily belong to the "epic" genre. Milton's "On the Late Massacre in Piedmont" or Yeats's "Nineteen Hundred and Nineteen" are not epic poems, yet each engages, or "contains," a historical subject. A more fundamental question also lies behind Pound's definition: *can* poetry "contain" history in a way that compels serious attention? Is Milton's sonnet essentially Puritan propaganda? Does Yeats's poem reduce the enormously complicated struggle for Irish independence to a series of emotionally charged images that obscure as much as they reveal about the history of that struggle? Can poets have anything to tell us about history that historians cannot tell us more authoritatively? Can poetry help us to think about the past? My contention in this book is that they can.

At first, history and poetry may appear to be mutually exclusive discourses: traditionally, history emphasizes the factual, objective world of public events—historians want to know "what really happened," and why it happened, and why it matters. Much of their work—names, dates, who did what when—is falsifiable in ways that poetry is not, and unlike poets, historians emphasize a rhetoric of detached exposition and disinterested analysis. Unlike poets, historians deploy an impressive critical apparatus: extensive notes and bibliographies citing manuscript and archival sources, as well as monographs and scholarly journals. Even those aspects of their work that are not falsifiable—disagreements on why the French Revolution unfolded as it did, or on its significance for contemporary and subsequent events—are subject to standards of rational, evidence-based argument that are rarely applied to poetry.

In *Democracy in America*, Alexis de Tocqueville suggests that American poets will be especially uninterested in history: "Democratic nations care but little for what has been, but they are haunted by visions of what will be. . . . Democracy, which shuts the past against the poet, opens the future before him."[2]

Dana Gioia confirms Tocqueville's prediction about American poets' lack of interest in history: "At its best our poetry has been private rather than public, intimate rather than social, ideological rather than political. It has discussed symbolic places rather than real ones, even when it has given the symbols real names. It dwells more easily in timeless places than historical ones."[3] Kevin Stein agrees, citing "a Modernist tradition that encouraged [poets] to turn their backs on larger historical forces," and concluding, "Twentieth-century American poets have generally run in fear of history."[4]

Such claims as Gioia's and Stein's are interesting in that even as we concede their legitimacy, we suspect that their opposite is also true, and in this case we can agree with Howard Nemerov when he writes that the fundamental "theme" of the work of Ezra Pound and T. S. Eliot is "the confrontation with the wonder and terror of history."[5] In fact, we find that confrontation with history running throughout American poetry. For example, Timothy Dwight's *The Conquest of Canaan* (1785) re-tells and amplifies the central chapters of the Old Testament Book of Joshua, in which Joshua leads the Israelites to victory over the Canaanites. The biblical story is meant to parallel Washington's victory over the British, as the new American nation is meant to parallel the nation of Israel along the lines of Puritan typological historiography such as Cotton Mather's *Magnalia Christi Americana* or Increase Mather's account of King Philip's War. Joel Barlow's *The Vision of Columbus* (1787), later revised as *The Columbiad* (1807), is built around an angel's appearing to Christopher Columbus near the end of his life. The angel shows Columbus the history of the Americas from the Incas to the present, as well as a vision of the utopian future: inexorable progress in science and the arts leads to the world-wide triumph of republican institutions, a universal language, and world peace. "I wish," Barlow wrote, "to encourage and strengthen, in the rising generation, a sense of the importance of republican institutions; as being the great foundation of public and private happiness, the necessary aliment of future and permanent ameliorations in the condition of human nature."[6] Just as Dwight imagined history's significance as the Puritan historiographers did, Barlow's romantic imagination of American history's significance parallels, in significant ways, George Bancroft's in his exuberantly optimistic *History of the United States* (1834–82). And just as Barlow's poem has fallen into critical disfavor, so Bancroft's approach to American history has been gently characterized by John Burrow as "somewhat naïve, parochial and uncritical,"[7] and less gently by Charles MacLean Andrews as "nothing less than a crime against historical truth."[8]

Other nineteenth-century American poets continue this confrontation with history, including the formerly canonical such as Bryant and Longfellow, as well as those acknowledged today as our strongest, such as Whitman, Melville, and Dickinson. These latter three are much more self-conscious of the ways in which their poems "contain" history, and in this self-consciousness they presage the ways in which twentieth-century American poets engage the past and sometimes challenge the hegemony American historiography increasingly claims over that subject matter as the discipline professionalizes itself at the end of the nineteenth century. In this book, I explore the ways in which nine twentieth-century American poets confront and "contain" history in their work. In chapter 1, I provide context and background for that exploration with a discussion of the long and tangled relationship between poetry and history, from Aristotle to Hayden White.

In the rest of the book, I organize these poets' engagements with history into three general categories: the first includes three poets who, broadly speaking, imagine poetry as ancillary to historiography. Stephen Vincent Benét (*John Brown's Body*, 1928), Archibald MacLeish (*Conquistador*, 1932), and Robert Penn Warren (*Brother to Dragons*, 1953, rev. 1979) acknowledge that they are writing poetry, not history, but Benét's poem is in part a response to the often highly partisan and recriminatory tone of much contemporary Civil War historiography. MacLeish finds in Bernál Díaz del Castíllo's *True History of the Conquest of New Spain* a metaphor for the pathos of the human experience of the "West," that dreamed-of future that we seek, discover, and then lose. Warren's *Brother to Dragons* presents the ghosts of Thomas Jefferson and others, so it is clearly a work of imagination—"I am trying to write a poem, not a history," Warren insists in his Foreword[9] (xiii)—but it challenges a central tenet of mainstream American historiography with its claim that Jeffersonian idealism was based on a profound misunderstanding of human nature and that its influence on the nation's history has been pernicious; Warren's poem is more iconoclastic and provocative in its challenge to mainstream history's truth-telling than Benét's or MacLeish's.

The second group includes three poets whose work suggests that history is meaningful insofar as it points beyond itself toward a spiritual order of reality. T. S. Eliot (*The Waste Land*, 1922, and *Four Quartets*, 1945) draws a very sharp distinction between these two orders of reality and articulates an orthodox Christian position on history. For Hart Crane (*The Bridge*, 1930) history grounds one end of the great Bridge that he imagines arching toward "Atlantis," a kind of island off the coast of history that is the site of that higher spiritual consciousness toward which Crane believed the human race was evolving. In *The Angel of History* (1994), Carolyn Forché reads the Holocaust and the atomic bombing of Hiroshima through the lens of a postmodern "weak" theology. Like Eliot and Crane, she challenges professional historiography's assumption that the past is best understood in strictly material terms.[10]

The final group includes three poets who challenge professional historiography directly on its own terms. Like the American Progressive historians who rebelled against the kind of uplifting, patriotic histories that Bancroft wrote, Ezra Pound seeks in his *Cantos* (1922–62) to expose the "real" economic forces at work in history and to use history as a tool for building a new society. Unlike those historians, however, Pound finds that new society in Mussolini's fascist Italy. In *Paterson* (1946–58) William Carlos Williams is suspicious of history's tendency to reduce its readers and writers to spectators, and to reduce the past to mere spectacle, distracting readers' attention from their present lives. Charles Olson, who was one of the first Ph.D. students in Harvard's American Civilization program, though he never completed the degree, writes colonial Massachusetts history in *The Maximus Poems* (1960–75) against the grain of mainstream colonial American historiography, first by focusing on the motivations that lay behind the kinds of communities that were organized in colonial New England, and later by imagining the past in terms of Whitehead's "event."

Other writers have approached the relationship of history and literature from different perspectives, such as the interface between fiction and history,[11] or the extent to which the nineteenth- or twentieth-century long poem may be considered "epic."[12] Mine is the first book to consider the interface between poetry and history among such a broad range of American poets. My selection of poets is admittedly somewhat arbitrary; other poets could have been included just as easily. H.D.'s *Trilogy* (1944–46), for example, would have fit quite well alongside the work of Eliot, Crane, and Forché, and John Neihardt's five-part poem on the conquest of the Plains Indians, *A Cycle of the West* (1949), would have fit well alongside the poems of Benét and MacLeish. Robert Duncan's *Ground Work* volumes (1984, 1987), as well as Susan Howe's *The Birth-Mark*, Sharon Doubiago's *Hard Country* (1982), or Rosemarie Waldrop's *A Key into the Language of America* (1994) could have been included alongside Olson or Pound. Barrett Watten's *Bad History* (1998) or W. D. Snodgrass's *The Führer Bunker* (1977) might also have been included, along with any of the late-twentieth-century American poets whose work "contains" history and who are discussed in Kevin Stein's *Private Poets, Worldly Acts*.[13] Finally, I chose these poets because, in my judgment, some are unfairly neglected (Benét and MacLeish), some are too important to leave out (Pound, Eliot, Crane, Warren), and some I simply love too much to leave out (Williams, Olson, Forché). These nine poets engage the past for widely varying reasons, and they come to widely differing conclusions regarding its significance, but they are all deeply serious in the attention they bring to the subject, and their work compels and rewards serious attention on the part of their readers.

Notes

1. The phrase occurs in his *Paris Review* interview with Donald Hall: Donald Hall, *Remembering Poets: Reminiscences and Opinions* (New York: Harper Colophon, 1979), 241. In his essay "Date Line," Pound uses this formulation: "An epic is a poem including history." See *Literary Essays* (New York: New Directions, 1968), 86.

2. Quoted in James Miller, *The American Quest for a Supreme Fiction: Whitman's Legacy in the Personal Epic* (Chicago: University of Chicago Press, 1979), 28.

3. Dana Gioia, *Can Poetry Matter?* (Minneapolis: Graywolf, 2002), 127.

4. Kevin Stein, *Private Poets, Worldly Acts: Public and Private History in Contemporary American Poetry* (Athens: Ohio University Press, 1996), xiii, 9.

5. Howard Nemerov, *Reflexions on Poetry and Poetics* (New Brunswick, NJ: Rutgers University Press, 1972), 52.

6. Quoted in James Woodress, *A Yankee's Odyssey: The Life of Joel Barlow* (Philadelphia: Lippincott, 1958), 248.

7. John Burrow, *A History of Histories: Epics, Chronicles, Romances and Inquiries from Herodotus and Thucydides to the Twentieth Century* (New York: Random House Vintage, 2009), 417.

8. Quoted in Russel Nye, "History and Literature: Branches of the Same Tree" (123–59) in *Essays on History and Literature*, ed. Robert Bremner (Columbus: Ohio State University Press, 1966), 129.

9. Robert Penn Warren, *Brother to Dragons* (Baton Rouge: Louisiana State University Press, 1979), xiii.

10. Outside the field of professional historiography, Reinhold Niebuhr's *The Irony of American History* (1952) remains a significant Christian interpretation of American history. Also writing from a Christian point of view, the philosopher R. A. Herrera offers a survey of philosophies of history in *Reasons for Our Rhymes: An Inquiry into the Philosophy of History* (Grand Rapids, MI: William Eerdmans, 2001).

11. Some of these include Linda Hutcheon, *A Poetics of Postmodernism: History, Theory, Fiction* (New York: Routledge, 1988); David Cowart, *History and the Contemporary Novel* (Carbondale: Southern Illinois University Press, 1989); David W. Price, *History Made, History Imagined: Contemporary Literature, Poiesis, and the Past* (Urbana: University of Illinois Press, 1999); Mark Carnes, *Novel History* (New York: Simon & Schuster, 2001); Amy Elias, *Sublime Desire: History and Post-1960s Fiction* (Baltimore: Johns Hopkins University Press, 2001); Timothy Parrish, *From the Civil War to the Apocalypse: Postmodern History and American Fiction* (Amherst: University of Massachusetts Press, 2008); and Beverley Southgate, *History Meets Fiction* (New York: Longman, 2009).

12. These include James Miller's *The American Quest for a Supreme Fiction: Whitman's Legacy in the Personal Epic* (Chicago: University of Chicago Press, 1979), Michael Bernstein's *The Tale of the Tribe: Ezra Pound and the Modern Verse Epic* (Princeton: Princeton University Press, 1980), and Jeffrey Walker's *Bardic Ethos and the American Epic Poem: Whitman, Pound, Crane, Williams, Olson* (Baton Rouge: Louisiana State University Press, 1989).

13. In addition to Stein's *Private Poets, Worldly Acts*, two very fine books on this topic are James Longenbach's *Modernist Poetics of History: Pound, Eliot, and the Sense of the Past* (Princeton: Princeton University Press, 1987) and Joseph Kronick's *American Poetics of History* (Baton Rouge: Louisiana State University Press, 1984).

Acknowledgments

I owe thanks to many people for help with this book. My editors at Lexington Books—Justin Race, Lindsey Porambo, and Megan Barnett—have been supportive throughout the process. I am grateful to Jeff Robbins, Art Ford, and my anonymous reader for their careful readings of all or parts of the manuscript, and to Mat Samuel for the wonderful cover art. My teachers Bonnie Costello, Michael McKeon, Ralph Maud, the late John Tagliabue, and my colleague Mike Day have been models of intellectual engagement. Donna Miller has been cheerfully and indefatigably resourceful, and Amy Mastrangelo, Mike Zeigler, and Todd Gamble gave me indispensable help in preparing the final manuscript. Lebanon Valley College provided resources without which the completion of this project would have proven far more difficult. Finally, and most importantly, I thank my wife Bridget and my children Timothy, Jessye, and Grace, who make everything matter.

An earlier version of chapter 4 appeared as "A Usable Past?: Poetry and History in Robert Penn Warren's *Brother to Dragons*," *Mississippi Quarterly* 62, nos.1-2 (Winter-Spring 2009), 117–36. I am grateful to the editor for permission to publish it here.
An earlier version of chapter 7 appeared as "Where Is Your God? Theophany in *The Angel of History*," *Renascence* 58, no. 4 (Summer 2006), 289–303. I am grateful to the editor for permission to publish it here.
An earlier version of chapter 9, "Getting the News from Poems: History, *In the American Grain*, and *Paterson*" appeared in *Rigor of Beauty: Essays in Commemoration of William Carlos Williams*, ed. Ian D. Copestake (Oxford, UK: Peter Lang AG, 2004), 339–64. I am grateful to the publisher for permission to publish it here.

Chapter 1
History and Poetry

Aristotle and Norman Mailer

Common sense holds that the difference between history and poetry (or history and fiction) is that history tells the truth, while poetry and fiction do not. Nor is this suspicion of poetry's ability to tell the truth limited to common sense. One finds it as well in the classic texts of non-Western cultures, such as the Koran—"And as to poets, those who go astray follow them"[1]—and of Western culture. Plato's suspicion of poetry is evident in such works as the *Ion* and in his banishing poets from his ideal republic because they pretend to know what they do not know; at times his suspicion seems to extend to language itself: "I should imagine that the name *Hermes* has to do with speech, and signifies that he is the interpreter (*hermēneus*), or messenger, or thief, or liar, or bargainer; all that sort of thing has a great deal to do with language."[2]

But we also find in the ancient world a suspicion of history's capacity to tell significant truths, especially in the theoretical distinction between history and poetry that Aristotle articulates in his *Poetics*:

> The poet's function is to describe, not the thing that has happened, but a kind of thing that might happen, i.e., what is possible as being probable and necessary. The distinction between historian and poet is not in the one writing prose and the other verse—you might put the work of Herodotus into verse, and it would still be a species of history; it consists really in this, that the one describes the thing that has been, and the other a kind of thing that might be. Hence poetry is something more philosophic and of graver import than history, since its statements are of the nature of universals, whereas those of history are singulars.[3]

For Aristotle, the difference between history and poetry consists, in part, in the difference between particular fact (what "has happened") and philosophical speculation (what "might happen"). Poetry, despite its fictionality, is closer to philosophical knowledge than is history because the truths of history are "singulars" or particular facts, whereas the truths of poetry reflect concepts or propositions such as "necessity" or "probability"—in other words, general laws or "uni-

1

versals." For Aristotle, historical knowledge is closer to *doxa* (opinion) than to *episteme* (theoretical knowledge, universally and eternally true), and thus Aristotle might agree with Dante when he calls his *Divine Comedy*, which is filled with things that are not facts, a treatise in moral philosophy, whereas Herodotus, who reports facts that various informants have told him, sometimes at second or third hand, would seem to be working with *doxa*.

This epistemological difference underlies what is, for Aristotle, the single most important element of poetry, and the key to the difference between the poet and the historian: plot. By *plot* (Greek *mythos*) Aristotle means the linguistic representation or imitation of an action or combination of incidents. For Aristotle a poetic plot (e.g., *Oedipus Rex*) represents a single action, complete in and of itself, and the elements of that plot are causally, i.e., necessarily, connected to one another—they form a coherent beginning, middle, and end. Historical plots are altogether different because "[a] history has to deal not with one action, but with one period and all that happened in that to one or more persons, however disconnected the several events may have been."[4] In other words, historical plots lack unity, or rather, they are unified not around an action, but around a period of time which involves multiple actions, some of which may have begun in an earlier period, or have yet to end in the period under review, and many of which will have no necessary connection with each other apart from the fact that they occurred around the same time.

But must the historian's plot, bound as it is to what "has happened," be merely a chronological listing of events whose connections may be accidental and not necessarily causal, or is Aristotle erecting a straw man? After all, both Herodotus and Thucydides work with much more sophisticated conceptions of *plot* than bare chronicle, and both are certainly as "poetic" or "philosophic," in Aristotle's sense, as Homer. Herodotus clearly states that his goal is not to describe "one period and all that happened in that [period]," as Aristotle puts it, and that his plot, or story, determines the material he includes: "If I do mention anything, it will be a necessary part of the story I am telling."[5] Given the profusion of "all that happened" within *any* period, no matter how brief, a historian must select and omit, emphasize and subordinate, on the basis of the plot that gives form and meaning to the "action" with which he is concerned. Like poetic plots, historical plots are concerned with necessary connections: with *propter hoc* as well as *post hoc*. But if Aristotle's definition of history is misleading in some respects, we can look to Herodotus for an alternative.

Herodotus, whom Cicero calls *pater historiae*, is the first writer to characterize his work as "history," and the word's etymology makes his meaning clear: *History* derives from the Greek *historia* (learning or knowing by inquiry), related to the Greek verb *historein* (to inquire into, to examine). As a historian, then, Herodotus travelled to many of the places he wrote about, conducted numerous interviews, and read widely—activities fairly similar to those of a good investigative reporter. So "history" names an activity—to inquire into what happened—and this activity distinguishes the work of the historian from that of other writers who take the past as their subject, such as Homer or Hesiod, who invoke the divine inspiration of the Muses to authorize the truth of what they say. Herodotus simply reports on his inquiries, sometimes giving us multiple variants of the same event—"That is how the Persians say it happened . . . The Phoenicians, however, do not agree with the Persians"—and sometimes telling us which variant, if either, he finds more plausible, and distinguishing what he does not know from what he does: "I am not going to say that these events happened one way or the other. Rather, I will point out the man who I know for a fact began the wrongdoing against the Greeks."[6]

But although Herodotus and Thucydides ground the truth of what they write in a methodology quite distinct from Homer's or Hesiod's, they nevertheless rely on what Aristotle would call "poetry" to transform their plots, as Nancy Partner puts it, "from a mere descriptive record of events in sequence to a level nearer philosophy, nearer to those permanently apt generalizations about human character, politics, and the causes of war so prized in Greek intellectual life."[7] Thucydides, for example, suggests that the primary cause of the Peloponnesian War was Athens's imperialist and overconfident foreign policy. He breaks from the Aristotelian definition of history by suggesting that such a will to power is not a particular trait of fifth-century Athenians, but rather a general trait to which all human beings are liable. A. W. Gomme suggests that the Athenians' *hubris* may be said to render them the tragic heroes of the drama of the Peloponnesian War.[8] Because of this "universal" element at work in history, the war becomes not merely an isolated particular, but an example of a kind of event that may recur in history, and it becomes possible to know history "philosophically," in Aristotle's sense. "Poetry" enables these ancient historians to invent speeches they never heard, and to imagine the details of events they never witnessed, or the thoughts and motives of persons they did not know. More importantly, the "poetry" of their plots, in Aristotle's terms, provides the causal explanation of the events they recount and illustrates the truths of human nature that are so central to both historians' books. Yet Thucydides implicitly contrasts his own work with that of Herodotus, whose *Histories* are filled with prophetic dreams, oracles, and traditional legends. Thucydides insists that he relies on "better evidence than that of the poets, who exaggerate the importance of their themes, or of the prose chroniclers [like Herodotus], who are less interested in telling the truth than in catching the attention of their public, whose authorities cannot be checked, and whose subject-matter, owing to the passage of time, is mostly lost in the unreliable streams of mythology."[9]

Interestingly Aristotle, despite the line he draws between poetry and history, is not at all averse to a poet choosing a historical (nonfictional) subject: "And if he should come to take a subject from actual history, he is none the less a poet for that; since some historic occurrences may very well be in the probable and possible order of things; and it is in that aspect of them that he is their poet."[10] In other words, insofar as the writer traces the "probable and possible" line of relationships in a historical subject, as opposed to merely relating the particulars of "what happened," he is engaging in a *poetic* treatment of history. Gomme suggests that Homer probably took from earlier chronicles such incidents as the quarrel between Achilles and Agamemnon, Achilles' love for Patroklos, Hektor's killing of Patroklos, and Achilles' killing of Hektor. In other words, Homer was bound to some extent by what he and most Greeks considered historical fact. However, he was free to give his plot the beginning and end that he desired, and to shape it according to the theme that he found illustrated by its incidents. We could say the same thing about Herodotus's depiction of the defeat of Xerxes, whose power and pride echo those of the legendary Croesus. Gomme remarks,

> Of Herodotos we may say that it is one of the most clearly marked features of his *History*, of its whole structure and "economy," that it is not a chronicle in Bywater's sense of the word, nor apparently in Aristotle's; that it is a triumph not of chronological but of *logical*, that is, for Aristotle in this context, *poetical* arrangement; that, as we should more probably say, it is a work of art, its author an accomplished artist, the "poet" of his plot.[11]

The distinction between poetry and history that Aristotle tries to draw is blurred and in many ways unpersuasive even when applied to Herodotus and Thucydides, yet it has proven remarkably durable over time, not only in its insistence on the difference between the two genres but also in its emphasis that one of the two is superior to the other. In his *Apology for Poetry* (1595), Sir Philip Sidney repeats Aristotle's argument that poetry is the superior genre because it deals with universal truths, whereas history is tied to particulars. Both history and poetry strive to illustrate philosophical, moral truths, but Sidney questions the value of history in that regard: "The historian in his bare *was* hath many times that which we call fortune to overrule the best wisdom. Many times he must tell events whereof he can yield no cause; or, if he do, it must be poetical," and thus despite his attempts to offer moral *exempla*, "the historian, being captived to the truth of a foolish world, is many times . . . an encouragement to unbridled wickedness."[12] Sidney's historian is a polemicist's caricature, poring over "old mouse-eaten records" and "authorizing himself (for the most part) upon other histories, whose greatest authorities are built upon the notable foundation of hearsay."[13] Percy Shelley takes up a different strategy in his *Defense of Poetry* (1840), simply subsuming the best historiography within poetry: "And thus all the great historians, Herodotus, Plutarch, Livy, were poets . . . filling all the interstices of their subjects with living images."[14] In *A Week on the Concord and Merrimack Rivers* (1849), Thoreau picks up Aristotle's distinction between universals and particulars and argues that the most valuable historians do not restrict themselves to particular truths. Punning on horticulture, he claims that the important truths of history are not "annals," but "*perennials*, which are ever without date. When out of history the truth shall be extracted, it will have shed its dates like withered leaves."[15] Thoreau writes as if he believes the "perennial" truths of history will be as apparent and as commonly agreed upon as are the particular truths, but of course that has never been the case.

In the twentieth century, Norman Mailer realigns Aristotle's distinction in his nonfiction novel *The Armies of the Night*, an account of his participation in the 1967 March on the Pentagon, probably the largest of the mass protests against the Vietnam War. Mailer concedes that the second part of his book, titled "The Novel as History,"

> while dutiful to all newspaper accounts, eyewitness reports, and historic inductions available, while even obedient to a general style of historical writing, at least up to this point, while even pretending to be a history . . . is finally now disclosed as some sort of condensation of a collective novel—which is to admit that an explanation of the mystery of the events at the Pentagon cannot be developed by the methods of history—only by the instincts of the novelist. The reasons are several, but reduce to one. Forget that the journalistic information available from both sides is so incoherent, inaccurate, contradictory, malicious, even based on error that no accurate history is possible. More than one historian has found a way through chains of false fact. No, the difficulty is that the history is interior—no documents can have sufficient intimation: the novel must replace history at precisely that point where experience is sufficiently emotional, spiritual, psychical, moral, existential, or supernatural to expose the fact that the historian in pursuing the experience would be obliged to quit the clearly demarcated limits of historic inquiry.[16]

For Mailer the distinction between literature and history lies in the "interiority" to which literature has access; history is confined to "exteriors," and because the real significance of the March lies in the "interior," and many of the exteriors are subject to profound disagreement, "a history of the March on the Pentagon which is not unfair will never be written, any more than a history which could prove dependable in details!"[17] But Mailer's distinction may be as fragile as Aristotle's, for surely a good biography of, say, Susan B. Anthony, could take account of her interiority. Mailer asserts that "no documents can have sufficient intimation" of interiority, but we may ask, "sufficient" for what? To make an informed, plausible guess at what Anthony's lived experience was like? If such an educated guess lies beyond "the clearly demarcated limits of historic inquiry," then the biographer's task is either hopeless or it lies outside history, and history is reduced to mere chronicle.

This is not to say that Mailer's or Aristotle's distinction is pointless, or that there exists no meaningful difference between Sophocles's *Oedipus Rex* and Thucydides's *The Peloponnesian Wars*. Most simply, the historian is committed to what actually happened in a way that the playwright is not, and other differences will be discussed later in this chapter. But the difference, as even Aristotle acknowledges when he states that a poet can take his plot from history, is not absolute. The two genres can blend into each other, to varying degrees. Without question, the historians we most admire—Herodotus, Thucydides, Tacitus, Gibbon, Parkman, Prescott, Carl Becker, C. Vann Woodward—are "philosophic" in Aristotle's sense of that term, i.e., they draw general conclusions or truths from the particular events with which they work. And equally without question, poetry can be about specific events: Lucan's *Pharsalia*, a remarkable poem on the civil war between Julius and Pompey, is perhaps the best known example from the ancient world, but Dante's account of Pope Boniface VIII and many dozens of other historical figures in his *Divine Comedy*, as well as poems like Milton's "On the Late Massacre in Piedmont" or Yeats's "Easter 1916," are plainly about "particulars" in Aristotle's sense. Even if Aristotle's distinction breaks down in certain ways, however, the points he makes about different kinds of truth and knowledge, and about different kinds of plots, are foundational to all later thinking about history and poetry.

Tales and Plots, or Two Senses of "History"

Most of us assume that an event from the past—an automobile accident, let's say—has an objective reality: it happened once, in one particular way, and in no other way. We know that the subjective perceptions and memories of the people who were involved in the accident, or the eyewitnesses, or the police officer who wrote a report of it, or its depiction by attorneys in the civil lawsuit that the accident inspired, may differ from that objective reality, and from one another, but we assume that the judge and/or jury can probably come to a decision regarding what happened that accords reasonably closely with the objective truth. History works like this as well, at its most basic level: we expect historians simply to tell us what happened, just as we expect a friend to be able to tell us simply what happened to her two days ago, or a newspaper reporter to tell us simply what happened at a school board meeting last night. This expectation is at least as old as Cicero: "For who does not know history's first law to be that an author must not dare to tell anything but the truth? And its second that he must make bold to tell the whole truth? That there must be no suggestion of partiality anywhere in his writings? Nor of malice?"[18]

Such expectations seem unremarkable, but if we return to the courtroom and the auto accident, we know that often there will be details that don't fit somebody's version of what happened, that witnesses sometimes misperceive or misunderstand certain things, and that apparently reliable witnesses may remember the same event in different ways. We want to understand what really happened, and we may overemphasize some evidence, de-emphasize other evidence, and speculate on what may have happened when we encounter gaps in the evidence, so that the evidence fits a plausible, coherent narrative of what really happened. This is not malicious—we constantly come to conclusions, in all aspects of everyday life, based of necessity on incomplete evidence. We know that judges' and juries' decisions are rarely grounded in total certainty, but rather on a sliding scale of probabilities—sometimes the innocent are found guilty, and sometimes the guilty are set free. To be wholly skeptical of our ability to know the truth about the past would remove the foundation from our justice system, as well as from most aspects of everyday life. Still, most of us would acknowledge that a gap exists, of indeterminate size, between what actually happened and our perceptions, memories, and narratives of what happened. Indeed, a large part of being human involves negotiating and evaluating the competing narratives that make up our experience of the world and its past.

Phrases like "competing narratives" may sound like postmodern posturing, but these are commonplaces of reflection on history. In *The Presuppositions of Critical History* (1874), for example, F. H. Bradley writes, "We ask for history, and that means that we ask for the simple record of unadulterated facts; we look, and nowhere do we find the object of our search, but in its stead we see the divergent accounts of a host of jarring witnesses, a chaos of disjoined and discrepant narrations, and yet, while all of these can by no possibility be received as true, at the same time not one of them can be rejected as false."[19] Bradley knows that some accounts of what happened are more coherent than others, or incorporate more of the available evidence, or seem less partisan or emotional. But he also knows that no single account of, say, the Glorious Revolution succeeds in holding the mirror up to history in a way that persuades all reasonable, well-informed readers that it tells "the whole truth," in Cicero's phrase. In his "Letters on the Study and Use of History" (1752), Lord Bolingbroke is even more skeptical: "the very best [of history] is nothing better than a probable tale, artfully contrived, and plausibly told, wherein truth and falsehood are indistinguishably blended together."[20] We find a similar point in Carlyle's essay "On History" (1830): any historical narrative is "at best . . . a poor approximation" to what actually happened, an oversimplification of the past itself, "that complex Manuscript, covered over with formless inextricably-entangled unknown characters" which finally "can be fully interpreted by no man."[21]

The distinction between the event itself and the narrative that describes the event is also a focus of Russian Formalist literary theory, for which the term "tale" refers to the actual event, and "plot" to any narrative account of that event. For the Formalists, even a fictional "plot" evokes in the reader's imagination a "tale" anterior to and independent of its narration, just as a historical narrative evokes a historical "tale" anterior to and independent of its narration, or emplotment. If Cicero is right, then a historical plot ought to be utterly contingent upon a historical tale, i.e., a historical plot ought simply to hold the mirror up to its tale. For instance, no matter how two different historians emplot the tale of the Battle of the Alamo, it must end with the massacre of the Texans. Unlike a poetic plot, a historical plot evokes a tale already constituted. However, without falsifying the facts, the tale of the Alamo can be emplotted as a story of hubris (Jim Bowie's refusal to carry out Sam Houston's order to remove the artillery and abandon the mission), as romantic tragedy (the heroic deaths of Bowie, Davy Crockett, and the other defenders of the mission), as an episode of American militarism and imperialism (prelude to the Mexican War and the annexation of a large part of Mexico, and the consequent expansion of slavery), as an episode of revolutionary self-determination (the fight to establish the Republic of Texas), or in other ways. These would be "divergent accounts," in Bradley's terms, that are neither simply true nor simply false. In history, as in poetry, the meaning of any tale depends finally upon the plot in which it is cast, and any tale is fully intelligible only in terms of a plot. Even the best historians concede that crafting a plot that fits the tale completely is impossible; Cicero's rules simply cannot be followed.

At this point in time we possess an enormous body of historical "plots," ranging over all of recorded history. The phrase "recorded history" suggests a second meaning of the noun "history," in that it implies the existence of another history that may be unrecorded. Used in this sense, history means simply "the past," i.e., everything that has happened since the dawn of time, regardless of what (if anything) has been written about it—this is the "tale" that the "plots" of historiography are meant to represent. The Oxford English Dictionary cites 1585 as the earliest usage of "history" in English to mean "events themselves"; the word had been used to mean "a narrative" since 1390 and as "that branch of knowledge which deals with past events" since 1482. Schiller makes this distinction in his inaugural lecture as professor of philosophy at Jena in May 1789—"What is Universal History and Why Do We Study It?"—when he distinguishes "der Gang der Weltgeschichte" (the course of world history, as it is written) from "der Gang der Welt" (the course of the world, or history as it happens),[22] as does Hegel when he points to the tension between history conceived as *historia rerum gestarum* as opposed to *res gestae*.[23]

Common sense holds that the accurate written depiction of an event is contingent on the event itself, but it is equally true that the event itself is always contingent on the narrative by which it is known. That is, an historical "event" does not exist as an object of knowledge unless and until it is organized in narrative form: knowing the "tale" depends upon knowing the "plot." An apocryphal remark attributed to Thucydides, that stories can only happen to people who are capable of telling them, speaks to this point: we organize our experience of the past after the fact in narrative form in order to make sense of it, to "know" it. But there remains inevitably, in Ernst Breisach's words, "an unbridgeable epistemological moat between account and past extralinguistic reality."[24]

The difference between history-as-tale and history-as-plot suggests that any plot's narrative form does not simply inhere in the tale itself. As Hayden White puts it,

> this value attached to narrativity in the representation of real events arises out of a desire to have real events display the coherence, integrity, fullness, and closure of an image of life that is and can only be imaginary. The notion that sequences of real events possess the formal attributes of the stories we tell about imaginary events could only have its origin in wishes, daydreams, rever-

ies. Does the world really present itself to perception in the form of well-made stories, with central subjects, proper beginnings, middles, and ends, and a coherence that permits us to see "the end" in every beginning? Or does it present itself more in the forms that the annals and chronicle suggest, either as mere sequence without beginning or end or as sequences of beginnings that only terminate and never conclude?[25]

Nietzsche quotes Schiller to similar effect: "one appearance after the other begins to withdraw from blind approximation, from lawless freedom, and as a fit member joins the ranks of a coherent whole—*which, of course, only exists in his* [the historian's] *imagination*."[26] Historical discourse promises to imitate, or represent, actual lived history accurately and objectively, but its capacity to do so is limited. If history were genuinely mimetic, we would never need another history of the same historical event. One history of the Civil War would be enough, and there would be no point in writing another. But as White points out, "every mimesis can be shown to be distorted and can serve, therefore, as an occasion for yet another description of the same phenomenon, one claiming to be more realistic, more 'faithful to the facts.'"[27]

Yet for many centuries historians and their readers have resisted the notion that historians must impose a plot upon the tale of the past. In *The Education of Henry Adams*, for example, Adams describes his attempt to write history without imposing a plot, his attempt to determine whether, "by the severest process of stating, with the least possible comment, such facts as seemed sure, in such order as seemed rigorously consequent, he could fix for a familiar moment a necessary sequence of human movement." But he admits that his attempt fails: "Where he saw sequence, other men saw something quite different, and no one saw the same unit of measure."[28] Adams's diction—"consequent," "necessary sequence"—recalls Aristotle's, and his failure would seem to support Aristotle's contention that consequential plots do not inhere, without a poet's intervention, in the bare tale of history.

This same shapelessness of the past marks the occasion of the onset of Roquentin's sickness in Sartre's *Nausea*. Roquentin, the novel's protagonist, is a historian whose work has come to a halt. He explains,

> In the first place, starting from 1801, I understand nothing more about his [Rollebon's, the subject of his historical research] conduct. It is not the lack of documents: letters, fragments of memories, secret reports, police records. On the contrary I have almost too many of them. What is lacking in all this testimony is firmness and consistency. They do not contradict each other, but neither do they agree with each other; they do not seem to be about the same person. And yet other historians work from the same sources of information. How do they do it? Am I more scrupulous or less intelligent? . . . I am beginning to believe that nothing can ever be proved. These are honest hypotheses which take the past into account: but I sense so definitely that they come from me, and that they are simply a way of unifying my own knowledge. . . . Slow, lazy, sulky,

the facts adapt themselves to the rigour of the order I wish to give them; but it remains outside of them.[29]

The dissonances among the particular truths Roquentin has uncovered about his subject, and between these particulars and the larger, general truths into which he tries to fit them, lead Roquentin to abandon his project. Roquentin concludes that what passes as history belongs to the orderly world of explanations and reasons, and not to the disorderly world of existence. And his claim that he has "almost too many" documents reminds us of Lytton Strachey's observation that the history of the Victorian Age cannot be written because "we know too much about it."[30]

To acknowledge the gap between tale and plot is not to claim that all plots are therefore equal, or that we have no way of determining good history from bad, or history from fiction or poetry. Instead, it simply suggests that no absolute difference exists between history and poetry, and that the border between the two genres is in places poorly marked, and may be easily crossed; in fact, it is regularly crossed by many of our greatest writers. The truths of history often take the form of Bradley's "divergent accounts"; in other words, historians regularly disagree with one another on how to interpret important aspects of the evidence before them. In this they are no different than economists, or art historians, or literary critics, or psychologists. Historians bring to the evidence their own assumptions about human nature and motivations, their own political or ideological convictions, their own values, and these affect what they "see" in the evidence they interpret. For their readers, similarly, there exists no value-neutral perspective from which the accuracy of an interpretation can finally be judged. Certainly skilled readers can identify errors of historical fact, or evidence that has been overlooked, or inconsistencies in an argument. But even when such errors are eliminated, some intelligent, well-informed readers will be persuaded by arguments and interpretations that others reject. As we will see later in this chapter, history is very much like a long conversation in which a variety of intelligent, well-informed people hold different interpretations of particular events, and different beliefs about why history matters.

Objective History and the Postmodern Challenge

As history developed into a professional discipline in the late nineteenth century, historians increasingly began to characterize their discipline as a science and to insist that it was not a genre of literature or rhetoric. In other words, history can provide genuine *epistemic* knowledge, while poetry is consigned to subjective *doxa*. Among the most intellectually ambitious attempts to address the structure of a scientific history is Carl Hempel's 1942 essay "The Function of General Laws in History," in which Hempel argues that historians, like scientists, ought to be concerned with general laws rooted in empirical observation.

To be truly scientific, history needs to deal with *kinds* of events rather than particular events, and to explain events in terms of general concepts rather than simply describing events in terms of unique incidents. These general laws would function as explanatory principles, and like all scientific laws, their validity would be tested (and the laws accordingly modified) on the basis of their ability to "cover" or explain actual historical events. Hempel's assertion that history is concerned with universal truths, not particular truths, inverts Aristotle's distinction between poetry and history, although to date, Hempel's "general laws" remain purely hypothetical. In the mid-twentieth century historians began to utilize the statistical methods of the social sciences, a step that Nietzsche anticipated and rebuked with his characteristic vigor: "What, statistics prove that there are laws of history? Laws? Yes, it proves how mean and disgustingly uniform the masses are: is one to call laws the effect of inertia, stupidity, aping, love and hunger? . . . . so far as there are laws in history, laws are worth nothing and history is worth nothing."[31] In fact, for Nietzsche the entire project of a scientific history is untenable: "Against that positivism which stops before phenomena, saying 'there are only facts,' I should say: no, it is precisely facts that do not exist, only interpretations."[32]

Somewhere between Hempel and Nietzsche we find Thomas Carlyle, who suggests in his essay "On History" that history-as-tale is always inevitably mediated by historiography. In effect, argues Carlyle, history-as-tale appears to us only as a text or "palimpsest," a manuscript marked by blanks, erasures, and rewriting, at once flawed and far too vast to be read in its entirety. Carlyle's figure—the past as text—will be altered by the anthropologist Clifford Geertz, for whom "culture" is a text,[33] and extended by Martin Heidegger, who asserts that history depends entirely upon language, that indeed only language makes possible the constitution of a world and its history. His student Gadamer elaborates: "Language is not just one of man's possessions in the world, but on it depends the fact that man has a world at all. . . . it [the world] is always, in whatever tradition we consider it, a human, i.e., a linguistically constituted world that presents itself to us."[34]

This claim may seem extreme, but upon reflection, the elements of "the past" that constitute the historian's primary sources—documents, letters, diaries, records, earlier histories, archeologists' reports—are linguistic artifacts, and the degree to which these various "plots" correspond with the "tale" of history may be difficult to determine. Our desire for a stable, objectively knowable past is like our desire that our words should represent our intended meanings unequivocally: too often unrequited. A historical event is like a text admitting many possibilities of meaning and open to endless re-reading and re-interpretation. Carlyle's figure of the past as text, and of the historian as reader/interpreter/rewriter of that text, has been restated in nonfigurative prose by later thinkers as divergent as Gadamer—"historical reality itself is a text that has to be understood"[35]—and Derrida: "The age already in the *past* is in fact constituted in every respect as a *text*."[36] And with that step the postmodern challenge to history, of which we find traces as early as Nietzsche, begins.

That challenge originates in its French form with the rise of structuralism in the mid-twentieth century. In *The Savage Mind*, for example, Claude Levi-Strauss dismisses history: "We need only recognize that history is a method with no distinct object corresponding to it to reject the equivalence between the notion of history and the notion of humanity that some have tried to foist on us with the unavowed aim of making historicity the last refuge of a transcendental humanism."[37] In "The Discourse of History" Roland Barthes argues that historiography employs a "referential illusion"[38] of objectivity, a rhetorical style that implies that the referent (the past) is speaking for itself. That is, the historian plays to our common-sense notion that history presents the "tale" without the mediation of a historian's "plot," and thus "historical discourse is in its essence a form of ideological elaboration."[39] For Barthes, and for postmodernism in general, language is never a neutral medium in which truth, historical or otherwise, may be plainly expressed.

Structuralism gave way to post-structuralism in the work of Jacques Derrida, for whom historiography, like all logocentric discourse, attempts to close off the free play of signifiers in a vain attempt to recover the "presence" of a stable truth. Derrida writes: "it could be shown that the concept of *episteme* has always called forth that of *historia*, if history is always the unity or the development of science or knowledge oriented toward the appropriation of truth in presence and self-presence, toward knowledge in consciousness-of-self."[40] Michel Foucault makes a similar observation:

> Continuous history is the indispensable correlative of the founding function of the subject: the guarantee that everything that has eluded him may be restored to him; the certainty that time will disperse nothing without restoring it in a reconstituted unity; the promise that one day the subject—in the form of historical consciousness—will once again be able to appropriate, to bring back under his sway, all those things that are kept at a distance by difference, and find in them what might be called his abode.[41]

For Foucault history unfolds in an aimless sequence of domination and oppression, opposition to that domination, and then a new order of domination and oppression, in an endless sequence of domination and opposition in which there must exist an oppressed "other." The challenge of postmodernism to our understanding of history is that "truth" can have no permanence, no stable foundation. Human consciousness is simply the site of an endless regression of linked signifiers that have no firm correspondence with a world "out there," historical or otherwise.

Louis Mink is among the first American intellectuals to take seriously the implications of postmodernism for history, and he boldly proposes that we simply "abandon the presupposition that there is a determinate historical actuality, the complex referent for all our narratives of 'what actually happened,' the *un-*

told story to which narrative histories approximate."[42] Hans Kellner suggests that although a single statement about a given historical event may be "true" or "false" as we typically understand those terms, historical narratives as a whole have "a truth more akin to the truth of a novel or painting than to that of a syllogism."[43] For Kellner, we have no unmediated view of the past—the past itself is *absent*.

In his magisterial *Metahistory*, Hayden White reads nineteenth-century historiography through a postmodern lens: "The historian performs an essentially *poetic* act, in which he *pre*figures the historical field and constitutes it as a domain upon which to bring to bear the specific theories he will use to explain 'what was *really* happening' in it." This "poetic act" lays the groundwork for the historian's explanatory argument, his ideological implications, and even the plot of his narrative. Perhaps most controversially, White argues that because "there are no apodictically certain theoretical grounds on which one can legitimately claim an authority for any one of the rhetorical modes over the others as being more 'realistic' . . . the best grounds for choosing one perspective on history rather than another are ultimately aesthetic or moral rather than epistemological."[44]

As one might expect, White's argument provoked a vigorous response: to his critics, White is a radical relativist who renders history meaningless, and some of White's supporters seem to agree. Beverley Southgate, for example, claims that White "utterly erodes" the distinction between history and fiction so that we can no longer speak about texts being "true" or "false," but only about their being more or less intelligible, persuasive, consistent, or coherent.[45] However, responding to his critics in *Figural Realism*, White does not go as far as readers like Southgate might wish. In claiming that our access to history is linguistic, that "our experience of history is indissociable from our discourse about it," White insisted that he was not implying "that past events, persons, institutions, and processes never really existed," nor "that we cannot have more or less precise information about these past entities."[46] Of course history in the sense of "extradiscursive entities" exists, and we can represent those entities in language. But "raw facts" have to be "described" by language, and once the historian embeds those facts in a narrative, they function as elements of a story, so that historiography does not give us raw facts, but rather various linguistic descriptions of events.

What White calls "events" are the raw experience of history as it happens; what he calls "facts" are historians' linguistically constituted descriptions of those events. Historians transform lists of facts into narratives, i.e., they "emplot" them, and different historians may emplot them in different ways "with equal plausibility and without doing any violence to the factual record." Different histories of the same events "can be assessed, criticized, and ranked on the basis of their fidelity to the factual record, their comprehensiveness, and the coherence of whatever arguments they may contain."[47] Still, no single history can ever tell the "whole" or "plain" truth about the events it describes because of what White calls "my own hobby-horse . . . the necessarily tropological . . . fig-urative nature of all descriptions of historical objects and their contexts."[48] For both White's critics and his more eager admirers, this ineluctable tropological nature of all historiography removes the possibility of objective truth and erases the line, as Southgate puts it, between history and fiction. For White, however, this poetic element not only gives the great histories their particular strengths, but it also provokes further historical inquiry: "It is the metaphoric nature of the great classics of historiography that explains why none of them has ever wrapped up a historical problem definitively; rather, they have always opened up a prospect on the past that inspires more study."[49]

The label "postmodern" has been a source of great mischief and confusion, not only because it lumps together thinkers as different as White and Baudrillard but also because it invites a kind of "for it" or "against it" simplification. As we have seen, ideas about the linguistic nature of history go back at least as far as the nineteenth century, and in the United States, Carl Becker argued in his semi-nal 1910 essay, "Detachment and the Writing of History," that historians essen-tially construct, rather than discover, "facts."[50] Becker was not arguing that his-torians simply invent the past, or that they cavalierly disregard the historical record, but rather that the truths they tell about the past are rarely authoritatively monolithic. Objective truths such as dates and names, which are falsifiable, are not like the truths we tell about, for example, the causes of the Civil War, or why it matters that Ann Hutchinson was excommunicated and exiled from the Massachusetts Bay Colony. Claims about such topics are not falsifiable in any simple objective sense, but they comprise the most important part of any histori-an's work.

Telling the truth about history is not easy. When Ronald Reagan and West German Chancellor Helmut Kohl made a formal visit in 1985 to the Bitburg cemetery where Waffen-SS officers lay buried, the significance of that visit led to heated discussions, a *Historikerstreit*, over the meaning, the "truth," the "facts," of Germany's Nazi past. Similar controversies over historical truth and facts are occasioned by many controversial events, such as the 1937 Nanjing Massacre, the Armenian Genocide, U.S. involvement in Vietnam, and the long conflict between Israel and the Palestinians. The distinction between objective and subjective truths turns out, at many points, to be as blurry as Aristotle's dis-tinction between poetry and history. The conservative philosopher Michael Oakeshott, whom no one would mistake for a postmodernist, concludes his 1958 essay "The Activity of Being an Historian" as follows:

> The activity of being an historian is not that of contributing to the elucidation of a single ideal coherence of events which may be called "true" to the exclusion of all others; it is an activity in which a writer, concerned with the past for its own sake and working to a chosen scale, elicits a coherence in a group of con-tingencies of similar magnitudes. And if in so new and delicate an enterprise he finds himself tempted into making concessions to the idiom of legend, that per-

haps is less damaging than other divergencies.[51]

We might think of it this way: we can agree that the Americans dropped an atomic bomb on Hiroshima on August 6, 1945. That is an objective historical truth. We know the name of the plane that dropped the bomb, and we can describe the bomb's design. But once the historian goes beyond that, and begins to think about the various reasons why it was dropped, and what its various consequences were (both short-term and long-term), and about what it *meant* to have dropped such a bomb, then quite plainly, well-informed and reasonable historians may tell quite different "stories," i.e., they may emplot the facts differently, and give the facts different kinds of significance, without denying or distorting those facts.[52] If historical narrative were entirely unattached to any extra-linguistic historical events, if it were simply afloat in a free-play of signifiers that have no discernible relation to a world "out there," which is admittedly what some postmodernists have argued, then history would be merely another genre of fiction.

But writers like Carl Becker and Hayden White do not make that claim. When White argues that all histories are inescapably poetic or ideological, or when Becker argues that all histories are relative, each still concedes that historians are constrained by the knowledge of particular historical truths, and that they may be judged by their fidelity to those truths. Unfortunately, the term "postmodern" seems to have encouraged a rigidly either/or kind of thinking: either historical truth is objective and authoritative, and any questioning of that truth is suspiciously "revisionist," or historical "truth" is merely a function of the writer's imagination, and we have no way of choosing among such "truths" apart from our aesthetic and ideological preferences. Writers occupy extreme positions on both sides of this argument, from Baudrillard and his *simulacra* to Roger Chartier and Gertrude Himmelfarb, who continue to defend a version of the "correspondence" model of objective historical truth.

A middle-ground position is laid out by Joyce Appleby, Lynn Hunt, and Margaret Jacob in their *Telling the Truth About History*, in which they acknowledge the importance of skepticism and the relativism that results from the historian's particular time, place, race, class, gender, and ideology. "No one argues any longer . . . that historical narrative in any way exactly mirrors past reality," they write, yet "We see no reason to conclude that because there is a gap between reality and its narration (its representation), the narration in some fundamental sense is inherently invalid. Just because narratives are human creations does not make them all equally fictitious or invalid."[53] They believe that the past is knowable, and that history affords methods by which more valid accounts of the past may be distinguished from less valid accounts. Still, they assert that "All histories are provisional. None will have the last word,"[54] an idea that reaches back in American history at least as far as Frederick Jackson Turner, who in "The Significance of History" wrote: "The first lesson the student of history has to learn is to discard his conception that there are standard ultimate histories. In the nature of the case this is impossible . . . they are not the final words."[55] I will suggest later in this chapter that the argument over the postmodern challenge to history is part of a much larger conversation about the nature and value of history—an unending conversation in which, in the motto of the Royal Society, *nullius in verba* ("nobody's word is final").

The Fact of Pluralism

Nobody's word is final because of what in another context John Rawls calls "the fact of pluralism"—the intellectual landscape of thinking about history reveals a diversity of positions regarding the meaning, purpose, and proper method of history, and as Rawls puts it, "[t]his diversity of doctrines—the fact of pluralism—is not a mere historical condition that will soon pass away; it is . . . a permanent feature."[56] In other words, it is not the case that over time the various historical interpretations of a given event—say, the Civil War—will grow gradually closer to the objective truth about the War and coalesce toward a single interpretation of the War's meaning. Historical interpretations do not unfold in a series of successive approximations that draw ever closer to the objective truth; instead, they simply continue to proliferate. Nor is this diversity of opinion the result of one historian having access to better data than another—historians basically work with the same set of data. However, they bring to their work different preconceptions, different political and economic beliefs, different beliefs about what drives human behavior, different beliefs about why the War matters and what it means—indeed, they may bring to their work different beliefs about why history in general matters. And this means that the histories they write usually cannot be disconfirmed in the way that a scientific hypothesis may be disconfirmed. A good history, like a good piece of literary criticism or economic theory, will persuade some intelligent, well-informed readers, while it may leave other equally intelligent, well-informed readers unimpressed or even move them to critical opposition. History has always been that way, and it will always be that way.

Here are some examples. One of the earliest beliefs about why history matters is that "history is philosophy teaching by examples," a remark attributed to Dionysius of Halicarnassus that reflects in varying degrees the beliefs of many of the great ancient historians, including Herodotus, Thucydides, Polybius, Livy, and Tacitus. In most cases, the examples that history illustrates involve wise or foolish instances of political conduct, and the implication is that we in the present can learn from these examples. Today, however, despite George Santayana's stern warning that "Those who cannot remember the past are condemned to repeat it," some historians believe that we are condemned to repeat it whether or not we remember it, and in general there exists widespread disagreement on what particular "lessons" history teaches, or whether it teaches any at all. Didacticism, especially in its cruder forms, has passed from fashion in both history and poetry.

The Christian interpretation of world history laid out by Eusebius in his *Chronicle* (ca. 325) or by Augustine in his *City of God*, in which history unfolds according to divine providence, offers a broader theoretical frame than Dionysius's model, and persists into the early Modern period in, for example, Bishop Bossuet's *Discours sur l'histoire universelle* (1681). But Enlightenment thinkers, such as Voltaire in his *Essay on the Manners and Character of the Nations* (1757), challenge that model and propose instead a secular history that traces the uneven progress of "enlightenment." Christian readings of history persist, however, even into the twentieth century with Berdyaev's *The Meaning of History* (1923) and Niebuhr's *The Irony of American History* (1952), though they remain a minority persuasion.

The Enlightenment suggests that human reason has the power to know all things, including history, and in his "Idea for a Universal History from the Cosmopolitan Point of View," Kant offers a teleological history: Nature drives the emergence of Reason toward a universal civic society. For Hegel, human history is simply the rationally necessary development of the World Spirit. In other words, history names the process of subjectivity's dialectical attainment of self-consciousness, and the *telos* of the historical dialectic promises the ultimate dissolution of objectivity: spirit will have become both subject and object of consciousness. Hegel shares with Augustine the idea of history as an order impelled by a transcendental force (the dialectic or God), the idea that historical events are finally meaningful only in the context of that transcendental reality, and the idea that at some point in the future, time and history will cease (when Spirit attains full self-consciousness or when Christ comes for the second time). He also shares with Augustine the idea that history involves the subject's apprehension or re-appropriation of itself; from the Christian perspective, man (who is the image of God) returns to God at the end of history—God recovers his image.

Of course, few practicing historians were Hegelians or Augustinians, but many were influenced by Leopold von Ranke, who repudiated both Hegelian teleology and any didactic function for history. One might say that Ranke's *a posteriori* approach to history turns Hegel's *a priori* approach on its head. In the Foreword to his first book, *Histories of the Latin and Germanic Peoples* (1824), Ranke writes, "To history has been attributed the function of judging the past, of instructing contemporaries for the profit of the future. To such lofty functions the present essay does not presume. It merely undertakes to show how things really took place."[57] To show "how things really took place," or "how it really happened"—*wie es eigentlich gewesen*—became the goal of many nineteenth-century historians, many of whom studied with Ranke at the University of Berlin, where from 1825 to 1871 he conducted seminars on the detailed, critical textual analysis of diplomatic reports and other official documents, and the patient, inductive historiography that such work could produce. The attraction of Ranke's method lay in its promise to separate the subjective—teleological speculation, moral judgment, didactic lessons—from the objective truth of what happened. Yet despite Ranke's opposition to Hegelianism, Fritz Stern points out that "at the same time Ranke conceived history as, in some strange manner, 'a revelation of God' . . . [and] imagined that man could see 'God's finger' in human affairs and dimly grasp God's handiwork in history."[58]

Ranke's was only one among several major voices in the nineteenth century's conversation on history. Arnaldo Momigliano suggests that "the most daring and perhaps most interesting historical thinking never cared too much" for Ranke's cautious approach, and that such great historians as Tocqueville, Marx, and Burckhardt "never treated evidence in a way to satisfy what Burckhardt called the 'viri eruditissimi,'" among whom he must have numbered Ranke.[59] In *Reflections on History*, Burckhardt makes the very un-Rankean claim that "After all, our historical pictures are, for the most part, pure constructions. . . . Indeed, they are mere reflections of ourselves."[60] Burckhardt's idea that the historian engages in a kind of sympathetic identification with the past is developed by Dilthey and Collingwood, for whom knowledge of the past is never simply empirical. Collingwood argues that "the historian must re-enact the past in his own mind"[61] and that this "web of imaginative construction . . . , [s]o far from relying for its validity upon the support of given facts . . . actually serves as the touchstone by which we decide whether alleged facts are genuine,"[62] which is quite far from the critical distance from the past that Ranke enjoins in the interest of objectivity.

Another nineteenth-century historian, Karl Marx, would challenge both Hegel's idealism and Ranke's claim to objectivity. Like Hegel, Marx conceives of the course of history as dialectical and teleological, but unlike Hegel, he is rigorously materialist, and he replaces the quasi-divine *Weltgeist*, or World Spirit, with the material forces of economics in *Capital* (1867), which remains the world's most systematic and influential materialist interpretation of history. Marx criticizes Ranke for accepting too readily the statements of his primary sources: "Whilst in ordinary life every shopkeeper is very well able to distinguish between what somebody professes to be and what he really is, our historians have not yet won even this trivial insight. They take every epoch at its word and believe that everything it says and imagines about itself is true."[63] For Marx, Ranke's emphasis on political documents as primary sources limits history to the level of the political "superstructure," and ignores the more fundamental economic forces that drive the formation of classes. Marx's confidence lies in the truth of the deep structure which he discerns beneath the empirical surface, the processes that lie behind what he calls "high-sounding dramas of princes and states," a confidence so great that he claims the ability to "conceive things thus, as they really are and happened,"[64] which sounds just like Ranke.

The nineteenth-century epistemological confidence that rigorous method, whether Rankean or Marxist or some other, can lead to objective historical truth persists into the twentieth: John Bury closes his 1902 inaugural address as Regius Professor of Modern History at Cambridge with the assertion that history is "simply a science, no less and no more,"[65] and because the discipline has attained that status, diverse schools of history will no longer exist. But once again, that confidence has its skeptics: G. M. Trevelyan, who succeeds Bury as Regius Professor in 1927, argues in *Clio, A Muse* (1913) that the analogy between history and science is false: it is impossible to isolate a historical event from its circumstances, to test causes and effects with controlled and uncontrolled variables.

Yet the appeal of the social sciences leads certain twentieth-century French historians to search for deep structures and long-term causes, and to dismiss what they called *histoire événementielle*, the narrative history of "events" that Fernand Braudel, in *The Mediterranean* (1949), would famously characterize as nothing but the foam on the waves of the sea of history. Braudel and his colleagues at the journal *Annales,* founded in 1929, focus instead on the *longue durée,* long periods of time in which they can analyze the gradual changes of a culture's fundamental social and economic structures. The *Annalistes* make heavy use of quantitative techniques and pay attention to things that historians like Marx or Ranke ignore, like the impact of geography, or shifts in population or agriculture, or the ways that a culture institutionalizes childhood or death or femininity.

What I am trying to show is that our sense of what history is, and why it matters, and how it ought to be practiced, changes regularly, and that the leading historians of any given period are likely to hold divergent views on these questions—in the mid-twentieth century, for example, serious historiography included *Annalistes*, Marxists, the so-called "consensus" historians of the United States, the Christian-inflected history of Niebuhr's *The Irony of American History*, and the beginnings of the heavily quantitative approach dubbed "cliometrics." Historians as different as Hegel, Augustine, and Marx imagine history moving toward a final redemptive climax, an *eschaton* or final event, while in *The Poverty of Historicism* (1957) Karl Popper attacks all such claims to any predictive power for history.

This same pluralism is evident if we narrow our focus to American historiography. If the first American history is John Smith's *A True Relation* (1608) or *General History of Virginia, New England, and the Summer Isles* (1624), with their focus on survival and adventure, and their promise of material prosperity, then almost immediately we find the rival millennialist, providential history of the Puritans, such as William Bradford's *History of Plimoth Plantation* (1646) or Cotton Mather's *Magnalia Christi Americana* (1702). In the nineteenth century, Prescott (*The Conquest of Mexico*, 1843) and Parkman (*History of the Conspiracy of Pontiac*, 1851) composed their great romantic narratives of conquest and exploration, while George Bancroft, whose twelve-volume *History of the United States* (1834–82) was perhaps the nineteenth century's most influential American history, saw the United States establishing a *novus ordo seclorum*, or "new order of the ages," ordained by Divine Providence to advance the linked causes of liberty, democracy, peace, and universal brotherhood. On the other hand, Bancroft's contemporary Richard Hildreth found no divinely ordained progress in America's history, but only groups of people pursuing their own material interests.

Unlike the romantic, unabashedly partisan Bancroft, who combined the inductive rigor of his teacher Ranke with the belief that America had been chosen by God as an instrument in the fulfillment of His providence, Henry Adams maintained what John Burrow calls a "pose of fastidious disillusionment"[66] and scholarly detachment. In 1870, Adams taught the first Harvard seminar ever devoted to the methods of German historical scholarship, and in *The Education of Henry Adams* he remarked on history's failure to keep pace with the natural sciences—"Since Gibbon, the spectacle was almost a scandal. History had lost the sense of shame. It was a hundred years behind the experimental sciences. For all serious purposes, it was less instructive than Walter Scott and Alexander Dumas"[67]—and looked forward to "an epoch when man should study his own history in the same spirit and by the same methods with which he studied the formation of a crystal."[68] In 1894, Adams recalled that "Those of us who read Buckle's first volume when it appeared in 1857, and almost immediately afterwards, in 1859, read the *Origin of Species* and felt the violent impulse which Darwin gave to the study of natural laws, never doubted that historians would follow until they had exhausted every possible hypothesis to create a science of history."[69] Yet Adams's great work, *The History of the United States of America during the Administrations of Jefferson and Madison* (1889–91), is remarkable for its belletristic excellence, not its scientific explanations of the past. Nevertheless Adams imagined historians "dreaming of the immortality that would be achieved by the man who should successfully apply Darwin's method to the facts of human history,"[70] and many historians have remained committed to that dream, from Adams's father Charles Francis Adams —"[History] closely allied to astronomy, geology, and physics . . . seeks a scientific basis from which the rise and fall of races and dynasties will be seen merely as phases of a consecutive process of evolution"[71]—to Jared Diamond, who concludes *Guns, Germs, and Steel* with an epilogue titled "The Future of Human History as a Science," in which he writes, "The challenge now is to develop human history as a science, on a par with acknowledged historical sciences such as astronomy, geology, and evolutionary biology."[72]

The establishment of the American Historical Association in 1884 marks the split between old-style literary historians who write for a broad public and professional academic historians who aspire to a scientific history written for other academics. Under the influence of the AHA, American graduate programs in history would follow the German *Geschichtswissenschaft*, with its insistence on strict evidence, archival research, textual criticism of written sources, research methodology, scholarly detachment, and educational credentials.

Almost immediately, however, the "scientific" nature of history would be called into question. In 1912, James Harvey Robinson borrowed Edward Eggleston's phrase the "New History" for the title of a manifesto commonly held to mark the initial phase of American Progressive historiography. The "New Historians" were scientific in the sense that they sought to uncover the "real" forces governing history, not only in political history but in sociology and espe- cially in economics. Where someone like Bancroft saw "liberty" as an autono- mous force at work in history, the New Historians tended to see ideas as prod- ucts of the social environment. But the New Historians' commitment to "sci- ence" was inconsistent, for they saw history as a tool of social activism and the advocacy of political reforms, and saw economic conflict between distinct groups—farmers or laborers against entrepreneurs and financial interests—as the "real" forces driving history. Their task was to expose the special interests that preserved the unjust status quo and to promote a truly democratic, egalitari- an society organized by means of rationalism and science instead of tradition and narrow self-interest.

Like Bancroft, the new progressive historians saw "progress" as inherent in human history, but unlike Bancroft, they saw progress as something to be ra- tionally and cooperatively planned. Progressive American history emerged alongside the muckraking tradition in American journalism and shared with that tradition the notion that the "truth" is typically concealed and needs to be re- vealed in order for us to see it—there is always an "inside story" that tells the "real" truth; there are "deep" forces at work in history that are not apparent on the surface of events. We find this same kind of thinking in Freud's psychology, in which the "real" forces at work within the unconscious are concealed from the conscious ego, and in Marxist historiography, in which the "real" economic forces driving history are masked by traditional historiography's "high-sounding dramas of princes." It is also at work in Darwin: natural selection is the "real" force at work in natural history, driving the evolution of species and species diversification. In exposing the "real" forces at work in American history, the progressives aimed to expose the reasons that actual American life fell short of our democratic ideals, and to promote political action that worked toward the realization of those ideals. Progressive history, in other words, was driven by a moral didacticism.

Despite the heavy influence of the "scientific" approach to history, Ameri- can historians for the most part paid little attention to epistemological issues or theoretical disputes. The Progressives saw no conflict between a "scientific" history and a history committed to the political goals of creating a more progres- sive democracy. American historians embraced the methods of Ranke alongside Buckle's contradictory idea that history ought to be practiced in the manner of the natural sciences. Ernst Breisach writes, "American 'scientific history' could accommodate German critical historical scholarship, Comtean positivism, Dar- winian evolutionism, and traditional faith in progress."[73] In their early careers, Carl Becker and Charles Beard were proponents of a scientific, objective histo- ry, but unlike most of their peers, they began to look more seriously at issues of truth and objectivity. Written in response to Theodore Clarke Smith's AHA pa- per in defense of objectivity, Beard's "That Noble Dream"[74] argued, in language that prefigures the later arguments of Louis Mink and Hayden White, that the past cannot be grasped as an external object, in part because the available evidence is always partial; that the multitude of past events has no intrinsic, coherent structure; and that historians cannot be truly impartial because they cannot avoid judgments of value in their selection and arrangement of the facts. For Beard history is an interpretation of the past, not a scientific re-creation, and the value of that interpretation may be measured by its usefulness to readers who are trying to create a more just and democratic society.

The Progressives dominated the conversation in American history from around the time of Robinson's "New History" to World War II, when the new "Consensus" school emerged and announced that, contrary to the Progressives' claims, conflict had been far less important in American history than the broad consensus of ideas and ideals within which those conflicts occurred and were contained. Books like Louis Hartz's *The Liberal Tradition in America* (1955) and Daniel Boorstin's 3-volume *The Americans* (1958–73) would emphasize the broad-based consensus rooted in the principles of the Declaration and Constitution, and supporting individualism, natural rights, private property, and a free market.

However, the "consensus" model grew increasingly unpersuasive during the socially turbulent and increasingly polarized 1960s, when neo-progressive historians once again began to emphasize conflict rather than consensus as typical of American history. Histories of women and minorities began to suggest the blind spots in the consensus school's approach, and "history from the bottom up" became a kind of rallying cry. Alongside this politically engaged history, however, there emerged something called cliometrics, or the New Economic history, which relied heavily on quantitative analysis and econometric models, as in Robert Fogel and Stanley Engerman's *Time on the Cross* (1974), which depicted American slavery as more efficient and profitable than most historians had believed. In the early years of the twenty-first century, American historiography remains the site of a vigorous conversation including neo-conservatives, their left-leaning opponents, quantitative historians, traditional narrative historians such as David McCullough, and those who have been called "postmodern" historians, such as Jill Lepore.[75] Some continue to endorse progressive versions of history, whether liberal, Marxist, or neo-conservative, but many remain skeptical of such models. No end of these contending, proliferating perspectives on history is in sight.

Yet despite this proliferation, or what Rawls calls the "fact of pluralism," there also exists within the discipline of history what Rawls calls an "overlapping consensus," a core of agreement on what it means to do history. Most contemporary historians would concede that their discipline lacks the conceptual rigor of the natural sciences, and that even the most rigorous application of method cannot yield complete objective knowledge of the past. Nevertheless, they remain devoted to the "facts," to archival research and primary sources, to methods for establishing the authenticity of documents or the reliability of witnesses, to considering both substantiating and countervailing evidence. They insist on accurate quotations and careful documentation. They believe in evidence. The "correspondence" between the past itself and what historians write about it will always be incomplete and perspectival, and history will never yield a final truth. Still, a good historian can provide her readers with truths about the past that are "authoritative" not in any absolute sense, but in what Ernst Breisach calls "a sufficiently proximate" or "optimal" sense.[76]

Breisach notes that historical truth is not simply a function of methodology, but also collegial critique. In other words, we may understand historical truth as an open-ended concept that is determined by the judgment of the professional community of historians and their shared criteria of plausibility. All historians begin their work on a subject by reading other historians on that subject, and their work is always in dialogue with other historians' work. Any good history is full of references to other histories, and to do history means in part to criticize, correct, and supplement the work of other historians. So history is always in flux, but disagreement is often more interesting than agreement, and like their colleagues in economics, political science, art history, or literary criticism, historians contend with different interpretations to which the evidence is open, and they join an unending conversation on the significance of that evidence.[77]

Aristotle, Walter Benjamin, and Genre Expectations

What, after all, do we mean when we claim to know, or to understand, history—even a small part of it? Do we mean that we know it in the sense that we *know* the quadratic formula, or the molecular structure of nylon? Or does knowing history have more in common with, say, knowing Keats's poems or *Moby-Dick*—the implication being that in history, as in literary studies, *knowing* does not mean the kind of right-or-wrong thinking characteristic of the sciences and mathematics. Obviously, we can know the date the tea was dumped into Boston Harbor, just as we can know the first sentence of *Moby-Dick* or the year in which it was first published—but to know *Moby-Dick* or to know the American Revolution in any serious sense is to move far beyond names and dates; it is to move into questions of human freedom and compulsion, power, desire, and morality, questions about the interplay of idea and contingency, intention and result.

Generally we bracket the truth-value of poetry, admitting that it renders emotion truthfully, or that it is true aesthetically. However, while we might nod our heads in assent to Keats's "Beauty is truth, truth beauty," we restrict our assent; confronted with today's newspaper, most of us would admit that it tells us the truth, and that the truth is often not beautiful. Even if the poet writes about "the real world," for example, Yeats's "Easter 1916," we tend to believe that the poem represents not so much the event of the rebellion as Yeats's private, artistic response to that event, whereas if we read an account of that revolt in an en-cyclopedia, we tend to believe we're getting the truth about the event, and not the writer's response to it.

Yet poems such as "Easter, 1916" or Milton's "On the Late Massacre in Piedmont" refer undeniably to extratextual history, just as historiography does, and both poem and historiography generate in the reader what Gadamer calls *Wahrheitsanspruch* (an expectation of truth). We expect poetic language to be more figurative than historiography, while we expect historiography to contain more explicit references to anterior discourse (source material). We expect that the "voice" in poetry may identify its location, attitude, feelings, and values; we are bothered if the "voice" in historiography does any of these things. We expect the poet to be eccentric, emotive, stylized—and if, like Williams in *Paterson*, he should insert a fragment from another text, we do not demand that he cite his source. We do expect the historian to cite his sources, and to write either a real-istic narrative or an expository argument.

We tend to be skeptical of poetry's claims about history. When Homer, for example, tells us that Apollo actually fought on the battlefield at Troy, we do not believe him, but that does not diminish our appreciation of the *Iliad*, and we smile knowingly when, in "Paul Revere's Ride," Longfellow depicts Revere riding successfully to Concord when in fact he was intercepted by a British pa-trol and forced to return to Lexington. On the other hand, if a historian tells us that God directed the outcome of the Battle of Chancellorsville, we are inclined to discredit his history. Northrop Frye writes, "The apparently unique privilege of ignoring facts has given the poet his traditional reputation as a licensed liar . . . the Norwegian word *digter* . . . is said to mean liar as well as poet. But, as Sir Philip Sidney remarked, 'the poet never affirmeth,' and therefore does not lie any more than he tells the truth."[78] What Frye calls a "privilege" masks the infe-rior status of poetry, just as the "privileges" of a lady mask the inferior status of a woman. When Keats places Cortez instead of Balboa "silent upon a peak in Darien," we accept the error because we tell ourselves that his poem is not about history. On the other hand, when Herodotus blends fact with rumor, tells us about ants the size of small foxes, and suggests that history can be divined via oracles, his title "Father of History" (bestowed by Cicero) is supplemented, in Plutarch's mean-spirited "On the Malignity of Herodotus," with the title "Father of Lies."

What we call the poet's license may consign his work to *muthos*, not *logos*. Here is Donald Davie on Ezra Pound's *Cantos*:

> Whatever more long-term effect Pound's disastrous career may have on Ameri-can and British poetry, it seems inevitable that it will rule out (has ruled out al-ready, for serious writers) any idea that poetry can or should operate in the di-mension of history, trying to make sense of the recorded past by redressing our historical perspectives. . . . History, from now on, may be transcended in poet-ry, or it may be evaded there; but poetry is not the place where it may be under-

stood.[79]

Davie is suspicious of Pound not simply because of his fascist sympathies but because poetry, unlike professional historiography, and especially in the aftermath of Romanticism, accepts the centrality of the author's subjective sensibility, which is fair enough, but *why* may history not be understood in poetry? We may grant that poets, like other writers, have often contributed to the misunderstanding of history, but why insist that history can never be understood in poetry? After all, historiography is often strongly colored by nationalist, sectarian, or ideological biases—one thinks of recent controversies over historians' accounts of the Armenian genocide, the Japanese occupation of China and Korea during World War II, the expulsion or voluntary emigration of Palestinians from their homes after the 1948 war, or the tempest surrounding the *Enola Gay* exhibit at the Smithsonian's Air and Space Museum. We may concede that poetry is particularly susceptible to subjective biases, or that the poet's subjectivity is unchecked by the disciplinary expectations of professional historiography, but that concession does not preclude poetry's serious treatment of history.

Yet to term any treatment of history "poetic" is to damn it with the faintest praise, and when Kenneth Burke used that adjective in his review of his friend William Carlos Williams's *In the American Grain*, Williams was peeved. On the other hand, the great Yale historian C. Vann Woodward once admitted that "our [historians'] kinship is actually much closer to novelists" than to political scientists or economists,[80] and if poetry did not tell the truth about the real world, we would be far less interested in reading it. In a speech given on May 9, 2001, in Jerusalem, in which she accepted the Jerusalem Prize for Literature, Susan Sontag said,

> The writer's first job is not to have opinions but to tell the truth . . . and refuse to be an accomplice of lies or misinformation. Literature is the expression of nuance and contrariness against the voices of simplification. The job of the writer is to help make us see the world as it is, which is to say, full of many different claims and parts and experiences. It is the job of the writer to depict the realities, the foul realities, the realities of rapture. It is the essence of the wisdom furnished by literature (the plurality of literary achievement) to help us to understand that, whatever is happening, something else is always going on.[81]

Telling the truth is complicated, and as Aristotle suggests, the poet and the historian go about that task in different ways. In his essay "The Story-Teller," Walter Benjamin suggests another way of thinking about the difference between poetry and history, which alters Aristotle's distinction:

> Every morning brings us the news of the globe, and yet we are poor in noteworthy stories. This is because no event any longer comes to us without already being shot through with explanation. In other words, by now almost nothing that happens benefits story-telling; almost everything benefits information. Actual-

ly, it is half the art of story-telling to keep the story free from explanation as one reproduces it. . . . The most extraordinary things, marvelous things, are related with the greatest accuracy, but the psychological connection of the events is not forced on the reader. It is left up to him to interpret things the way he understands them, and thus the narrative achieves an amplitude that information lacks.[82]

In Benjamin's sense, historical narrative is "informational," suffusing each event with explanation, looking backward toward its causes and antecedents, as well as forward toward its ramifications and effects. Historical narrative resists the aleatory and strives to be thorough enough to account for each turn of events as it occurs. Poetic narrative, on the other hand, is anti-informational precisely because it sometimes refuses to explain the connections between events, although it may offer partial or ironic explanations, or competing explanations, or explanations from some particular point of view. The "amplitude" of poetic narrative is a result of the wealth of possible interpretations adumbrated by its unfolding of events. If Shakespeare had *explained* the events of *Hamlet*, the drama would have failed. Conversely, if Thucydides had failed to offer an explanation of the Peloponnesian War, or if he had offered inconsistent or inadequate explanations, his history would have failed.

Van Wyck Brooks diagnoses the effects of an information-saturated sense of history in his 1918 essay "On Creating a Usable Past," in which he argues that "our professors continue to pour out a stream of historical works repeating the same points of view to such an astonishing degree that they have placed a sort of Talmudic seal upon the American tradition . . . [and] put a gloss upon it which renders it sterile for the living mind." But the past need not remain sealed or sterile, suggests Brooks; indeed, the most "vital" writers can discover or invent another, more "usable" past:

> The past that Carlyle put together for England would never have existed if Carlyle had been an American professor. And what about the past that Michelet, groping about in the depths of his own temperament, picked out for the France of his generation? We have had our historians, too, and they have held over the dark backward of time the divining-rods of their imagination and conjured out of it what they wanted and what their contemporaries wanted—Motley's great epic of the self-made man, for instance, which he called "The Rise of the Dutch Republic."[83]

Both poets and historians, if they find existing accounts of the past unpersuasive or unusable, can create others. And despite the genre distinctions formulated by Aristotle and others, a writer's poetic and historical imaginations, the activities of *poiein* and *historein*, are reciprocal rather than exclusive, as even Plato at times admits. In the *Symposium*, Diotima tells Socrates, "By its original meaning poetry meant simply creation, and creation, as you know, can take very various forms. Any action which is a cause of a thing emerging from non-existence into existence might be called poetry, and all those who are engaged in them poets."[84] The act of inquiry calls forth the reciprocal act of shaping or making the experience of that inquiry into a form, just as the impulse to create calls forth an impulse to inquire into the world and its history.

The poet is a curious being, at once trusted and distrusted. After hearing Odysseus's story of his wanderings, King Alkinoos says, "You speak with art, but your intent is honest. / The Argive troubles, and your own troubles, / You told as a poet would, a man who knows the world."[85] The "but" in the first line reflects the king's suspicion of the mimetic, transformative power of language, while the apposition of "poet" and "man who knows the world" suggests a healthy revision of Plato's suspicion of poets in the *Republic* and *Ion*. Poets know the world and its history, just as historians do. Their differences in method are well known, but their similarities are equally important, and the results of their inquiries can be both enlightening and provocative.

Notes

1. Qur'an, Surah 26: 224.
2. Plato, *Cratylus*, 407e, trans. Benjamin Jowett.
3. Aristotle, *Poetics*, in Richard McKeon, ed., *Introduction to Aristotle* (New York: Random House: Modern Library, 1947), 635–36.
4. Aristotle, *Poetics*, 657–58.
5. Herodotus, *The Histories*, trans. Walter Blanco (New York: Norton, 1992), 75.
6. Herodotus, *Histories*, 5.
7. Nancy Partner, "Historicity in an Age of Reality-Fictions," in *A New Philosophy of History*, eds. Frank Ankersmit and Hans Kellner (Chicago: University of Chicago Press, 1995), 27.
8. A. W. Gomme, *The Greek Attitude to Poetry and History* (Berkeley: University of California Press, 1954), 139.
9. Thucydides, *The Peloponnesian War*, trans. Rex Warner (Baltimore: Penguin Classics, 1954), 24. The professionalization of history in the nineteenth century served to formalize the distinction between serious history and other kinds of writing about the past. In his inaugural lecture as Regius Professor of History at Cambridge in 1902, J. B. Bury declared that "history is a science, no less and no more," and announced the severance of its "time-honored association with literature" (quoted in Fritz Stern, ed., *The Varieties of History*, 2nd ed. (New York: Random House, 1972), 210–11).
10. Aristotle, *Poetics*, 636.
11. Gomme, *Greek Attitude*, 76.
12. Quoted in Hazard Adams, ed., *Critical Theory Since Plato* (New York: Harcourt Brace, 1971), 162, 163.
13. Quoted in Adams, *Critical Theory*, 160.
14. Quoted in David Perkins, ed., *English Romantic Writers* (New York: Harcourt Brace, 1967), 1075.
15. Henry David Thoreau, *A Week on the Concord and Merrimack Rivers* (New York: Harper & Row, 1961), 272.

16. Norman Mailer, *The Armies of the Night* (New York: New American Library, 1968), 284.

17. Mailer, *Armies*, 292.

18. Cicero, *De Oratore* II. 62–64.

19. Quoted in Robert Holton, *Jarring Witnesses: Modern Fiction and the Representation of History* (New York: Harvester Wheatsheaf, 1994), 11.

20. Quoted in Beverley Southgate, *History Meets Fiction* (New York: Pearson, 2009), 29.

21. Quoted in Stern, *Varieties*, 96.

22. Robert Canary and Henry Kozicki, eds., *The Writing of History: Literary Form and Historical Understanding* (Madison: University of Wisconsin Press, 1978), 19.

23. G. W. F. Hegel, *Lectures on the Philosophy of World History*, trans. H. B. Nisbet (New York: Cambridge University Press, 1975), 135.

24. Ernst Breisach, *On the Future of History: The Postmodernist Challenge and Its Aftermath* (Chicago: University of Chicago Press, 2003), 77.

25. Hayden White, *The Content of the Form: Narrative Discourse and Historical Representation* (Baltimore: Johns Hopkins University Press, 1990), 24.

26. Friedrich Nietzsche, *On the Advantage and Disadvantage of History for Life*, trans. Peter Preuss (Indianapolis: Hackett, 1980), 35.

27. Hayden White, *Tropics of Discourse* (Baltimore: Johns Hopkins University Press, 1986), 3.

28. Henry Adams, *The Education of Henry Adams* (Boston: Houghton Mifflin, 1973), 382.

29. Jean-Paul Sartre, *Nausea*, trans. Lloyd Alexander (New York: New Directions, 1964), 13.

30. Lytton Strachey, *Eminent Victorians* (London: Chatto & Windus, 1928), vii.

31. Walter Kaufmann, ed., *The Portable Nietzsche* (New York: Penguin, 1977), 55.

32. Kaufmann, *Portable*, 458.

33. In, for example, *Local Knowledge: Further Essays in Interpretive Anthropology* (New York: Basic Books, 1983).

34. Hans-Georg Gadamer, *Truth and Method* (New York: Crossroad, 1982), 401, 405.

35. Gadamer, *Truth*, 174.

36. Jacques Derrida, *Of Grammatology*, trans. Gayatri Spivak (Baltimore, Johns Hopkins University Press, 1974), lxxxix.

37. Claude Levi-Strauss, *The Savage Mind* (Chicago: University of Chicago Press, 1966), 262.

38. Roland Barthes, "The Discourse of History," trans. Stephen Bann, *Comparative Criticism* 3 (1981): 9.

39. Barthes, "Discourse," 16.

40. Jacques Derrida *Writing and Difference*, trans. Alan Bass (Chicago: University of Chicago Press, 1978), 291.

41. Michel Foucault, *The Archeology of Knowledge*, trans. A. M. Sheridan Smith (New York: Harper & Row, 1972), 12.

42. "History and Narrative," in Canary and Kozicki, eds., *Writing*, 13.

43. Ankersmit and Kellner, *New Philosophy*, 1.

44. Hayden White, *Metahistory: The Historical Imagination in Nineteenth-Century*

Europe (Baltimore: Johns Hopkins University Press, 1973), x, xii.

45. Southgate, *History*, 32.

46. Hayden White, *Figural Realism: Studies in the Mimesis Effect* (Baltimore: Johns Hopkins University Press, 1999), 1, 2.

47. White, *Figural*, 28.

48. White, *Figural*, 51.

49. White, *Figural*, 7.

50. Carl Becker, "Detachment and the Writing of History," *Atlantic Monthly* 106 (Oct 1910): 526–28.

51. Michael Oakeshott, "The Activity of Being an Historian," in *Rationalism in Politics and Other Essays* (Indianapolis: Liberty Press, 1991), 182–83.

52. See Edward Linenthal and Tom Engelhardt, eds., *History Wars: The Enola Gay and Other Battles for the American Past* (New York: Henry Holt, 1996).

53. Joyce Appleby, Lynn Hunt, and Margaret Jacob, *Telling the Truth about History* (New York: Norton, 1994), 234, 235.

54. Appleby, Hunt, and Jacob, *Telling*, 11.

55. Quoted in Stern, *Varieties*, 201.

56. John Rawls, "The Idea of an Overlapping Consensus," 1987, in *The American Intellectual Tradition*, 6th ed., volume 2, ed. David Hollinger and Charles Capper, (New York: Oxford University Press, 2011), 548.

57. Quoted in Emery Neff, *The Poetry of History* (New York: Columbia University Press, 1947), 190.

58. Stern, *Varieties*, 318.

59. Arnaldo Momigliano, "The Introduction of History as an Academic Subject and Its Implications," in *The Golden and the Brazen World: Papers in Literature and History, 1650–1800*, ed. John M. Wallace (Berkeley: University of California Press, 1985), 203.

60. Quoted in Linda Orr, "The Revenge of Literature," in *Studies in Historical Change*, ed. Ralph Cohen (Charlottesville: University of Virginia Press, 1992), 100.

61. R. G. Collingwood, *The Idea of History* 1946 (New York: Oxford University Press, 1994), 282.

62. Collingwood, *Idea*, 244.

63. Karl Marx and Frederick Engels, *The German Ideology*, ed. C. J. Arthur (New York: International Publishers, 1970), 67.

64. Marx and Engels, *German*, 57, 62.

65. Stern, *Varieties*, 223.

66. Burrow, *History*, 417.

67. Quoted in Bremner, *Essays*, 130.

68. Quoted in Bremner, *Essays*, 131.

69. Henry Adams, "The Tendency of History," *Annual Report of the American Historical Association for the Year 1894* (Washington DC, 1895), 17–18.

70. Adams, "The Tendency of History," 19.

71. Quoted in Bremner, *Essays*, 129.

72. Jared Diamond, *Guns, Germs, and Steel: The Fates of Human Societies* (New York: Norton, 1998), 408.

73. Breisach, *Future*, 290.

74. Charles Beard, "That Noble Dream," *American Historical Review* 41 (October 1935): 74–87.

75. See, for example, Gordon Wood's review of Lepore's *In the Name of War* in *The New York Review of Books* (April 9, 1998), 41–45.

76. Breisach, *Future*, 116, 119–20.

77. For Kenneth Burke's famous "parlor image" of this conversation, see his *The Philosophy of Literary Form* (Berkeley: University of California Press, 1967), 110-11. See also David Hollinger, "T. S. Kuhn's Theory of Science and Its Implications for History," *American Historical Review* 78.2 (1973): 370–93, which remains among the most cogent and clearheaded discussions of historical knowledge and the work that historians do.

78. Northrop Frye, *Anatomy of Criticism* (Princeton: Princeton University Press, 1957), 75–76.

79. Donald Davie, *Ezra Pound: Poet as Sculptor* (New York: Oxford University Press, 1964), 244.

80. Quoted in Cushing Strout, *The Veracious Imagination* (Middletown, CT: Wesleyan University Press, 1981), 10.

81. Susan Sontag, "In Jerusalem," *The New York Review of Books* (June 21, 2011), 22.

82. Benjamin, "The Storyteller," in *Illuminations*, trans. Harry Zohn, ed. Hannah Arendt (New York: Schocken, 1969), 89.

83. Van Wyck Brooks, "On Creating a Usable Past," *Dial* 64 (April 11, 1918): 337, 339.

84. Plato, *The Symposium*, trans. Walter Hamilton (New York: Penguin, 1951), 85.

85. Homer, *Odyssey*, trans. Robert Fitzgerald (Garden City, NY: Doubleday Anchor, 1963), 197.

Chapter 2
Stephen Vincent Benét:
John Brown's Body and the Meaning of
the Civil War

Stephen Vincent Benét's *John Brown's Body* (1928) appears after Ezra Pound's "Hugh Selwyn Mauberley" (1920) and the early *Cantos*, T. S. Eliot's *The Waste Land* (1922), Wallace Stevens's *Harmonium* (1923), William Carlos Williams's *Spring and All* (1923), and Marianne Moore's *Observations* (1924), but Benét's poem belongs only marginally within this modernist tradition. Like his modernist contemporaries, Benét uses multiple and fragmented narrative perspectives, cutting abruptly from one storyline to another, and from fictional storyline to historiography, but each fictional narrative is clearly demarcated, and all of the storylines fit neatly into a single master narrative, the stability of which is never questioned. Benét's narrative experiments are more tepid or tentative than Dos Passos's or Faulkner's, and many of his meters and rhyme schemes are premodernist. In some ways, *John Brown's Body* is closer in spirit to the great narrative poems of the American nineteenth century, such as Longfellow's *New England Tragedies* or *Evangeline*, than to its modernist contemporaries.

In *John Brown's Body*, Benét recounts the history of the Civil War from Harper's Ferry to Appomattox, weaving several fictional storylines through accounts of the war's major battles: Fort Sumter, Bull Run, Shiloh, the Peninsula campaign, Antietam, Chancellorsville, Vicksburg, Gettysburg, and Sherman's March to the Sea. Although poor eyesight kept Benét out of active military service in World War I and he was deeply unhappy in the military academy in which his parents briefly enrolled him as a child, he spent most of his youth on the various military bases at which his father, a colonel, served. His grandfather had been a Brigadier General in the Army Ordnance Corps, and Benét absorbed and retained his family's genial patriotism throughout his adult life. The poem's two main fictional characters—Jack Ellyat of Connecticut and Clay Wingate of Georgia—serve in their respective armies, and each is admirable and sympathetic; indeed, although Ellyat's character is more fully developed, they might be taken as mirror images of each other. Other fictional characters represent particular geographic regions or social classes, and function as types rather than fully realized characters. Trying to be fair to the perspectives of both North and South, Benét presents one fictional slave who is treated poorly and flees to the North, and another who is treated well and remains loyal to his masters throughout the war. Essentially Benét sees the meaning of the war as Lincoln saw it: the war results in "a new birth of freedom," a redeemed nation, a re-unified people. From our perspective in the twenty-first century, it is easy to forget how important such an attitude toward the War was, even in 1928. The divisiveness spawned by the War was bitter, deeply recriminatory, and enduring. In order to read the War as producing the kind of reconciliation he proposes, however, Benét emphasizes certain romantic, even sentimental elements and marginalizes certain troubling questions, and these aspects of his poem lend a peculiar shape to its "containing" of the war's history.

In 1926, Benét (1898–1943), a Yale graduate who had also studied at the Sorbonne, won a Guggenheim grant—the first ever awarded for poetry—to research and write a long poem on the American Civil War. He moved to Paris, where the cost of living was more manageable, and wrote *John Brown's Body*, a poem of over three hundred pages and almost 15,000 lines, in less than two years. Benét was unsure of its quality; after 135 manuscript pages, he wrote to his brother, "Sometimes I think it will be the most colossal flop since Barlow's *Columbiad*."[1] But many of the book's first readers felt otherwise. The Book of the Month Club selection for August 1928, *John Brown's Body* proved incredibly popular. It was Doubleday's biggest moneymaker between 1924 and 1934, selling over 130,000 copies in its first two years, and well over 200,000 copies to date,[2] numbers that Williams, Stevens, Eliot, Pound, and even Robert Frost could only envy. In 1929 the book was awarded the Pulitzer Prize for Poetry, and at that time Benét was probably the most widely read poet in the United States. Writing at the time of Benét's death in 1943, Henry Seidel Canby claimed, "It seems probable that no writer of poetry in English has ever been read by so many in his lifetime—not even Longfellow."[3] Sinclair Lewis mentioned *John Brown's Body* in his 1930 Nobel Prize acceptance speech as evidence of an American literary renaissance, and Allen Tate called it "the most ambitious poem ever undertaken by an American on an American theme." As late as 1962, Parry Stroud called the poem "decisively the closest approach to Homer and Vergil that an American poet had ever made."[4]

To his credit, Benét was more modest than some of his critics. "A poet of greater faculties," he wrote to his publisher, John Farrar, "would have avoided my failures in it and my superficialities—and there are many of both."[5] And later: "If the poem is to stand eventually, in any sort of way, it will do so because of a few passages in each Book and the mass-effect of the whole. The faults are many and glaring. But I could do no better, given such brains as I had."[6] Benét's judgment has proven more accurate than Parry Stroud's: although his poem has remained in print, it is rarely assigned in high school or college classes, and Benét is difficult to find in either American literature anthologies or the MLA bibliography.

The poem is most effective in its cataloguing of vivid emotional images: Ulysses Grant seeing that the Confederates have lit bonfires to celebrate the birth of George Pickett's son, and ordering his Union troops to do the same, then sending the baby a silver service several days before attacking the Confederate position; the secessionist Edmund Ruffin, who fired the first gun against Fort Sumter, walking in his garden after hearing the news of Lee's surrender, draping a Confederate flag around his shoulders, and shooting himself in the heart; Lincoln visiting Pickett's widow in Richmond, just before the surrender at Appomattox; a fictional Confederate cavalryman, surrounded and outgunned by Union soldiers, late in the course of the war, suddenly standing up from behind his cover and

> Walking out like a duelist
> With his torn coat buttoned up at the throat
> As if it were still the broadcloth coat
> Duellists button to show no fleck
> Of telltale white at the wrists or neck.
> He stepped from his cover and dropped his hat.
> "Yanks, come get it!" he said and spat
> While his pistols cracked with a single crack,
> "Here we go on the red dog's back!
> High, low, jack and the goddam game."
> And then the answering volley came.[7]

In early reviews, both Allen Tate, who refers to its "motion picture flashes," and Harriet Monroe, who calls the poem "a kind of cinema epic,"[8] praise Benét's powerful juxtaposition of images. The content of those images is as important as their cinematic form: each of them reflects an established moral order that transcends the war itself and is expressed by both Northerners and Southerners. Of course a gentleman would send a gift to another gentleman's newborn son, just as he would express in person his condolences to a widow. Ruffin's suicide carries about it the nobility of the Roman or the Japanese, while the cavalryman's suicidal emergence reflects the kind of reckless physical courage and honorable death evident in those men who, when given the chance, refused to abandon the Alamo. In some ways this emphasis on honorable, heroic conduct amid the horrors of civil war is similar to what Michael Shaara achieves in his Civil War novel, *The Killer Angels*, although Benét comes much closer to melodrama than does Shaara.

Benét is a good storyteller, especially in terms of his ability to tell the tale of a complicated war in a coherent and engaging manner—the major battles, the broad political issues involved, character sketches of the chief figures on both sides (similar to John Dos Passos's short biographies in the *U.S.A.* trilogy). *John Brown's Body* can be absorbing reading, almost novel-like in its ability to pull the reader along. Benét read voluminously as he worked on the poem—

regimental histories, diaries, memoirs, autobiographies—and complained that he wanted still more to read. Both Samuel Eliot Morison, who wrote to Benét for permission to quote from *John Brown's Body* in his *The Growth of the American Republic*, and Lee's biographer Douglas Southall Freeman praised the poem for its historical accuracy.[9] The historian Bruce Catton has called it the single best book, in some respects, ever written on the Civil War,[10] a judgment shared by Henry Steele Commager.[11]

Benét, however, insists he is not a historian; in a note prefaced to the book, he writes, "this is a poem, not a history," explaining the absence of notes and bibliography. However, he protests too much, for he then goes on to cite his chief sources and to explain his approach to history: "In dealing with known events I have tried to cleave to historical fact where such fact was ascertainable. On the other hand, for certain thoughts and feelings attributed to historical characters, and for the interpretation of those characters in the poem, I alone must be held responsible."[12] For Benét, history seems to be essentially a matter of fact, while interpretation belongs to speculation or poetry. In a *Saturday Review* essay of 1932, he complains,

> A good many of our recent biographies—or biografictions—whatever you choose to call them, have [been] rather like Mark Twain's reconstruction of the dinosaur, "three bones and a dozen barrels of plaster." The author might not always take the trouble to find out just what his subject did and when he did it—for that often requires a tiresome amount of research. But, as regards what the subject thought and felt, there the author was not merely all-wise but all-seeing.[13]

The sharp distinction between "what his subject did and when he did it" and "what his subject thought and felt," and Benét's preference for the former, suggests that history ought to be comprised primarily of ascertainable fact, and that interpretation ought to be minimal. At another point Benét writes, only half in jest, "I wish prominent historians wouldn't contradict each other as much as they do. How's a poor poet to know which is right."[14] If they'd take the time to do the "tiresome research" and resist the temptation to speculative interpretation, Benét implies, the contradictions might disappear.

A number of Benét's early reviewers faulted him on this point; Max Eastman, for example, asserted that the poem "as a whole . . . lacks idea. It lacks attitude. It lacks the unity that is imparted by an intention,"[15] while Frank Jones wrote that Benét "can tell a first-rate story when not wrestling with attitudes towards history."[16] Newton Arvin suggested that the book lacked "the higher virtues . . . partly because it is not organized and controlled, as such a [grand historical poem] would be, by a clear and sweeping philosophic vision."[17] But "attitude" and "philosophic vision," for Benét, are the stuff of Mark Twain's "plaster," as well as the stuff of the partisan, blame-assigning historiography against which he was reacting.

John Griffith places Benét's depiction of the war in the context of what he calls the conflict between American "scientific" historians and their rivals, the relativists. For Griffith the scientific historians, exemplified by Herbert Baxter Adams, who founded the American Historical Association in 1884, work in the Rankean positivist tradition, while the relativists, exemplified by Frederick Jackson Turner, Charles Beard, and Carl Becker, are more epistemologically sophisticated. Benét, suggests Griffith,[18] follows the epistemological assumptions of the scientific historians. Griffith is right as far as he goes, but for Benét, epistemology is not the central issue, i.e., whether our "knowledge" of the War can best be described as positivist or relativist is not the central issue. The central issue concerns the war's meaning, and this is also the issue of central concern to Civil War historians between 1865 and the time that Benét wrote *John Brown's Body*.

The earliest historians of the War were highly partisan and especially interested in assigning responsibility for the War's cause to either the North or the South. The North's partisans included such influential historians as George Bancroft and Hermann Von Holst, who depicted the War as a moral struggle between good and evil (freedom and slavery), and John Draper, who interpreted the War as the result of a conspiracy on the part of a small group of Southern oligarchs desperate to cling to power and wealth. The South's partisans, such as Alexander Stephens, Albert Bledsoe, and Bernard Sage, insisted that because the states were sovereign, secession was a constitutional right, and the Union's invasion of the Confederacy had been wholly unjustified. For roughly twenty years after 1865, historians tended to assign all of the virtue to one side and all of the vice to the other, and to place responsibility for the war entirely on one side or the other.

This began to change with historians like James Schouler and John Burgess, who despite their Unionist sympathies substituted the term "Civil War" for "War of the Rebellion," dismissed the rhetoric of "treason" and "conspiracy," and expressed admiration for individual Confederates such as Robert E. Lee. James Ford Rhodes produced the most influential of these balanced, "neither side was fully right or wrong" approaches; although Ford was clear on the immorality of slavery, he argued against most of the work of Reconstruction, including suffrage for African Americans. Indeed, one might argue that only the dismantling of Reconstruction in the late nineteenth century and the North's acquiescing to white Southerners' disfranchisement and suppression of African Americans enabled white Americans to reconcile and embrace a new American nationalism. Northern historians played significant roles in validating the white racism that underlay reconciliation: William Dunning, who taught at Columbia University and served as President of the AHA in 1913, was plainly racist and deeply critical of Reconstruction in his *Reconstruction, Political and Economic, 1865–1877* (1907). Dunning's student Ulrich Phillips, who taught at Michigan in the 1920s and would go on to teach at Benét's alma mater, Yale, was similarly critical of Reconstruction and, in his influential *American Negro Slavery*

(1918), deeply sympathetic toward Southern plantation owners. Around the turn of the century, reunions of Blue and Gray veterans became popular, with each side extolling the courage of the other and ignoring African Americans and the question of why the war was fought. Reconciliation was further bolstered by historians like Frederick Jackson Turner, Frederic Paxson, and John McMaster, who argued that large, impersonal forces such as physiography, economics, and societal structures and values, rather than the decisions of particular human beings, had led to the War. At the time Benét wrote *John Brown's Body*, in other words, the dominant mood among American historians and the American public (or at least the white American public) was that we ought to see the War as Lincoln saw it, "with malice toward none," as something for which both sides bore some responsibility, but more importantly as the result of large, impersonal, irrepressible forces (God, for Lincoln in his Second Inaugural, or economics, social structures, or physiographic, sectional conflicts for other historians). And nobody was especially interested in thinking about black Americans, who were no longer slaves but were far from full equality. Benét's depiction of the War in *John Brown's Body* fits securely within this tradition.[19]

Benét imagines history as essentially a stable, linear narrative whose objective meaning is accessible to the patient inquirer. That meaning is a function of accuracy, massive detail—what Ezra Pound called "the method of multitudinous detail," in contrast to his own "method of Luminous Detail"[20]—and a variety of points of view subsumed within a coherent narrative. Benét works hard to tell a story that both North and South can agree is true; to be objective, for Benét, is to be non-partisan, and he treats both Northern and Southern historical characters with respect, depicting heroic behavior motivated by sincere ideals on both sides of the conflict. His fictional storylines are sentimental and sometimes simply unbelievable, and we might wonder why Benét, with his insistence on the supremacy of the fact, would include them. The answer lies in his inability to get the historical facts by themselves to generate the kind of meaning he wants to impart to the war. The fictional storylines tell accessible, romantic tales that end happily, tales in which suffering and destruction become redemptive and purposeful. In other words, Benét can make the War meaningful in his fictional storylines in a way that he cannot in the historiographic parts of the poem. Benét's scrupulous adherence to the particular truths of the War prevents him from twisting history to suit his thematic goals, and so he relies on fictional narratives. But the war itself, in all its complications and refusal to conform to neat or simple meanings, keeps getting in his way.

Benét's difficulty with the War's meaning becomes clear early in the book when he considers the question of the War's cause. He points to the usual factors, especially the slavery question—the poem's preface describes a Bible-quoting New England sea captain carrying a cargo of slaves from Africa to North America (emphasizing that the South was not solely responsible for the institution of slavery), and book one describes John Brown's raid on Harper's Ferry. But rather than represent the War as the result of political, economic, and moral decisions made by particular human beings, Benét depicts the war as the inevitable consequence of large forces beyond human comprehension, thereby mystifying the War's causes. Early in the poem, both Jack Ellyat, the main Northern fictional character, and Clay Wingate, the main Southern fictional character, experience supernatural premonitions of an imminent upheaval, so the war is presented as something like an act of God, the product of fate or destiny rather than human decisions. In this way, Benét aligns himself with historians like Turner and Paxson, who assign the War's causes to large, impersonal forces rather than to individuals on one side or the other. Such impersonal causes may be non-partisan, but they raise other difficulties.

Benét's representation of the war as the inevitable shedding of blood necessary for redeeming the nation from the sin of slavery is similar to the rhetoric of John Brown, whose favorite Bible passage was Hebrews 9:22, "Without shedding of blood is no remission [of sin]," and whose final handwritten note stated plainly: "The crimes of this guilty, land: will never be purged away; but with Blood."[21] It is also similar to Lincoln's language in the Second Inaugural: "If God wills that it [the War] continue, until all the wealth piled by the bond-man's two hundred and fifty years of unrequited toil shall be sunk, and until every drop of blood drawn with the lash, shall be paid by another drawn with the sword, as was said three thousand years ago, so still it must be said 'the judgments of the Lord, are true and righteous altogether.'"[22] For Lincoln, the War is mandated by God as punishment for America's sin: "American slavery is one of those offences which, . . . having continued through His appointed time, He now wills to remove, and . . . He gives to both North and South, this terrible war, as the woe due to those by whom the offence came."[23] Such rhetoric, though it places responsibility for the sin on both North and South and is thus non-partisan, also serves to remove the War's justification and its consequences from human responsibility. Lincoln had no choice, he claims, but to go to war and to continue the war—God has given this war to the United States as a just punishment for its sins, and God determines its duration and the suffering it causes. Benét picks up on Lincoln's mystification because it furthers his thematic goal (similar to Lincoln's political goal) of a non-partisan depiction of the war's causes and a redemptive depiction of its results. Some readers might argue, however, that the assumption that the War redeems the sin is facile, particularly in the light of segregation, lynchings, and the bitter history of racist violence and persecution in the post-1865 United States.

It is clear, however, that Lincoln did not go to war against the Confederacy in order to abolish slavery, but rather to preserve the Union, and the Emancipation Proclamation, as Garry Wills persuasively argues in *Lincoln at Gettysburg*, is a military rather than a political or moral document, i.e., abolition in the rebelling states is necessary and justifiable primarily in order to put down the insurrection and preserve the Union. John Brown sides with abolitionists like William Lloyd Garrison or Wendell Phillips who, writes Benét, "would have broken the Union as blithely as Yancey[24] / for his own side of abolition."[25] Lincoln, on the other hand, although he believes "the last slave should be forever free," also says, ". . . But I put / The Union, first and last, before the slave. / . . . [and] should such freedom mean / The wreckage of the Union that I serve / I would not free a slave."[26] For Benét, too, the preservation of the Union takes priority over the abolition of slavery as the ultimate purpose for which the War is fought. But why is the preservation of the Union so important? The poem offers no explicit answer, and elsewhere Benét offers only a vague notion of manifest destiny: "My sense of the union," writes Benét, "is of two majestic and continuing phases, the preservation of the Union and the continual restless movement of its people."[27] The Civil War is essential to the fulfillment of that second phase, westward expansion, which is the subject of Benét's unfinished long poem *Western Star*, the first volume of which won him a posthumous Pulitzer Prize in 1944. But Benét never explains why the preservation of the Union and its overspreading the continent is necessary, or good, or worth more than 600,000 deaths. For some of his readers, this may be a claim that needs no justification, a self-evident truth; for others, however, this kind of unexamined acceptance of dogmatic assertions diminishes the power of Benét's engagement with history.

If Benét is unclear on the War's causes, or more importantly its justification, he is able with his fictional storylines to tell coherent, meaningful tales associated with the War. His fictional characters, however, tend to be flat; they are closer to stereotypes than to individuals (especially his minor characters), and in some of them his Unionist bias seeps out. The Georgian Clay Wingate, for example, loves Sally Dupré, but the rigid class structure of the South drives him instead into the arms of the beautiful but vain and shallow Lucy Weatherby, a crudely stereotypical Southern belle. The War is thus a good thing because it destroys the class system of the Old South, enabling the love of Clay and Sally to flower. Like the un-American Tories after the Revolutionary War, Lucy goes off to Canada, suggesting that the antebellum South was un-American in its Anglophilic, aristocratic pretensions. Jack Ellyat of Connecticut, who unrealistically participates in every major battle of the war, from Bull Run to Shiloh to Gettysburg, and is even incarcerated in the notorious Andersonville POW camp, falls in love with and impregnates Melora Vilas in Tennessee. After the war's end Melora, like Longfellow's Evangeline, travels the country in search of Ellyat, whom she finally finds and marries. Luke Breckinridge is a Southern Appalachian backwoodsman so stereotypically ignorant that he believes—literally, not figuratively—that the Yankees are the Redcoats, and the Civil War a reprise of the Revolutionary War. Cudjo, the slave who remains loyal to the Wingates even after Wingate Hall is burned by Sherman's troops, is counterbalanced by Spade, the runaway slave who makes the difficult journey north and eventually crosses the Potomac. He encounters racist taunts and exploitation even in the North, but eventually is hired by the Pennsylvanian Jake Diefer, who has lost an arm in the war and can no longer manage his farm by himself. With that image of racial harmony, Benét evades the failure of Reconstruction and the very painful history of African Americans between 1865 and the poem's publication in

1928, as well as the question of the depth of the nation's redemption from the sin of race-based slavery. The fictional happy endings—Melora re-united with Ellyat, Sally Dupré winning Wingate from Lucy, Spade working with Jake Diefer in an idyll of interracial harmony, Luke Breckinridge going home with the chambermaid Sophy—do for Benét what history alone cannot: they justify the suffering wrought by the war, and turn the War into a Romantic tale of redemption. When Benét turns to history itself for such justification, however, he cannot find it because, to his credit, he is scrupulously faithful to the historical record in all its tangled complexity.

Benét is in control of his material and its meanings, either fictional or historical, when he presents vignettes or images calculated to evoke a particular emotional response. Indeed, his historical vignettes are effective because they are not reduced to the melodrama of the fictional storylines. When Benét moves away from romance and emotion, however, he sometimes loses control of his material and its meanings. This is most clear in his treatment of the abolitionist John Brown, whose presence hovers over the entire poem. Readers have disagreed over the significance of Brown in the poem. John McWilliams claims that Abraham Lincoln, and not "the murderous John Brown," is the hero of the poem,[28] while Henry Seidel Canby asserts that Brown, not Lincoln, is the poem's protagonist.[29] Parry Stroud writes, "The gigantic myth of the corporeal death and spiritual rebirth of Brown . . . becomes an American version of the ancient Egyptian myth of Osiris and the Greek myth of Dionysus,"[30] the kind of wildly exaggerated claim we might expect from a critic who is such a careless reader that he mistakenly identifies Spade as a Wingate slave.[31] But if Brown is not Osiris or Dionysus, the terms "protagonist" and "hero" are also misleading. What are we to make of Benét's treatment of John Brown? Allen Tate writes, "The symbol of John Brown becomes an incentive to some misty writing, and instead of sustaining the poem it evaporates in mixed rhetoric. Mr. Benét sees that the meaning of the war is related to the meaning of Brown; yet what is the meaning of Brown?"[32] Because Benét never clearly answers that question, argues Tate, the War itself "has no meaning" in the poem. This is fair up to a point: Benét never reduces Brown or the War to one single meaning, which is what Tate seems to want; instead, each is a signifier of multiple and sometimes contradictory meanings.

Benét treats Brown ironically as well as romantically, but his irony is inconsistent. In the Prelude, the words of a Negro spiritual ask for a prophet or angel to free the slaves,[33] and Brown sees himself as an instrument of God: he calls himself "Jehovah's rod" and refers to himself and his followers metonymically as "pikes and guns / In God's advancing war."[34] Recalling his murder of five unarmed pro-slavery settlers at Pottawatomie, Kansas, Brown states, "Lord God, it was a work of Thine, / And how might I refrain?"[35] Although this language is disturbingly similar to Lincoln's in the Second Inaugural, and although Benét admires Brown's idealism, he is uncomfortable with Brown's violence and fanaticism, and he notes the irony that the first man killed by Brown's Harper's

Ferry raiders was the black baggagemaster, Shepherd Heyward. He notes also Brown's curious refusal, after seizing the armory's weapons, to retreat before the Virginia militia and federal troops could seize the Potomac bridge and then surround him. Benét can be harsh in his depiction of Brown:

> He was a stone,
> A stone eroded to a cutting edge
> By obstinacy, failure and cold prayers.
> Discredited farmer, dubiously involved
> In lawsuit after lawsuit, Shubel Morgan [an alias Brown used]
> Fantastic bandit of the Kansas border,
> Red-handed murderer at Pottawattomie,
> Cloudy apostle, whooped along to death
> By those who do no violence themselves
> But only buy the guns to have it done,
> Sincere of course, as all fanatics are,
> And with a certain minor-prophet air,
> That fooled the world to thinking him half-great
> When all he did consistently was fail.[36]

But then Benét's speaker corrects himself, returning to the image of John Brown as a "stone eroded to a cutting edge," and asserting that despite his unreasoning and destructive temperament, Brown was also "Heroic and devoted" in a stone-like manner, and that he was a passive instrument of a large historical force beyond his comprehension: "Call it the *mores*, call it God or Fate, / Call it Mansoul or economic law, / That force exists and moves. And when it moves / It will employ a hard and actual stone."[37] These lines echo the supernatural premonitions that Wingate and Ellyat experience early in the book, as well as Lincoln's Second Inaugural, in their suggestion that the war is the product of something like fate or destiny rather than human decisions. However, they also seem to suggest that what we call "That force" is unimportant, and that suggestion is unpersuasive. If we call it "God," then history unfolds as Lincoln suggests in the Second Inaugural, or as Augustine suggests in *City of God*; if we call it "economic law," then history unfolds as Marx suggests it does, or Charles Beard. The difference is hardly insignificant, particularly with regard to the meaning of the Civil War. Yet Benét evades the question, largely, I think, because such mystification of John Brown and the war's origins makes it easier to be nonpartisan (neither side is finally responsible for the war; destiny is responsible, and thus the war is neither good nor bad, but rather something simply to be endured) and to effect the redemptive reconciliation between North and South that is, for Benét, the war's signal achievement.

In his failure and execution, John Brown becomes the catalyst that ignites the War, a "swift fire whose sparks fell like live coals / On every State in the Union."[38] Benét's dominant tone toward Brown, however, remains ironic, as in this description of contemporary accounts of the days before his execution:

The North that had already now begun
To mold his body into crucified Christ's,
Hung fables about those hours—saw him move
Symbolically, to kiss a negro child,
Do this and that, say things he never said,
To swell the sparse, hard outlines of the event
With sentimental omen.
                                        It was not so.[39]

Was Brown successful? Not at this point, according to the poem's narrator: "The slaves have forgotten his eyes. / . . . / Cotton will grow next year, in spite of the skull. / Slaves will be slaves next year, in spite of the bones. / Nothing is changed, John Brown, nothing is changed." But Brown's ghost replies, "There is a song in my bones / . . . / And God blows through them with a hollow sound," and the poem's narrator admits, "I hear it."[40] That song, of course, faint as it is at first, will become "John Brown's Body," the tune of which will later be used for "The Battle Hymn of the Republic." And early in book two, which opens with the fall of Fort Sumter, Benét recalls Brown: "The stone falls in the pool, the ripples spread."[41]

At this point in the poem, John Brown disappears, and the War takes center stage. He re-appears in 1862, at the end of Book Four, nearly three years after his execution, with the war in stalemate. The poem's narrator reports that certain Union soldiers claim to have seen him walking "in front of the armies."

A dead man saw him striding at Seven Pines,
The bullets whistling through him like a torn flag,
A madman saw him whetting a sword on a Bible,
A cloud above Malvern Hill.[42]

"But these are all lies," insists the narrator. Brown is dead, his goals unrealized. "The South goes ever forward, the slave is not free, / The great stone gate of the Union crumbles and totters, / The cotton-blossoms are pushing the blocks apart."[43] Nonetheless, the narrator affirms for Brown a crucial role in the war, invigorating Union morale and providing a sanctifying justification of the war effort: "His song is alive and throbs in the tramp of the columns."[44]

Yet Benét's discomfort with Brown persists. He is at pains to distinguish the man, who was a violent fanatic willing to engage in terrorism, from the symbol. "But his song and he are two,"[45] Benét insists, and addressing the man, he says, "You did not fight for the union or wish it well, / You fought for the single dream of a man unchained." Benét aligns Brown with those radical abolitionists who would sooner dissolve the union than countenance slavery, whereas for Benét, the preservation of the union is the primary justification of the war. For Benét abolition, which has led to the South's secession, becomes at the nadir of Union morale the means to the end of the Union's preservation. Addressing

Brown directly, Benét says, "You fought for a people you did not comprehend, / For a symbol chained by a symbol in your own mind, / But, unless you arise, that people will not be free."[46] So the man—failure, murderer, and fanatic—is transformed into and invoked as a symbol:

> Your song goes on, but the slave is still a slave,
> And all Egypt's land rides Northward while you moulder in the grave!
> Rise up, John Brown,
> (A-mouldering in the grave.)
> Go down, John Brown,
> (Against all Egypt's land)
> Go down, John Brown,
> Go down, John Brown,
> Go down, John Brown, and set that people free![47]

Casting black slaves in the role of the captive Israelites, the American South as Egypt, and John Brown as the people's Great Deliverer, Moses, is an analogy that breaks down in several key respects. God spoke with Moses directly, while Brown's claim that he acted under divine guidance is at best problematic. Moses was an Israelite, and his people's acknowledged leader, whereas Brown was not black, and far from being black Americans' acknowledged leader, his followers in the raid on Harper's Ferry included seventeen whites and only five blacks; Frederick Douglass, among others, had refused to join him. When Brown sent some of his men to the plantation of George Washington's grandson Louis, where they captured Washington and seized a sword that had belonged to the first president, the plantation's slaves did not rush to join their liberator, as Brown had assumed they would. Finally, the Israelites eventually reached the Promised Land; whether American blacks have done the same, despite Benét's sunny depiction of Spade on Diefer's farm, is a far from settled question. Benét's attempt to separate, via irony, the man from the symbol remains problematic; Brown's moral intensity cannot be separated from his violence and fanaticism.

Brown indirectly accomplishes his goal: the thirteenth amendment finally abolishes slavery. But the means to that end—the Civil War—bring about much more than abolition and the preservation of the Union. Does the War effect the "new birth of freedom" that Lincoln prophesies at Gettysburg? Does it establish a nation committed to the moral ideals articulated by Jefferson in the Declaration of Independence? Having purged the nation of its sin (slavery), does it re-establish a covenantal relationship with God? Benét makes no such claims. In fact, on the consequences of the War he is in some ways remarkably close to Edmund Wilson, who describes

> the whole turbid blatant period that followed the Civil War—with its miseries of an industrial life that was reducing white factory workers to the slavery which George Fitzhugh had predicted, with its millionaires as arrogant and bru-

tal as any Carolina planters, with the violent clashes between them as bloody as Nat Turner's rebellion or John Brown's raid upon Kansas, with its wars in Cuba and Europe that were our next uncontrollable moves after the war by which we had wrested California from the Mexicans and the war by which we had compelled the South to submit to the Washington government.[48]

Similarly, Robert Penn Warren writes that the War's consequences include "not only the Union sanctified by blood, but also Gould and Cook and Brady and the Crédit Mobilier and the Homestead blood and the Haymarket riot. . . . the uncoiling powers of technology and finance capitalism, the new world of Big Organization."[49] At the end of his poem, Benét makes remarkably similar points about what the war destroys, in addition to the institution of slavery and the agrarian values of the Old South, and what it brings about. Focusing on the irony inherent in the kind of nation the Civil War produced, Benét reminds us that Brown had been a shepherd and a farmer, not at home in towns or cities, and was a man more interested in the things of the spirit than in material prosperity. And yet ironically,

> Out of his body grows revolving steel,
> Out of his body grows the spinning wheel
> Made up of wheels, the new, mechanic birth,
> No longer bound by toil
> To the unsparing soil
> Or the old furrow-line,
> The great, metallic beast
> Expanding West and East,
> His heart a spinning coil,
> His juices burning oil,
> His body serpentine.
> Out of John Brown's strong sinews the tall skyscrapers grow,
> Out of his heart the chanting buildings rise,
> Rivet and girder, motor and dynamo,
> Pillar of smoke by day and fire by night,
> The steel-faced cities reaching at the skies,
> The whole enormous and rotating cage
> Hung with hard jewels of electric light,
> Smoky with sorrow, black with splendor, dyed
> Whiter than damask for a crystal bride
> With metal suns, the engine-handed Age,
> The genie we have raised to rule the earth,
> Obsequious to our will
> But servant-master still,
> The tireless serf already half a god—[50]

Benét sees the kind of society, the kind of nation, the Civil War engendered, but he refuses, finally, to judge or to evaluate those consequences. In "Ars poetica," Archibald MacLeish writes, "A poem should not mean / But be," summarizing what the New Critics called "the heresy of paraphrase," according to which a poem's "meaning" depends entirely on its particular combination of formal literary elements. Any attempt to paraphrase or interpret the poem's meaning involves an inevitable reduction of that combination of formal elements and a distortion of the poem's meaning, which exists only as the complete poem itself. Benét treats history as the New Critics treat poetry, and the "heresy of paraphrase" becomes for him the heresy of historical interpretation or judgment. In a sense Benèt falls into the kind of naïve realism that calls for history to give us "just the facts," and assumes that a non-partisan presentation will allow the facts to speak for themselves, and to speak the same thing to any fair-minded listener. In the poem's final lines, he warns his readers about "prophets," partisan historians who look at what America has become and either "Bawl out their strange despair / Or fall in worship there." Cautioning his reader against either approach, he continues, in the poem's final four lines:

> If you at last must have a word to say,
> Say neither, in their [the prophets who either "bawl" or "worship"] way,
> "It is a deadly magic and accursed,"
> Nor "It is blest," but only "It is here."[51]

For Benét, in interpreting the history of the Civil War and its consequences, our choices are limited to (1) the partisan reductivism of cursing or blessing, or (2) silent acceptance. He chooses the latter, and he advises his reader to do so as well. But this false choice is a version of the either-or fallacy: after all, we can imagine interpretations of the Civil War that are neither curse, blessing, nor laconic acceptance. In adopting the posture of the moderate anti-extremist, the non-partisan who simply and objectively recounts what happened, making what he takes to be the war's significance clearer and more accessible in the themes of his fictional storylines, Benét presents a meaningful tale of suffering, sacrifice, heroism, redemption, and reconciliation. But that meaningful tale pushes hard, intractable questions about the War to the margins, where they are "contained" beneath the inert observation "It is here." Benét wants the historical meaning of the War to align with the meaning of his fictional storylines, and at some level he believes that it does. Unlike the other poets considered in this book, Benét is not interested in problematizing what we might call mainstream or established understandings of history. Neither a revisionist nor a skeptic, Benét stands in the political mainstream; he is of the party of Lincoln, and *John Brown's Body* effectively dramatizes Lincoln's conception of the war. One may take issue with Lincoln's conception of the war, as Warren and Wilson have done, but Lincoln's conception, after all, has become the nation's conception. Most Americans want to believe what Lincoln believed about the War; the Second Inaugural is among the nation's most revered speeches, and Benét reiterates its claims.

Benét is caught between his thematic goal—to depict the war as effecting a tragic yet redemptive reconciliation of North and South that enables the reborn nation to fulfill its destiny—and his adherence to an historical record that fails in places to align with that goal. He cannot deny what Wilson and Warren observe about the War's effects, and he is honest enough to include similar observations in his poem, yet he cannot bring himself to concede that such observations, at least implicitly, undermine the theme of his fictional storylines. The War and its hugely complicated history cannot be reduced to the thematic meaning that Benét wants to give it, and although at one level Benét resists this truth, at another level his poem embodies it. Allen Tate has been this poem's most astute critic, but when he identifies Benét's failure to assign a clear "meaning" to John Brown and the War as a weakness, he may be wrong: the unresolved tensions in Benét's depiction of Brown mirror the tensions between fictional theme and historical record, between Lincoln's idealism and Wilson's dour realism, and those tensions save the poem from Benét's apparent intention; indeed, they are what give the poem its contemporary interest.

Notes

1. Quoted in Charles A. Fenton, *Stephen Vincent Benét: The Life and Times of an American Man of Letters* (New Haven: Yale University Press, 1958), 192.

2. Fenton, *Benét*, 219.

3. Henry Seidel Canby, "Stephen Vincent Benét," *Saturday Review of Literature* (March 27, 1943), 14.

4. Parry Stroud, *Stephen Vincent Benét* (New York: Twayne, 1962), 46.

5. Fenton, *Benét*, 199.

6. Fenton, *Benét*, 209.

7. Stephen Vincent Benét, *John Brown's Body* (Chicago: Ivan R. Dee, 1990), 321.

8. Allen Tate, "The Irrepressible Conflict," *The Nation* 127 (19 September 1928): 274; Harriet Monroe, "A Cinema Epic," *Poetry* 33 (November 1928): 91.

9. Fenton, *Benét*,182.

10. John Griffith, "Narrative Technique and the Meaning of History in Benét and MacLeish," *The Journal of Narrative Technique* 3, no. 1 (January 1973): 14.

11. Frederick H. Jackson, "Stephen Vincent Benét and American History," *The Historian* 17 (Autumn 1954): 73.

12. Benét, *John Brown's*, vii.

13. Fenton, *Benét*, 184–85.

14. Fenton, *Benét*, 348.

15. Max Eastman, "America Attempts an Epic," *The Bookman* 68, no. 3 (November 1928): 362.

16. Frank Jones, "Bon Voyage, S.V.B." *The Nation* 155 (12 September 1942): 218.

17. Newton Arvin, "A Minor Epic," *New York Herald Tribune Books* (August 12, 1928), 2.

18. Griffith, "Narrative Technique," 4.

19. For a good discussion of the historiography of the Civil War in the late nineteenth and early twentieth centuries, see Thomas B. Pressly, *Americans Interpret Their*

Civil War, (Princeton: Princeton University Press, 1954).

20. Ezra Pound, *Selected Prose, 1909-1965*, ed. William Cookson (New York: New Directions, 197), 21.

21. James M. McPherson, *Battle Cry of Freedom: The Civil War Era* (New York: Random House Ballantine, 1988), 203; Merrill D. Peterson, *John Brown: The Legend Revisited* (Charlottesville: University of Virginia Press, 2002), 20.

22. David A. Hollinger and Charles Capper, eds., *The American Intellectual Tradition*, 6th ed., vol. 1, (New York: Oxford University Press, 2011), 537.

23. Hollinger and Capper, *American Intellectual*, vol. 1, 536–37.

24. William Yancey of Alabama, "the Orator of Secession," led the Southern withdrawal from the Democratic Convention and split the party, ensuring victory in 1860 for Lincoln and the Republicans.

25. Benét, *John Brown's*, 207.

26. Benét, *John Brown's*, 188.

27. Fenton, *Benét*, 344.

28. John McWilliams, "The Epic in the Nineteenth Century," *The Columbia History of American Poetry* (New York: Columbia University Press, 1993), 61.

29. Benét, *John Brown's*, xii.

30. Stroud, *Benét*, 70.

31. Stroud, *Benét*, 54.

32. Tate, "Conflict," 274.

33. Benét, *John Brown's*, 12–13.

34. Benét, *John Brown's*, 23, 25.

35. Benét, *John Brown's*, 24.

36. Benét, *John Brown's*, 47.

37. Benét, *John Brown's*, 48.

38. Benét, *John Brown's*, 48.

39. Benét, *John Brown's*, 51.

40. Benét, *John Brown's*, 52–53.

41. Benét, *John Brown's*, 55.

42. Benét, *John Brown's*, 183.

43. Benét, *John Brown's*, 184.

44. Benét, *John Brown's*, 183.

45. Benét, *John Brown's*, 183.

46. Benét, *John Brown's*, 184.

47. Benét, *John Brown's*, 185.

48. Edmund Wilson, *Patriotic Gore: Studies in the Literature of the American Civil War* (New York: Oxford University Press, 1962), 794.

49. Robert Penn Warren, "Edmund Wilson's Civil War," *Commentary* 34 (August 1962): 153.

50. Benét, *John Brown's*, 335.

51. Benét, *John Brown's*, 336.

Chapter 3
MacLeish's *Conquistador*:
History as Metaphor

In 1933, four years after *John Brown's Body* was awarded the Pulitzer Prize, Archibald MacLeish won the same prize for another long narrative poem containing history, *Conquistador*. While MacLeish's poem never enjoyed the popularity that Benét's did, it attracted significant critical attention. R. P. Blackmur's response to the poem is typical of the poem's detractors: "unintegrated, fragmentary, disjunctive."[1] Cleanth Brooks, on the other hand, called it "one of the finer accomplishments of modern American poetry,"[2] and Allen Tate, praising its "finely sustained tone" and "flawless craft," asserted that "in versification, in diction, in the quality of the narrator's point of view, it stands alone. There is no other poem in English with which it may be compared."[3] Both Tate and Harriet Monroe praised MacLeish's adaptation of terza rima, and as late as 1977 Hayden Carruth claimed, "[*Conquistador*] is our best epic (and I do not except *The Bridge*), it is coherent, complete, and strongly conceived, and it contains many, many magnificent passages. It merits a good deal more attention than it has been given lately."[4]

Benét and MacLeish respected each other's work—in his review Benét called *Conquistador* "a magnificent and sustained achievement"[5]—but the two poems differ in important ways. Where Benét sees the Civil War as redemptive, leading on the whole to a better present and future, MacLeish sees Cortés's conquest of Mexico as destructive, both for the Native Americans and for the Spanish. Benét writes from an omniscient point of view, but MacLeish uses the first-person voice of Bernál Díaz del Castillo. Benét does extensive research on the Civil War, while MacLeish relies on a single source: "I should have done a lot of things that I didn't do. I should have collected every book I could about the Aztecs and, above all, the Mayan civilization, which surrounded them and qualified theirs. I should have done a great deal of reading. I just didn't do it."[6] Benét states that *John Brown's Body* "is a poem, not a history," but he adds, "I have tried to cleave to historical fact where such fact was ascertainable. On the other hand, for certain thoughts and feelings attributed to historical characters, and for the interpretation of those characters in the poem, I alone must be held responsible."[7] MacLeish, on the other hand, states, "Where I have followed the historical chronicles of the Conquest of Mexico I have, in general, followed the account given by Bernál Díaz del Castillo. . . . I have however altered and transposed and invented incidents,"[8] leaving it to the reader to determine what, precisely, has been altered or invented. Finally, although both poems depict sympathy for each of the warring sides, including instances of extraordinary courage, tenacity, loyalty, and heroism, in *Conquistador* those traits are backlit by a cruelty and violence far darker and more brutal than anything we find in *John Brown's Body*. MacLeish's characters are more selfish, fearful, avaricious, and treacherous—in short, harder to admire—than Benét's.

MacLeish had begun to think about the topic in the summer of 1927 while living in Paris: "I'd started work on *Conquistador* in the Bibliothèque Saint Janvier. . . . They had very little in English, but one of the things they had was a set of Hakluyt Society publications. And one of those was Bernál Díaz del Castíllo's *True History of the Conquest of New Spain*."[9] Serious work on the poem, however, occurred only after his trip to Mexico in February 1929. From Vera Cruz, where he "spent quite a lot of time down on the coast on the beaches trying to figure out more or less where the ships put in," MacLeish travelled by automobile to Jalapa, where he hired a guide/translator. Travelling by automobile, mule, and foot, with "the maps provided in the Hakluyt book . . . and the automobile map put side by side,"[10] MacLeish retraced the route taken by Cortés across the Sierra to Tlaxcala and Tenochtitlán (Mexico City). MacLeish completed the poem in November 1931 and published it in March 1932.[11]

Bernál Díaz del Castíllo (1492–1584), whose *Historia Verdadera de la Conquista de la Nueva España* (*True History of the Conquest of New Spain*) is the framework around which MacLeish builds his poem, travelled to the West Indies in 1514 and claimed to have been the only man to participate in all three of the first major voyages from Cuba to the mainland: in 1517 with Francisco Hernandez de Córdoba to the Yucatán, in 1518 with Juan de Grijalva, also to the Yucatán, and finally in 1519–21, on the great expedition with Cortés. He had begun his memoir in the 1550s and then put it aside until 1564, when his anger over what he perceived as the inaccuracies of Francisco López de Gómara's *Crónica de la Nueva España* led him to resume his work. Bernál completed the first draft of his history in 1568, though it would not be published until 1632, long after his death.

MacLeish's poem is around two thousand lines long, composed in a terza rima based more often on terminal assonance than on rhyme, in a loose pentameter. It begins with a prologue in which the narrator, alluding to Odysseus's journey to Hades, invokes the voices of the dead conquistadors—a clear borrowing from Pound's early *Cantos*, which also begin with the *neukia* of Odysseus. From this point on, the poem's speaker is Díaz, one of the dead invoked in the prologue, who begins with a "Preface to His Book" in which he recounts his participation in the voyages of 1517 and 1518 from Cuba to the Yucatán, and his anger with Gómara, who had never been in the Western Hemisphere, never mind taken part in the Conquest, and who in his *Crónica* ignores, Díaz feels, the important roles played in the Conquest by individuals besides Cortés. The rest of the poem, called "The True History of Bernál Díaz," is made up of fifteen short "books" which follow the narrative of the *True History*.

MacLeish's "True History" differs in certain ways from Bernál's *Historia*. For example, the Díaz of *Conquistador* focuses on the sensory details of the journey's landscapes far more than the Díaz of the *True History*, and on what he and his companions felt as opposed to what they did. *Conquistador's* Díaz leaves out important names and dates, and in general compresses much of the narrative so tightly that it is sometimes difficult to follow. By confining himself to Bernál's point of view, MacLeish limits the breadth of the poem's narrative as well as its capacity to "contain" history. Grover Smith is one of several readers who have argued that the poem is in fact *not* a narrative: ". . . it is kaleidoscopic, a fantasia of emotions . . . not primarily a narrative at all but a series of tableaux with subjective coloring."[12] For readers unfamiliar with the historical figures and place-names of the Conquest, the story can be confusing. But as MacLeish points out, "[Bernál's *True History* is] not a history, really, at all. It's a very personal apology—'apologia.'"[13] In other words, Díaz wants to justify his anger with Gómara, and with his own poverty-stricken old age. He is a *conquistador* without recognition and without wealth, and he affirms the truths of his own memory over those of historiography. In the preface, Díaz characterizes himself as "an ignorant old sick man" living in poverty in Guatemala and unskilled in writing: "unused to the combing of / Words clean of the wool while the tale waits."[14] Gómara, on the other hand, "with the school-taught skip to his writing / The pompous Latin,"[15] is young, healthy, and well educated. But, concludes Díaz, "I / Fought in those battles! These were my own deeds! / . . . / These were my friends: these dead my companions."[16] Díaz knows what he must sound like—"The tedious veteran jealous of his fame!"[17]—but he feels his anger is justified, for he and his companions have been forgotten, their names ignored as they live out their lives in obscurity. For Díaz, Gómara is simply one more of the powerful and privileged who appropriate to and for themselves the fame, the wealth, and even the memories of the men who actually did the difficult and dangerous work of the Conquest. After his first trip to the Yucatán, says Díaz, in which he was wounded in an Indian attack, the Cuban Governor Diego Velás-quez took all credit for the discovery of land in the West rich in gold, and Fonséca, the powerful Bishop of Burgos, made no mention of the men's deeds in his report on the discovery to King Charles.[18]

As readers, we can sympathize with Bernál, and for the most part he comes across in the body of the poem as a reliable, honest, and perceptive narrator. In the end, however, as Cleanth Brooks[19] and others have pointed out, Bernál limits MacLeish's ability to say anything particularly interesting or profound about history. Allen Tate writes,

> The melancholy of the hero's resentment against the "taught tongues of fame" is obscure and meaningless. It does not at any point emerge as criticism of the

avowed purposes of the "conquest"; and so, instead of a classical irony, we get something like sentimental regret on the part of Bernal, whose anger rises at the failure of the official histories to recreate the sensuous correspondence to his own part in the action. . . . The poem recovers Bernal's perceptions but it does not place them against the objective stream of events. His personal significance is impenetrable; the meaning of the course of outside events is obscure.[20]

I will return to this point later in this chapter, but first some background on the "objective stream of events": Cortés arrived in the Spanish Caribbean in 1504, and in 1511 he joined Diego Velásquez in the conquest of Cuba. As Governor of Cuba, Velásquez sponsored the 1517 and 1518 expeditions to the Yucatán, and he planned to send Cortés on a third expedition. However, relations between the two strong-willed men had soured, and after Cortés began organizing and planning the trip, Velásquez changed his mind and ordered the voyage halted. Cortés ignored the order, and sailed around the Yucatán and westward up the Mexican coast, halting at the site of present-day Vera Cruz. Native Americans had told Grijalva in 1518 that their gold came from "Méjico" in the west, and Cortés was determined to get there. In order to squelch the idea that marching west with him might not be a good idea, he sank his ships, and in August 1519, Cortés and an army of around 500 Spaniards marched west, over the Sierra Madre Oriental and into the Aztec capital of Tenochtitlán (present-day Mexico City), which they reached in early November. Along the way, Cortés alternately fought and formed important alliances with tribes hostile to the Aztecs, such as the Tlaxcalans and the Cempoalans. Montezuma, both alarmed and intrigued by the strangers, reluctantly invited them into his city. Cortés and the Spanish were in awe of what they found: here was a massive city of causeways, canals, and floating gardens, with an architecture and social organization as sophisticated as any in Europe. However, suspicions on both sides quickly grew so high that the Spanish took Montezuma hostage. In April 1520, Cortés learned that Velásquez had sent an army to the coast to arrest him for treason. Leaving roughly half his men in Tenochtitlán, Cortés led the other half to meet the much larger force of Pánfilo de Narváez. With a nighttime surprise attack, Cortés managed to win the initial battle, and in the parley that followed, he persuaded Narváez's men to join him. In late June, he returned to Tenochtitlán. However, in his absence his lieutenant, Pedro de Alvarado, had perpetrated a massacre during a religious ceremony, and the Aztecs had had enough. They attacked in force, and on the night of June 30, *la noche triste*, Cortés and his men had to fight their way with heavy losses out of the city and up into the surrounding mountains. There he re-grouped and re-established his alliances with the Tlaxcalans and other tribes, and in the winter and spring of 1521, he and his allies subdued the towns around Tenochtitlán. In May, they surrounded and besieged the city itself, which held out until August 1521, when Cortés and his army fought their way into the city and razed most of it.

To say that the poem illustrates the abuses of colonialism and the horrors of

war, as Scott Donaldson does,[21] is correct to a point, but it omits Bernál's repeated descriptions of pride in his own and his comrades' ability as soldiers—
not only is a company of a few hundred men able to defeat the entire Aztec nation (with the important help of Indian tribes unallied with the Aztecs, a point
which Díaz de-emphasizes, and with the devastating effects of smallpox, a dis-
ease the Spanish brought with them), but Cortés is also able, with only about
half of his men, to defeat and then enlist as allies Narváez's force of almost 1000
men. In true epic fashion, MacLeish has Díaz begin his "True History" with the
line "Of that world's conquest and the fortunate wars"[22]—if Donaldson's reading is correct, "fortunate" is a curious adjective unless we are meant to take the
entire narrative ironically, a claim that no reader has made.

Of the relatively recent responses to *Conquistador*, the two that take the poem's treatment of history most seriously are Michael Cavanagh's and John Griffith's. Cavanagh claims that the conquest was the ideal vehicle for "MacLeish's
thoughts about history" because it allows him to depict clearly the conflict between the East—"the secure past"—and the West—"the life of exploration."
Cavanagh believes that for MacLeish, "History is a journey westward, or at least
should be."[23] MacLeish, continues Cavanagh,

> wanted to argue the existence of a real historical process in which the human
> race is driven by some unknowable powers . . . periodically to renounce the
> mythologies of the immediate past in order to better realize the "otherness" of
> the world. The "otherness" of the world . . . is emblematized by the "west" and
> the journey toward it is also a journey backward into time, toward a kind of
> prelapsarian Eden of effort, adventure, and danger.[24]

In this case, he might have added, it proved to be a journey into massacre, rape,
plunder, and the brutal destruction of a civilization. However, Cavanagh sees the
poem celebrating "the sense of communal adventure—the thrill of living dangerously in unknown places," and he argues that Díaz, despite the fact that he
offers no analysis of battles or military strategy, and "no real insight" into the
purposes or significance of the expedition, nevertheless "sees history, MacLeish
would seem to imply, as primitive man saw it and as all men should see it." In
other words, *Conquistador* depicts history as "a journey westward" that "takes
one back to a simpler—yet more mysterious—and radical existence, one which
all men under their veneer of civilized mores strongly desire to reassume."[25]
Cortés's error, for Cavanagh, is that he stops exploring: "colonization brings an
end to exploration. In seeking security, the Spanish abandon their own values.
The journey should have gone on; the way was not *to* the city but *through* the
city to the west."[26] This is an odd and finally unpersuasive view of both history
and *Conquistador*, for of course the Spanish did go west (as well as north and
south), throughout Latin America and, in the voyages of Coronado and De Soto,
throughout much of what is now the United States, where they encountered not a
prelapsarian Eden but long-established indigenous peoples. The results of their

trans-hemispheric explorations were almost always violent and bloody, and their goals were plainly "colonization" rather than the "radical existence" Cavanagh extols. Far from abandoning their own values, the Spanish pursued with a furious intensity the "values" they placed on gold and silver, and on the imposition of Catholicism and Spanish cultural and political mores. Cavanagh's observation that the bulk of the poem concerns the journey itself, and not the military conflict, is valid, but the poem makes clear that the goal of the journey is gold, fame, and conquest. The poem's title, after all, is *Conquistador*, not *Explorador*.

John Griffith reads the poem quite differently. He picks up on Tate's point about the limiting effects of Díaz as narrator: although Díaz speaks with the authority of the "intimate participant," his narrative is "adulterated with nostalgia and a numbing sense of loss," and the Conquest's historical meaning is reduced to "the projection of a fictive mind, a self-defining, self-limiting complex of impressions. Larger contexts are neither affirmed nor denied."[27] The only "interpretive thesis" that MacLeish imposes on the *True History* is "the notion that the Spanish conquests were a manifestation of man's westering instinct." Unlike Cavanagh, however, Griffith reads this "romantic conception" of the West in terms of Cortés "trying to rouse enthusiasm for a faltering crusade" and Díaz "trying to recapture the grandeur of his youth."[28] In fact, the historical Cortés had stronger incentives with which to rouse enthusiasm: primarily the promise of gold and fame, and secondarily the spiritual value of converting the natives to Christianity. Similarly, the historical Díaz mentions the lure of the West only briefly—he too is more concerned with gold and fame. "The westering motif," Griffith concludes, "is thus an aspect of the poem's mood of mildly boastful elegy; it is to be understood not historically but dramatically, as the rhetoric of an anxious captain and a nostalgic old survivor."[29] Griffith tries to defend MacLeish by arguing that "*Conquistador* is history told in the only way MacLeish could tell it in 1930" because MacLeish sees the poet's primary function as social, giving aesthetic form to his people's spiritual truths. Because the twentieth century has reduced our stock of spiritual truths, MacLeish's Díaz embodies the kind of inner life still available to us: "little else than blank submission to emotion and sensation." "*Conquistador*," Griffith concludes, was MacLeish's "heroic effort to find meaning in the uncertain past."[30] However, if the "westering motif" is merely a device of dramatic rhetoric, and if "blank submission to emotion and sensation" is what passes for an inner life, then we are left asking, to paraphrase another American poet, what to make of a diminished thing.

Signi Falk finds in Bernál a greater awareness of history than does Griffith, but she reads the present into the past when she claims that Bernál is aware of the awful tragedy for which he and his comrades are responsible.[31] From a mid-twentieth-century point of view the conquest may look awful and tragic, and it is possible to read regret into the poem's last lines—"O day that brings the earth back bring again / That well-swept town those towers and that island"[32]—but Bernál does not regret what has happened so much as he wishes, sentimentally and nostalgically, to relive the glamour of his youth. Similarly, it is a mistake to

read guilt into such lines as "And none of us but had his heart foreknown the /
Evil to come would have turned from the land then,"[33] for the "Evil" that Bernál
describes refers not to the actions of the conquistadors, but to the Indians. Bernál
refers repeatedly to the Spaniards' fear of the Indians and to their horror of the
Indians' practice of cutting the hearts out of living victims, including captured
Spaniards, and cannibalizing them. Bernál is angry that he and his comrades did
not receive what he feels is their just portion of wealth or fame, but he never
suggests that the conquistadors were wrong to do what they did. Even in his
account of the massacre at Cholúla, he anticipates and rebuts his reader's criticism: "*And who are ye to be judge of us?*"[34] Bernál has much to say about his
own experience with Cortés, but he has nothing to say about the historical meaning, tragic or otherwise, of the conquest.

Like Bernál, MacLeish has little to say about the strictly historical meaning
of the conquest; instead, he finds in the conquest a metaphor for a universal human experience. Dissatisfied with William Prescott's *History of the Conquest of
Mexico* (1843), which in a letter to Hemingway he calls "fine and rhetorical and
obviously false as bloody hell,"[35] MacLeish turns to Bernál's *True History* because he

> was immediately struck by the metaphor in a way that I had not been in reading
> Prescott. I mean the obvious metaphor of the unknown West, the difficult and
> dangerous journey into the West, the wonders of that, the scene at the beach be-
> low when Cortés burned his ships, cut himself off from Europe, cut himself off
> from Cuba, made it impossible for anyone to go anywhere else but West with
> him. All these things subsume and clarify the whole experience of the Ameri-
> cas to the Europeans, including the disastrous ending—the *noche triste*—and
> the destruction of the city and the miserable, horrible, beastly decay and degra-
> dation that set in afterward. What white men have done to the land was made
> pretty explicit. And it was that, the metaphoric sense of the thing, which more
> than anything else carried me away.[36]

The metaphor appears in the poem in Cortés's speech to a group of his men who
had attempted to steal some of the group's ships and sail back to Cuba instead of
marching inland to Tenochtitlán. Cortés orders the feet of the ringleader cut off
and all the ships but one sunk. He then speaks to the men who had tried to leave,
in a passage that MacLeish invents, telling them to take the remaining ship and
return to the east:

> Why should you waste your souls in the west! You are young:
> Tell them you left us here by the last water
> Going up through the pass of the hills with the sun:
>
> Tell them that in the tight towns when you talk of us!
> The west is dangerous for thoughtful men:
> Eastward is all sure: all as it ought to be:

> A man may know the will of God by the fences:
> Get yourselves to the ship and the stale shore
> And the smell of your father's dung in the earth: at the end of it
>
> There where the hills look over and before us
> Lies in the west that city that new world
> We that are left will envy your good fortune![37]

The west stands for the unknown, for risk, for promise, for hope; in the European imagination, somewhere in the "west" lie the Islands of the Blessed, the Garden of the Hesperides, Tír na nÓg, Atlantis, and Avalon. In the preface, MacLeish's Bernál writes of its attraction—after his first voyage to the Mexican coast, in which he was badly wounded and saw fifty of his comrades killed by Indians, he nonetheless wants to return:

> But as for us that returned from that westward country—
> We could not lie in our towns for the sound of the sea:
> We could not rest at all in our thoughts: we were young then:
>
> We looked to the west . . . .[38]

The quest possesses the men. In an essay on how one begins or decides to become a writer, MacLeish tells an imaginary interlocutor that Hemingway resigned from the *Toronto Star* not "to become a writer," but "because he was a writer—because he had to write." And when his interlocutor doesn't understand him, MacLeish continues, "Do you remember Cortés on the beaches when he burned his ships? He burned them because he had to go on—because he had heard of Tenochtitlán beyond the mountains. He had never heard of that city before but now he had to go there. He belonged to the journey. Writers belong to the journey. They belong to the work before it is written."[39] Such belonging, suggests MacLeish, "clarif[ies] the whole experience of the Americas to the Europeans," i.e., the meaning of America is bound up in European dreams and desires that are so powerful that men belong to them, rather than vice versa.

"Belonging to the journey," however, implicates the conquistadors in "the disastrous ending" as well. *Conquistador* opens with a "Dedication" drawn from Dante's *Inferno* (XXVI, 112–13) in which Odysseus describes his last voyage into the west; as he passes the Strait of Gibraltar and sails into the Atlantic Ocean, Odysseus addresses his crew: "'Brothers,' I said, 'who through a hundred thousand / perils have made your way to reach the West.'" The poem's prologue continues the allusion, with its journey to the underworld to invoke the dead, and Odysseus may be figured as a prototype of the conquistador. Yet in drawing his dedication from Dante, MacLeish implicitly reminds his reader that Odysseus speaks from the eighth circle of Hell, the circle of fraud, and more precisely from within that circle's eighth bolgia, the bolgia of deception. Odysseus's skill at deception is legendary; Dante mentions his theft of the Palladium from Troy and his tricking Achilles out of his disguise as a girl so that he will join the Greek expeditionary force, and we recall as well the episodes with the Cyclops and the suitors in the *Odyssey*. Cortés is also a consummate deceiver: he deceives the Governor of Cuba before embarking on his unauthorized trip to Mexico, and he deceives both Montezuma and the Native American tribes whom he enlists as his allies before the final battle. But the greatest deceptions are those practiced not upon others, but upon oneself, and as readers we recall the old Bernál of the preface, living in poverty in Guatemala, complaining of his lack of gold and fame, bitter at the Spanish settlers who followed the conquistadors—"They came like nettles in dry slash: like beetles: / They ran on the new land like lice staining it." "And the west is gone now,"[40] says Bernál, and we see that like Dante's Odysseus, who deceived himself into thinking that all he wanted was to go home, the conquistadors were also most great in their capacity for self-deception.

MacLeish's working notes for the poem make more explicit his understanding of the metaphor embodied in the Conquest:

> The Conquest of the New World . . . is the metaphor not only of our continent but of our time—as "America" is the metaphor of all human hope—as "west" is the metaphor of the dreamed-of future. . . . The heroism and the nobility and the pathos of an indestructible belief in that kingdom in the west, our search for it, our discovery of it, our conquest and its forever loss. . . . The material of the poem . . . compels me because it is a symbol . . . of the life of our race on this earth. That sailing westward into the unknown bay, those reports of riches and wonders . . . to the west, the will to seize them, the long marches, the endless battles, the finding of the beautiful city (and then its capture and destruction) . . . . it is like the life of a man with its first enchantment—the universal dream of happiness and glory beyond—the laborious and dangerous attempt to seize it— the success which destroys the dream itself. . . .[41]

In these notes, MacLeish imagines American history—indeed, world history— as inevitably tragic: we have suffered, and will continue to suffer, the "forever loss" of "the dreamed-of future," of "all human hope." Certainly Bernál seems to feel that he has suffered this, at the end of the poem, but are we to take Bernál's experience, as MacLeish seems to suggest, as emblematic of "our time," of "our race on this earth," of "the life of a man [any man] in its first enchantment"? If we do, then a kind of fatalism is the result: the Spaniards, once they "belonged to the journey," were bound to search for Tenochtitlán, to discover it, to conquer it, and to lose/destroy it. Cavanagh suggests something like this, with his "unknowable powers" that drive the human race, and Donaldson reads the poem in this way, stating that the Spaniards were "driven . . . by the hypnotic pull of the journey westward that history demanded."[42] But "history" demands no such thing, and such rhetoric asks its readers to take a trope as much more than a trope. This mystificatory fatalism also cuts against the grain of MacLeish's well-known and extensive involvement in national and international politics, as well as his polemical poems and essays of the 1930s and 1940s, which are the work of a man who believes passionately in human hope and in a future in which dreams are not necessarily destroyed. In his radio play *The Fall of the City* (1937), MacLeish uses the Aztecs' permitting Cortés to enter their city peacefully as analogous to contemporary events leading to the *Anschluss* between Austria and Nazi Germany. There the implication is that the Spaniards were not necessarily fated to conquer—no more than the Nazis were—and that the Aztecs and Austrians should have offered a far more spirited resistance. It is a mistake to read the metaphor too deterministically: yes, human lives and history often unfold tragically or ironically—we work to realize our dreams, and somehow in the act of realizing them, we destroy them. But MacLeish was far too supple and progressive and Jeffersonian a thinker to apply that metaphor in a crudely determinist manner.

In the poem's prologue, MacLeish asks and does not answer an important question:

> What are the dead to us in the world's wonder?
> Why (and again now) on their shadowy beaches
> Pouring before them the slow painful blood
>
> Do we return to force the truthful speech of them
> Shrieking like snipe along their gusty sand
> And stand: and as the dark ditch fills beseech them
>
> (Reaching across the surf their fragile hands) to
> Speak to us?[43]

In other words, what is the value of history? Why read it? Why listen to Bernál for two thousand lines? Odysseus travels to Hades for instruction on how to return home, but Bernál offers no such instruction. History cannot teach him how to live in the present or move toward the future.[44] But for MacLeish, Bernál's "True History" carries a "metaphoric sense" in which the poet recognizes an important truth that no other history of the Conquest captures.

The metaphor embodies a tension that most historians might reject as inconsistency or contradiction: the Conquest unfolds as it does because (1) the conquistadors and the Indians make particular choices (history is open-ended, and our free will shapes its course) but also (2) because the human condition is always and inherently tragic, so that certain fundamental patterns recur in both individual lives and in history. Tenochtitlán is the archetypal terrestrial paradise in the West, like California or the Seven Cities of Gold. The conquistadors believe it exists, embark on a heroic quest for it, and actually discover it. Díaz and his comrades are in awe of the city's size and beauty. They are given gold and women, and for a short time they live like heroes or gods. But they are men, not gods, and their heroic stature is undermined by their all too human fear and avarice, which lead to the violent destruction of the city, along with the destruction of what they had hoped to attain. The Conquest embodies both the heroic and the base. As individuals and as a species, MacLeish suggests, we repeatedly search for, discover, attain, and then destroy or lose what we most value. What we love always vanishes, and Díaz always ends his life old, alone, forgotten, and in poverty.

But can the history of the Conquest be reduced to an archetypal or mythic pattern of search, discovery, and loss? Does the metaphor embodying that pattern actually "clarif[y] the whole experience of the Americas to the Europeans"? Or is MacLeish indulging in the same sort of hyperbole evident in his glib remark to Hemingway that Prescott's *History of the Conquest of Mexico* is "false as bloody hell"? Why, after all, is he so quick to dismiss Prescott and to ignore the other historians who have written on the Conquest and the events surrounding it? Unlike Benét, who pays scrupulous attention to the historiography of the Civil War and humbly concedes that his poem is not a history, MacLeish strikes an almost combative pose toward historians, somewhat similar to the pose that Díaz strikes toward Gómara. In a curious attempt to place himself on the side of those, like Díaz, who actually experienced the events of the Conquest, as opposed to the historians who weren't there, MacLeish writes in a note appended to the end of the poem: "My account of the topography of the march from the seacoast to the Valley of Mexico is based upon my own experience of the route and the country by foot and mule-back in the winter of 1929 and differs from that of the historians."[45] The precise differences between his "account of the topography" and "that of the historians," along with the identities of "the historians," are left to the reader's imagination, but it seems important to MacLeish that he distance himself from "the historians" and speak from the privileged position of "my own experience." Explaining to Hemingway why his trip to Mexico was necessary, MacLeish writes, "I want to write a poem about the Conquest . . . and you once told me . . . never to write about anything I didn't know all about."[46]

To "know all about" the Conquest might well involve the physical experience of re-tracing, as nearly as possible, Cortés's journey from Veracruz to Mexico City, but why would it not also include doing the kind of extensive reading that Benét did on the Civil War? And why would it mean dismissing as "false" the most prestigious American account of the Conquest? After all, Prescott made careful use of extensive documentary source materials in his writing, and in terms of the facts of what happened, it is difficult to see where he was "false as bloody hell." Some readers find that Prescott overplays the romance of the Conquest, as well as its "drama of Western progress" aspect. He clearly sees the Conquest as a good thing, as the following quotations suggest: "In this state of things it was beneficently ordered by Providence that the land should be delivered over to another race, who would rescue it from the brutish superstitions that daily extended wider and wider with extent of empire."[47] "The Aztecs not only did not advance the condition of their vassals, but, morally speaking, they did much to degrade it. How can a nation where human sacrifices prevail, and especially when combined with cannibalism, further the march of civilization?"[48] "The empire of the Aztecs did not fall before its time."[49] On the other hand, Prescott also depicted the cruelties and treacheries perpetrated by the Spanish, and at the end of his account of the Conquest, his treatment of the Aztec leader Guatemozin, who fought bravely to the very end, is sympathetic.

So does MacLeish tell the truth about history while Prescott is "false as bloody hell"? A simple "yes" is as misleading as a simple "no." MacLeish dismisses Prescott not because he distorts what really happened, and not because he was too romantic or too ethnocentric or too Christocentric or too progressive, but simply because Prescott's narrative obscures the metaphor that MacLeish finds so plainly evident when he reads Díaz, whose elegiac lament transcends his quarrel with Gómora. The historical event matters to the poet because of the metaphor adhering to Díaz's account of it, and the truth of the metaphor is more profound than the truths of historians like Prescott. The archetypal pattern conveyed by the metaphor illuminates the meaning of the Europeans' encounter with the Americas during the period of discovery and colonization, and as readers, we can find the pattern repeated in the Puritan settlement of New England, the Spanish conquest of the Inca, and many other episodes the history of the Americas. In this poem, MacLeish revives the ancient quarrel between poetry and history. His critics find his focus on Díaz too narrow, and his poem's grasp of history consequently inadequate, but MacLeish suggests that poets and historians tell different kinds of truth, and that the poets' is more philosophically significant. Unlike his friend Stephen Vincent Benét, MacLeish comes down firmly on the side of Aristotle in the *Poetics*.

Notes

1. R. P. Blackmur, "Mr. MacLeish's Predicament," *The American Mercury*, April 1934, 507.

2. Cleanth Brooks, *Modern Poetry and the Tradition* (Chapel Hill: University of North Carolina Press, 1939), 119.

3. Allen Tate, "Not Fear of God," *The New Republic*, June 1, 1932, 77–78.

4. Hayden Carruth, "Homage to A. MacLeish," *Virginia Quarterly Review* 53, no. 1 (Winter 1977): 150.

5. Stephen Vincent Benét, "High Achievement," *The Saturday Review of Literature*, April 2, 1932, 630.

6. Archibald MacLeish, *Reflections*, ed. Bernard A. Drabeck and Helen E. Ellis, (Amherst: University of Massachusetts Press, 1986), 75–76.

7. Benét, *John Brown's*, vii.

8. Archibald MacLeish, *Collected Poems, 1917–1982* (Boston: Houghton Mifflin, 1985), 261–62.

9. MacLeish, *Reflections*, 73.

10. MacLeish, *Reflections*, 74.

11. Scott Donaldson, *Archibald MacLeish: An American Life* (Boston: Houghton

Mifflin, 1992), 208, 215.

12. Grover Smith, "Archibald MacLeish," in *Seven American Poets*, ed. Denis Donoghue (Minneapolis: University of Minnesota Press, 1975), 37.

13. MacLeish, *Reflections*, 75.

14. MacLeish, *Poems*, 174.

15. MacLeish, *Poems*, 173.

16. MacLeish, *Poems*, 174.

17. MacLeish, *Poems*, 176.

18. MacLeish, *Poems*, 179.

19. Cleanth Brooks, *Modern Poetry*, 119–20.

20. Tate, "Not Fear," 78.

21. Donaldson, *MacLeish*, 215.

22. MacLeish, *Poems*, 184.

23. Michael Cavanagh, "The Problems of Modern Epic: MacLeish's *Conquistador*,"
Papers on Language and Literature 17, no. 3 (Summer 1981): 299. A revised version of
this essay may be found in Michael Cavanagh, "*Conquistador*: An American Epic," in
The Proceedings of the Archibald MacLeish Symposium, May 7–8, 1982, ed. Bernard A.
Drabeck and Helen E. Ellis (Lanham, MD: University Press of America, 1988), 105–14.

24. Cavanagh, "Problems," 302.

25. Cavanagh, "Problems," 296.

26. Cavanagh, "Problems," 298.

27. John Griffith, "Narrative Technique," 14.

28. Griffith, "Narrative Technique," 16.

29. Griffith, "Narrative Technique," 16.

30. Griffith, "Narrative Technique," 17.

31. Signi Lena Falk, *Archibald MacLeish* (New York: Twayne, 1965), 63.

32. MacLeish, *Poems*, 261.

33. MacLeish, *Poems*, 181.

34. MacLeish, *Poems*, 228.

35. Archibald MacLeish, *Letters of Archibald MacLeish: 1907–1982*, ed. R. H.
Winnick (Boston: Houghton Mifflin, 1983), 225.

36. MacLeish, *Reflections*, 73.

37. MacLeish, *Poems*, 213–14.

38. MacLeish, *Poems*, 180.

39. Archibald MacLeish, *Riders on the Earth: Essays and Recollections* (Boston:
Houghton Mifflin, 1978), 72.

40. MacLeish, *Poems*, 261.

41. Donaldson, *MacLeish*, 215–16.

42. Donaldson, *MacLeish*, 215.

43. MacLeish, *Poems*, 170–71.

44. Cavanagh disagrees, as does Eve Stoddard, who sees Bernál in the role of Virgil
in Dante's *Inferno* and reads *Conquistador* in the light of Dante: MacLeish's narrator is
educated by Bernál, just as Dante is educated by Virgil. See "Dante's *Inferno* as Allusive
Context for MacLeish's *Conquistador*," *Notes on Modern American Literature* 6, no. 3
(1982). I find her argument, like Cavanagh's, strained.

45. MacLeish, *Poems*, 262.

46. MacLeish, *Letters*, 225.

47. William Prescott, *History of the Conquest of Mexico*, vol. I, ed. Wilfred Harold Munro (Philadelphia: J. B. Lippincott, 1904), 101.

48. Prescott, *History*, vol. IV, 112–13.

49. Prescott, *History*, vol. IV, 114.

Chapter 4
A Usable Past? Robert Penn Warren's
Brother to Dragons

> ... the historian is a poet and the poet is a historian; history is poetry and po-
> etry is history. . . .
> —Lewis Simpson, on Warren's *Brother to Dragons*

> The trouble is, it is very difficult, to be both a poet and, an historian.
> —Charles Olson, *Mayan Letters*, October 1953

In 1807, Thomas Jefferson's sister, Lucy Jefferson Lewis, left Virginia and crossed the Appalachian Mountains with her husband Charles, their children, and their slaves. One of their sons, Lilburne, had purchased 1500 acres in western Kentucky on the Ohio River, around ten miles east of present-day Paducah, on which he built a large house that he called "Rocky Hill." On the night of December 15, 1811, Lilburne and his younger brother Isham murdered one of Lilburne's slaves, a sixteen- or seventeen-year-old boy named George, with an axe. During or after the murder, Lilburne may have dismembered George, whose offense was to have broken a pitcher given to Lucy Jefferson Lewis by her brother Thomas. Lilburne's other slaves had been called to witness the murder, and some of them may have been ordered to dismember and burn the body. Around 2:00 a.m., the first tremor of the New Madrid earthquake struck, collapsing the fireplace in the room in which George's corpse was being burned. Several days later, Lilburne may have ordered his slaves to conceal the bones in the rebuilt fireplace. Rumors of the crime began to circulate, and Lilburne and Isham were indicted for murder. Before the trial, and before Lilburne and Isham could execute a mutual suicide pact, Lilburne shot himself, perhaps accidentally. Isham fled, and according to some accounts was one of only two Americans killed at the Battle of New Orleans in 1815.

Although Jefferson almost certainly heard of this crime, nowhere among his papers is there any mention of it, and this refusal to address his nephews' action is the germ of Robert Penn Warren's *Brother to Dragons* (1953, revised 1979). The poem has generated far more critical discussion than any of Warren's other poems, and much of it has been favorable. Randall Jarrell, for example, calls the original version Warren's "best book."[1] Reviewing the revised version, Harold Bloom admits to being uneasy with Warren's "ideological ferocity" and unpersuaded by the poem's "implicit theology and overt morality," but nonetheless calls Warren "our most impressive living poet."[2]

In his foreword, Warren traces the poem's inception to "bits of folk tale, garbled accounts heard in my boyhood"[3] that related the brutal murder of a slave by Lilburne and Isham Lewis. In the 1940s, Warren traveled to Smithland, Kentucky, to read the courthouse records of the case, and his work at the Library of Congress afforded him access to newspaper files and abolitionist tracts that mentioned the case. In the poem, he recounts two visits to the site of the ruins of Lilburne's house. What intrigued him about the story, he says, was the irony that "The philosopher of our liberties and the architect of our country and the prophet of human perfectibility had this in the family blood."[4]

In form, the poem is close to drama; subtitled "A Tale in Verse and Voices," all of its lines are spoken by particular characters, one of whom is called "R.P.W., the writer of this poem," who engages in a dialogue located outside of history (in "no place," at "any time," Warren writes) with the characters involved in the crime, all of whom exist in a kind of extra-historical limbo.

Considerable attention has been focused on the historical accuracy, or inaccuracy, of the poem. Warren admits in his foreword to having "altered certain details," such as omitting any mention of Lilburne's first wife and their children, substituting Lilburne's mother's grave as the site of Lilburne's death, instead of his first wife's grave, "for thematic reasons," and inventing the character of the slave Aunt Cat.[5] Typical of those critics who catalogue the poem's historical errors, C. Hugh Holman cites not only those that Warren admits to in the foreword, but also points out that (1) Letitia (Lilburne's wife) did not leave Lilburne on the night of the murder, but remained at the house until after Isham's indictment as accessory to murder; (2) George was murdered and dismembered not in the meathouse on a butcherblock, but in the kitchen cabin on the floor; (3) Lilburne did not trick Isham into shooting him, but killed himself, probably accidentally. "Indeed," he writes, "one is forced to the conclusion that the suggestions of deranged motives for Lilburne—the Oedipal struggle, Letitia's sexual frigidity, the suggestions of class hatred between her family and the Lewises, and Lilburne's dominance of Isham—all have little or no support in historical fact."[6] Richard Law is more equivocal about the historical accuracy of the account, stating that Warren "discovers (or invents) in the background of the slaying all the elements of a psychological case study: an unhappy, loveless marriage in which the mother seeks companionship in her son, the Oedipal rivalry in her two sons, the nursemaid who competes with the mother for the son's love, and the son's wife who is unwittingly a surrogate for his mother."[7] The extent to which Warren engages in invention, as opposed to discovery, is more than an academic question; it is central to the reader's response to the argument on American history that the poem makes.

Boynton Merrill, the author of what Warren calls "a conscientious and scholarly account of the general subject,"[8] *Jefferson's Nephews: A Frontier Tragedy* (1976), writes,

> In regard to the historicity of *Brother to Dragons*, Warren states in the preface: "I am trying to write a poem and not a history, and therefore have no compunction about tampering with the facts." Warren succeeded admirably, both in his poem and in tampering with the facts. However, it might be ventured that facts usually do stand in the way of poetic expression and artistic triumph, such as Warren has achieved.[9]

For his part, Warren claims that Merrill's book, "fascinating and reliable as it is, does not change the basic thematic or dramatic outline of my tale."[10] Moreover, Warren suggests that history, and our response to it, must involve more than simply knowledge of specific facts. Near the end of the poem he notes that we know the names, ages, sex, and prices of the slaves who were present at the murder: "We know that much, but what is knowledge / Without the intrinsic mediation of the heart?"[11]

Like many of Warren's critics, Merrill stresses the distinction between history and poetry, while Warren blurs the distinction. In the revised edition of the poem, he inserts the adjective "non-essential" before the noun "facts" in the passage Merrill cites, suggesting that his tamperings are insignificant. In the case of the Lewis crime, however, both the essential and non-essential "facts" are difficult to establish. After providing a detailed narrative account of the murder, Merrill admits,

> This account of the murder may well be inaccurate. None of the available sources are, at the same time, both detailed and of unquestionable reliability. The four major sources of information about the murder contradict each other on so many points that a true and factual description of George's death will probably never be achieved. This reconstruction . . . is a combination of what appear to be the most plausible parts of the four written statements. . . .[12]

Merrill's description of the historical record exposes the naivete behind Irvin Ehrenpreis's claim that "a plain historical account [would be] . . . more absorbing than Warren's self-indulgent, highly reflexive work."[13] Such a "plain account" simply cannot be written, so Warren takes advantage of what he calls "the ambiguous opacities of history"[14] to fill in the blanks in the historical record by imagining, in Aristotle's terms, "what might have happened." For Aristotle, the poet differs from the historian because he works with universal as opposed to particular truths; the "universal" from which Warren deduces the action of his poem is human nature. For Warren, the historical event germinates in "the blind nutriment of Lilburne's heart," and the human heart contains "the rich detritus of all History."[15]

Many of Warren's supporters have been sensitive to the charge of historical inaccuracy, and in defending Warren against that charge, their general strategy has been to insist that the poem is not about history at all. Holman, for example, argues that "the change of the victim's name [in the revised edition] from the historical George to John is a quiet but emphatic declaration to Clio, in the guise of Boynton Merrill, of 'non serviam.'" This might be persuasive if Warren had not, after the publication of Merrill's book, corrected the spellings of "Letitia" and "Lilburne," and altered Charles Lewis's title from the historically question-able "Dr." to the more firmly established "Colonel," hardly the kind of revisions we might expect from a writer who refuses to serve Clio. Holman goes on to argue that the poem "takes people and events from history and uses them to a most unhistorical, very mythic purpose, to state a universal truth about the nature of man and his world and not a local or temporal truth about a crime in Kentucky in 1811."[16] Warren's use of history, claims Holman, is parallel to Shakespeare's in *Hamlet* or *Julius Caesar*: to revert to the language of Aristotle, both Warren and Shakespeare are concerned with universal rather than particular truths, and therefore any historical inaccuracies in the poem are inconsequential. But Holman neglects to mention that Shakespeare, in *Julius Caesar*, advanced no argument about why Roman history unfolded as it did, whereas in *Brother to Dragons* Warren does make such an argument about American history.[17]

This insistence that the poem is not about the historical event but rather about permanent or mythic meanings suggests a misleading either/or dichotomy. Holman is correct: Warren's poem *is* an inquiry into universal truths about human nature. However, it is also about a specific historical event. One of the poem's central themes concerns what Warren sees as a recurrent problem in American history, or what he calls "the symbolic implication of the event for the Jeffersonian notion of the perfectibility of man and the good American notion of our inevitable righteousness in action and purity in motive."[18] Clearly the event itself gives rise to the implication, and any serious distortion of the event would also distort its implication.

Unlike some of his readers, Warren refuses to draw a sharp distinction between the truths of history and those of poetry. In his foreword, he writes:

> I know that any discussion of the relation of this poem to its historical materials is, in one perspective, irrelevant to its value; and it could be totally accurate as history and still not worth a dime as a poem. I am trying to write a poem, not a history, and therefore have no compunction about tampering with non-essential facts. But poetry is more than fantasy and is committed to the obligation of trying to say something, however obliquely, about the human condition. Therefore, a poem dealing with history is no more at liberty to violate what the writer takes to be the spirit of his history than it is at liberty to violate what he takes to be the nature of the human heart. What he takes those things to be is, of course, his ultimate gamble.
>
> This is another way of saying that I have tried in my poem to make, in a thematic way, historical sense along with whatever kind of sense it may otherwise be happy enough to make.
>
> Historical sense and poetic sense should not, in the end, be contradictory,

for if poetry is the little myth we make, history is the big myth we live, and in our living, constantly remake.[19]

That last sentence is often quoted by critics with finality, as if it clarifies once and for all the question of the poem's historicity. It is an elegantly phrased sentence, certainly, but its truth is open to question, for the little myths we make, such as poems, regularly contradict the big myths we live, such as history. Indeed, one of the burdens of *Brother to Dragons* is to argue that Jefferson's little myth, the Declaration of Independence, is fundamentally and repeatedly contradicted by the big myth of the nation's history as it has been lived out by its people.

Nor is it entirely clear why, in order to say something "about the human condition," a poem must "therefore" not violate the "spirit" of whatever historical material the poem touches upon. It is difficult to imagine why, if "the issues that the characters here discuss are, in my view at least, a human constant,"[20] as Warren writes in explaining the "unspecified place and unspecified time" in which the poem's characters meet, the author or reader need be concerned with the poem's making historical sense. A human constant—the "universal" truths that Aristotle describes, or the "mythic" truths that Holman claims are depicted by Warren and Shakespeare—holds true across all periods of history, so in literature focusing on universal themes, errors of "historical sense" such as the anachronisms in Shakespeare's *Julius Caesar* or Keats's mistaking Cortés for Balboa in "On First Looking into Chapman's Homer" become insignificant. But Warren wants to make "historical sense" as well as "poetic sense," i.e., in Aristotle's terms, he wants to tell the truth about both universal issues, such as the nature of the human heart, as well as particular historical issues such as the impact of Jeffersonian idealism on American history.

The question of the poem's treatment of history is focused most clearly in Warren's depiction of Thomas Jefferson. Early in the poem Jefferson's spirit, haunted by his nephews' brutal crime, is so disgusted with the "human" that he cannot force himself to drink from Lethe because each time he bends to do so, he confronts his own reflection. Everything he believed and stood for, he claims, is wrong. He was wrong to believe that evil could be resolved in time, and wrong in his "towering / Definition" of man as "angelic, arrogant, abstract, / Greaved in glory, thewed with light, the bright / Brow tall as dawn." He was wrong to imagine the American West as "great Canaan's grander counterfeit."[21] He was wrong to believe "That man must redeem nature," wrong to believe that "If we might take man's hand, strike shackle, lead him forth / From his own nightmare—then his natural innocence / Would dance like sunlight over the delighted landscape," wrong to believe "the old charade where man dreams man can put down / The objectified bad and then feel good."[22] His "old definition of man" is only defensible now, says Jefferson, "in senility / And moments of indulgent fiction," and his famous epitaph is only "One more lie in the tissue of lies we live by."[23] All kinds of human love, he claims, are "but a mask / To hide

. . . / the un-uprootable ferocity of self."[24] In *Brother to Dragons*, then, Jefferson's vision of man is as dark and unforgiving and sin-besmirched as the most intense Puritan's, but his lacks the Puritan's promise of a divine redeemer. "There's no forgiveness for our being human," he tells his sister Lucy. "It is the inexpungable error."[25]

This depiction of Jefferson, crucial to one of the poem's major themes, does not reflect Warren's thinking about American history so much as it reflects his thinking about the human condition. The poem's "traumatic subject," writes Jarrell, is "sin, Original Sin, without any Savior," and that sin is rooted in the "ignoble truth of man's depravity." Reviewing the poem shortly after its publication, in the wake of the Second World War, Jarrell continues, "Most of us know, now, that Rousseau was wrong: that man, when you knock his chains off, sets up the death camps."[26]

Later critics have followed Jarrell's lead. James Justus, for example, finds Jefferson representing "the philosophical failure of the Enlightenment," and many critics[27] have remarked on the similarities between Warren's critique of Jefferson and his critiques of John Brown and Ralph Waldo Emerson. All three engage in a self-righteous, absolutist idealism that, in its denial of the merely human, borders on extremism. Driven by what Justus calls "the pride to err massively" or "ideological vanity,"[28] Warren's Jefferson blinds himself to human nature's violent, irrational aspect and thereby makes himself vulnerable to its irruption.

If Warren were simply using Jefferson as a mouthpiece to present a particular brand of ideological rigidity, the question of historical accuracy would be of minimal importance. But Warren uses Jefferson's intellectual flaws to emblematize those of the nation throughout its history. Hugh Ruppersburg develops this point most fully, arguing that "romantic humanism blinded Jefferson to certain inevitable aspects of human character and reality. So too . . . has America been blinded by belief in its own exalted cause to the possibility of its own error, corruption, and even malicious intent."[29] Thus for Ruppersburg, Jefferson's enormous intellectual influence lies behind America's inability to confront, or even to recognize, the moral corruption evident in such issues as slavery or the removal of the Native Americans.

Still, many of Warren's critics, even those who praise the poem enthusiastically, are nevertheless uneasy with the poem's depiction of Jefferson. Harold Bloom, for instance, complains of the "massive drubbing" that Jefferson receives "for being an Enlightened rationalist" and concludes that Warren is "dreadfully unjust to Jefferson."[30] The only critics to come close to defending Warren's Jefferson as historically accurate are Lesa Carnes Corrigan, who claims that "The Thomas Jefferson that Warren introduces in the poem is in many ways the historical personage revered in the annals of American greatness" and that "the Jefferson of history provides the contextual referent of the poem"[31] and William Bedford Clark, who writes, "From Jefferson's own writings, both public and private, we can see that these sentiments attributed to him by Warren have at least a psychological validity." But Clark quickly slips into arguing that the historical verisimilitude of Warren's Jefferson is less important than the character's symbolic function: "the Jefferson of *Brother to Dragons*, however convincing and well-drawn he may be, is less important as an individual reconstructed from the past than as a symbol embodying Warren's critique of America's history and his hopes for America's future."[32]

Most critics, however, do not find Jefferson to be at all "convincing and well-drawn." Holman, for example, labels Warren's Jefferson "totally unhistorical," but he agrees with Clark that the historical accuracy of Warren's depiction is unimportant: "Warren's intention is clearly not to describe an historical Jefferson but to criticize the view of man and human possibility which Jefferson is generally considered to embody, and which the Lewis atrocity teaches him . . . to call a 'lie.'"[33] We find the same argument in William Van O'Connor's review: "He is dealing with the spiritual consequences of Jefferson's idealism, not with the man Jefferson . . . he is Jefferson's shade, a fictional character, a projection of a view of human conduct. It may be closest to the truth to say that Jefferson is the sort of idealist-gone-sour that one finds in Conrad. . . . He is hardly the sage of Monticello"[34]

The problem with such analysis is that, in conceding the historical inaccuracy of Warren's depiction of Jefferson, these critics seriously undermine their claims that Warren's Jefferson embodies a critique of American history. Warren wants to have it both ways, and most of his critics are willing to let him: he wants to write a poem that makes a serious argument that Jeffersonian idealism restricts the nation's ability to comprehend its capacity for corruption, malice, and error, but instead of adhering to the rigorous standards of historical evidence, he asserts the poet's prerogative to "tamper with the evidence." In the light of Warren's foreword, it is difficult to believe that his depiction of Jefferson constitutes "non-essential evidence." John Burt makes a point complementary to mine: Warren

> creates his Jefferson by adopting apparently reasonable surmises about how he
> might have reacted to the Lewis tragedy had he allowed himself to comprehend
> it fully. Those surmises, however, cause him to produce a Jefferson who not
> only is different from his historical counterpart but is also absolutely and sys-
> tematically counterfactual, opposite to the historical Jefferson in every respect.
> In the figure of Jefferson, that is, the concept of historical plausibility runs in
> circles, for in him Warren has plausibly imagined a historically implausible
> character, a character whom, did he not identify himself by name, we would not
> recognize. By means of the figure of Jefferson, the imagination that moves the
> poem calls attention to its liberty, even as it denies taking liberties and accounts
> for its deviations from historical expectation.[35]

The most fully developed, interesting, and believable character in the poem is Lilburne Lewis, perhaps because the paucity of historical evidence regarding Lilburne gives Warren's imagination free reign. Lilburne is a monster, but every monstrous thing he does is a result of a sadly twisted love for his mother, whose love for her son, perhaps displaced from the husband who fails her repeatedly, is not quite what he needs. Lucy says, "the human curse is simply to love and sometimes to love well, / But never well enough,"[36] language that twists Othello's "one that loved not wisely, but too well." Lilburne lacks Othello's heroic stature, but he shares his capacity to twist love into brutal violence, and he needs no Iago to poison his perception of the world and the people in it. He sets sweet-gum leaves in Letitia's hair, telling her they are golden stars and she is an angel. And then his face darkens, and he tells her, "Go back to Heaven if you can, / And if you can't, then try the Other Place, / For . . . / I tell you, even Hell would be better than this sty." He comes home drunk, forces Letitia to perform a sex act that horrifies her, then the next day forces her to describe the act, to say that she enjoyed it, and to say that she enjoyed describing it, and then concludes, "now I see when angels / Come down to earth, they step in dung, like us. / And like it." When his mother sends the slave John to bring Lilburne home from a three-day drunk, Lilburne beats the boy's face bloody. When Aunt Cat tries to comfort Lilburne after his mother's death, reminding him that she nursed him, he replies, "All right, I sucked your milk, but now-- / . . . . / . . . I'd puke the last black drop, / I'd puke it out . . . ."[37]

In his desolate and hysterical love for his dead mother, he berates or humiliates everyone alive who loves him: Letitia, Aunt Cat, his brother Isham. After the murder and the indictment, Isham tries to convince Lilburne to run off, but Lilburne refuses: "Where'er you go the world all stinks the same." Lilburne's disgust with the world, with the people in it, and with himself is projected and focused on the black boy John, who is clumsy and slow, who runs away for days at a time, who breaks Lilburne's mother's china. In dismembering John, in full view of Isham and of the other slaves, Lilburne strikes at all that he believes is wrong with the world, all that is degraded and foul and dark, all that he has recognized within himself. His mother tells Jefferson that Lilburne, in attacking John, was trying to defend "himself against the darkness that was his. / He felt the dark creep in from all the woods. / He felt the dark fear hiding in his heart. / . . . / He saw poor John as but his darkest self / And all the possibility of dark he feared."[38]

In his foreword, Warren calls Lilburne a "light-carrier";[39] like Conrad's Kurtz, he carries the light of civilization into the savage wilderness, and like Kurtz, he discovers the savage wilderness within himself. For Warren, Lilburne's kinsman Meriwether Lewis was also a "light-carrier," and both were among the nation's "founding fathers."[40] Lilburne's story—moving west to the frontier, building Rocky Hill, carrying the refined values and beliefs of Virginia's best families, and then sinking into a cynical disgust with himself and the world that ends in murder and, perhaps, suicide—parallels Meriwether's. In Warren's poem, Meriwether Lewis is the son Jefferson never had, and he believes what he calls Jefferson's "lie." But after his journey to the Pacific and his appointment as Governor of the Louisiana Territory, he is accused of fraud. The poem assumes that he was unjustly accused, and that his acceptance of Jefferson's idealized notion of human nature and the new republic left him totally unprepared to face his attackers. He turns as bitter and cynical as Lilburne and the Jefferson of the poem, and finally commits suicide:

> For suddenly I knew there was no Justice.
> For the human heart will hate Justice for its humanness.
>
> Had I not dreamed that Man at last is Man's friend
> And they will long travel together
> And rejoice in steadfastness.
> Had I not loved, and lived, your lie, then I
> Had not been sent unbuckled and unbraced—
> Oh, the wilderness was easy!—
> But to find, in the end, the tracklessness
> Of the human heart.[41]

Warren uses the almost wholly fictional character of Lilburne as his pattern for re-imagining the historical characters Meriwether Lewis and Thomas Jefferson. In a poem that makes an argument about American history, however, the wisdom of patterning historical characters after a fictional character is questionable. Ehrenpreis quotes the historical Meriwether Lewis to point out his extreme difference from Warren's character: "I hold it an axiom incontrovertible that it is more easy to introduce vice in all states of society than it is to eradicate it, and this is more strictly true when applied to man in his savage than in his civilized state"[42]—hardly the kind of thinking Warren's romantic idealist would engage in.

In his notes on the poem, Warren writes that Jefferson's "crime" parallels Lilburne's.[43] By "crime" he means Jefferson's denial of humanity, expressed in his repudiation of his relationship to Lilburne and his wish, in the poem, that "They should have thrown / It [the infant Lilburne] out where the hogs come to the holler, out with the swill." Lucy accusingly tells her brother that "what poor Lilburne did in madness and exaltation, / You do it in vanity," and that "in virtue and sick vanity / You'd strike poor Lilburne down."[44] Although Jefferson's "Crime" is never enacted physically, as Lilburne's is, the parallel holds on the ethical or spiritual plane: each denies the humanity of another; each denies the essential brotherhood of human being.

Warren and some of his readers, however, want to push the parallel from the spiritual plane onto the plane of history, and on that plane the parallel breaks down. Early in the poem Jefferson suggests that all human beings carry deep within their labyrinthine psyches a monster, a minotaur; John Burt asserts that "Jefferson's Declaration of Independence, no less than Lilburne's murder, is a destructive attempt to achieve transcendence, an attempt to strike down the minotaur which transforms the self into one."[45] Burt's equating of a brutal axe-murder with the writing of the Declaration of Independence may sound extreme, but the poem invites the equation. Richard Law draws a similar conclusion, claiming that the murder is "an image of the tragic core of American history,"[46] and Ruppersburg sees the murder as emblematic of the "American capacity for inhumanity and violence. Such a capacity is innately human, but American democracy, predicated on Jeffersonian humanism and its belief in original virtue, was defenseless against its existence. . . . The murder represents not merely the invalidation of Jeffersonian humanism but the American republic's failure to honor the ideals its founders meant it to embody and their repeated violation throughout its history."[47] Such interpretations make Lilburne's crime bear too great a burden.

Perhaps because he recognizes that burden, Warren blurs the crime's implications for American history with its implications for human nature. The poem's climax has virtually nothing to do with history. Lucy and Meriwether Lewis help Jefferson to acknowledge Lilburne's act, as Richard Law puts it, "as a fulfillment of qualities latent in himself."[48] Over the course of the poem, Jefferson comes to recognize that man is not merely the monster, or minotaur, that he believes him to be early in the poem, just as he is not the angel that he believed him to be while writing the Declaration of Independence. Once he recognizes his relationship to Lilburne, his complicity in what Lucy calls "the shade of the human condition," Jefferson is able to take his nephew's hand in a gesture of reconciliation and acceptance, and to agree with Meriwether that "All is redeemed, / In knowledge."[49]

At the moment of climax, just before Jefferson takes Lilburne's hand, Lucy and Meriwether claim not only that Jefferson's "dream" remains, but that a "nobler" dream is now possible, "nobler because more difficult / And cold, in the face of the old cost / Of our complicities. And— / —knowledge of that cost is, / In itself, a kind of redemption." Jefferson replies by recalling a letter he wrote late in his life to John Adams, in which he said "That the dream of the future is better than / The dream of the past. / How could I hope to find courage to say / That without the fact of the past, no matter / How terrible, we cannot dream the future?"[50] Hugh Ruppersburg, trying mightily to apply the poem's theme to American history, argues that the climax calls for a pragmatic idealism, a fusion of Jeffersonian ideals with an acceptance of the limitations of human nature. Such a pragmatic idealism would imply the continued pursuit of the ideals of the country's founding, tempered by the knowledge that those ideals are unattainable. The poem "seeks from the past a glory which will restore meaning to a diminished present."[51]

Ruppersburg's is a hopeful vision, but the poem does not support it. Far from providing "glory" with which to restore meaning to the present, the past can at best afford us what Jefferson calls the "bitter bread"[52] of a knowledge which is often terrible. Delmore Schwartz is more persuasive when he argues that the poem's characters never finally answer the question of how it is possible to believe in any human ideal or aspiration after facing the actuality of evil; the only answer is "the courage to live with the consciousness that we are all guilty."[53] Echoing Schwartz, Burt concludes that the poem "provides no solution to its motivating difficulty. At best, it provides a way of facing the fact that there will never be one."[54]

The climax of *Brother to Dragons*, in which Jefferson recognizes his complicity in sin, forgives Lilburne, and begins his moral regeneration, is part of a story about ethics, not about American history. Yet Warren understands history as an essentially ethical enterprise. At the Fugitives' Reunion in 1956, he says,

> The past is always a rebuke to the present. . . . It's a better rebuke than any dream of the future. It's a better rebuke because you can see what some of the costs were, what frail virtues were achieved in the past by frail men. And it's there, and you can see it, and see what it cost them, and how they had to go at it. . . . And that is a much better rebuke than any dream of a golden age to come, because historians will correct, and imagination will correct, any notion of a simplistic and, well, childish notion of a golden age. The drama of the past that corrects us is the drama of our struggles to be human, of our struggles to define the values of our forebears in the face of their difficulties.[55]

In other words, the past is a "rebuke" to the kind of arrogance Warren depicts in Jefferson's idealistic, naive vision of human nature. Such language—"rebuke," "virtues," "values," "corrects us"—suggests that history performs an educative function. However, in his essay "The Use of the Past," Warren is quite clear that history cannot give us the answers to current problems or "a formula for making right decisions," nor can it help us avoid the kinds of errors committed in the past or reveal the laws that govern human events. Instead, its value is similar to the ineffable value of literature: history can give its students "insight" or a feeling for "the medium in which action can be undertaken. . . . That feeling for the medium—it is the indefinable, untranslatable thing."[56]

Twenty years after the Fugitives' Reunion, Warren tells Bill Moyers:

> I don't know how you can have a future without a sense of the past. A real future. And we have a book like [John Harold] Plumb's book, *The Death of the Past*, which is a very impressive and disturbing book. . . . He says only history keeps alive the human sense, history in the broadest sense of the word. It might be literary history or political history or any other kind of history. It's man's long effort to be human. And if a student understands this or tries to penetrate this problem, he becomes human.[57]

In other words history, like poetry, teaches us what it means to be human. "The deepest value of history keeps alive the sense that men have striven, suffered, achieved, and have been base or generous—have, in short, been men."[58]

In our reading of both literature and history, writes Warren,

> The truth we want to come to is the truth of ourselves, of our common humanity, available in the projected self of art. We discover a numinous consciousness and for the first time may see both ourselves in the world and the world in us.

This drama of the discovery of the self is timeless. Costume and décor do not matter. In it, the past becomes our present—no, it becomes our future. So far as we understand ourselves, that is, we may move freely into a future and need not be merely the victims of the next event in time that happens to come along.[59]

In *Brother to Dragons*, both Jefferson and Meriwether Lewis suffer from the lack of self-knowledge Warren describes, and precisely because they do not understand themselves or other men, they become "mere victims" of events: "and I come back to the study of the past," writes Warren, "as a way of discovering the self."[60]

Yet for Warren the discovery of the self in history involves also the creation of the self, for he admits that an "absolute, positive past" does not exist; the past is always "an inference, a creation."[61] Self-discovery and self-creation are at once antithetical and complementary phenomena. We might also say that historians must inevitably both discover and create the men and women they write about and that Warren does this in his poem with Thomas Jefferson, Meriwether Lewis, and Lilburne Lewis. But a historian's "creation" can be tested in a way that a poet's or novelist's cannot, as, for example, when Irwin Ehrenpreis quotes the historical Meriwether Lewis in a way that strongly suggests the fictional quality of Warren's Meriwether.

As a fictional character, Jefferson is a highly effective embodiment of the theme of complicity in evil, but as a historical character he is much less effective. Ruppersburg argues that the poem's theme is "the corruption of the American Dream in the nineteenth century as the nation moved inexorably away from the ideals of the Declaration and the Revolution" and that the root causes of the Dream's corruption are "centered in the emblematic figure of Jefferson, who recognized the nation's potential for greatness and was most fatally blind to its potential for blunder." Jefferson "embodies the forces which left the nation vulnerable to its own corrupt nature."[62] Such an argument grants Jefferson far more influence and responsibility than is fair. In fact, the ideals of Jefferson's Declaration were regularly criticized in the early days of the Republic. To cite but one example, John C. Calhoun writes, "[I]t is a great and dangerous error to suppose that all people are equally entitled to liberty. It is a reward to be earned, not a blessing to be gratuitously lavished on all alike;—a reward reserved for the intelligent, the patriotic, the virtuous and deserving—and not a boon to be bestowed on a people too ignorant, degraded and vicious, to be capable either of appreciating or of enjoying it."[63] Ruppersburg's argument is also unpersuasive because the poem suggests very clearly that Jefferson's vision, as embodied in the Declaration, was deeply flawed from its inception; that is, the poem argues, the nation did not "move away" from those ideals—it never embodied them in the first place. In other words, the "American Dream" was not gradually corrupted over the course of the nineteenth century; human beings have always behaved like Lilburne Lewis, and human history has always been made up of that "rich detritus" comprising the "blind nutriment of Lilburne's heart."[64] When

Ruppersburg argues that, for Warren, Jefferson's "idealism, disillusionment, and readjustment . . . is the archetypal pattern of American history,"[65] he offers us on the one hand a pattern so abstract as to be applicable to the history of almost any individual or nation and on the other hand so narrow as to be grossly reductive of the very complicated thing American history is. It makes more sense to read the poem in the context of its composition shortly after World War II and in the early years of the Cold War and America's emergence as a world superpower. In *The Burden of Southern History* C. Vann Woodward suggests that the South's historical experience of failure, defeat, and human fallibility can offer a corrective to a nation convinced of its exceptionalism and its triumphalist role as leader of the free world (a nation soon to become caught up in what another Southerner, J. William Fulbright, would call "the arrogance of power"). Read alongside the pronouncements of John Foster Dulles and Richard Nixon, *Brother to Dragons* becomes an example of a poet speaking truth to power.[66]

Lewis Simpson offers a reading of the poem's implications regarding American history somewhat subtler than Ruppersburg's, suggesting that *Brother to Dragons* shows that "the underlying motive of American history is . . . the assertion of the connection between intellect and self-will" and that Jefferson and Lilburne embody "the willful self as a central, and at times destructive, force in American history." But Simpson concedes that the theme of intellectual willfulness applies not only to "the specific conditions of American history" but also to "the character of the self in modern history generally";[67] he cites Marlowe, Shakespeare, Donne, Francis Bacon, and Joseph Conrad—none of whom dealt with "the specific conditions of American history"—as other writers whose work develops that theme in important ways. Intellectual willfulness may be evident "in modern history generally," but whether it is "*the* underlying motive of American history" (my italics) is open to question.

Finally, the effectiveness of the poem's argument on American history pivots on whether the historical Jefferson was nearly as blind to the nation's "potential for blunder" as is Warren's Jefferson. In the poem Jefferson says, "And as history divulged itself, / I saw how the episode in the meat-house / Would bloom in Time,"[68] and then cites a slave child's crying as its mother is sold, a Christian Cherokee on the Trail of Tears, several horrific Civil War battles, the Haymarket Riot (1886), and violence between labor organizers and "Henry's goons" at the Ford Motor Company, as "ample documentation" in support of his cynical vision of human history. The problem here is that Warren implies that Jefferson, while he was alive, was ignorant of history. The only evidence that Warren's Jefferson cites, apart from the crying child, is drawn from history after Lilburne's murder. But it would have been just as easy for Jefferson, or for anyone with a reasonable knowledge of history, to come up with an equally horrifying catalogue of events from before 1811.

Warren is enough of a scholar to know that Jefferson was widely read in history; in fact, in "Query XIV" of *Notes on the State of Virginia* (written well before Lilburne's act of murder) Jefferson mentions a Roman slavemaster, "a certain Vedius Pollio, who, in the presence of Augustus, would have given a slave as food to his fish, for having broken a glass"[69]—an incident not so very different from Lilburne's murder of a slave for having broken a pitcher. Indeed, if we take seriously Warren's "The Use of the Past," we might wonder why Jefferson's understanding of the human condition, despite his wide reading in history, is so deeply flawed. The historical Jefferson may sometimes seem to ignore "man's capacity for evil" or the tragic dimension of history, as Gordon Wood argues in "The Trials and Tribulations of Thomas Jefferson" (in his *Revolutionary Characters*), especially if we contrast Jefferson with a hard-headed realist like John Adams. But Jefferson is not simply a foil to Adams, and his thinking is not reducible to mere "Jeffersonian idealism." He concludes "Query XVII" of his *Notes* with a prediction that is at once prescient and remote from the facile optimism of Warren's Jefferson:

> But is the spirit of the people an infallible, a permanent reliance? . . . the spirit of the times may alter, will alter. Our rulers will become corrupt, our people careless. A single zealot may commence persecutor, and better men be his victims. It can never be too often repeated, that the time for fixing every essential right on a legal basis is while our rulers are honest, and ourselves united. From the conclusion of this war [i.e., the American Revolution] we shall be going down hill. It will not then be necessary to resort every moment to the people for support. They will be forgotten, therefore, and their rights disregarded. They will forget themselves, but in the sole faculty of making money, and will never think of uniting to effect a due respect for their rights. The shackles, therefore, which shall not be knocked off at the conclusion of this war, will remain on us long, will be made heavier and heavier, till our rights shall revive or expire with convulsion.[70]

Ruppersburg tries to explain Jefferson's traumatic shock over the fact that a slave-owner might murder one of his slaves by arguing that "the historical reality which John as slave represents . . . was too grim and dark for Jefferson or his contemporaries to acknowledge," and that "slavery and the mistreatment of the American Indian were two manifestations of brutality whose moral implications the nation was unprepared to confront,"[71] both of which claims are simply false. Jefferson and his contemporaries may not have confronted the moral implications of slavery and the treatment of American Indians in the same way that Ruppersburg and his contemporaries do, but to suggest that these issues were simply unacknowledged or not confronted is inaccurate. In "Query XVIII" of the *Notes* Jefferson argues, despite his own slaveholding, that "The whole commerce between master and slave is a perpetual exercise of the most boisterous passions, the most unremitting despotism on the one part, and degrading submissions on the other" and concludes that "The man must be a prodigy who can retain his manners and morals undepraved by such circumstances." Despite his racism, Jefferson concedes that blacks as well as whites are endowed by their Creator with the inalienable right of liberty, and reflecting on the history of slavery in America, he concludes, "Indeed I tremble for my country when I reflect that God is just."[72]

In short, Warren's Jefferson is far more ignorant of history and of the moral shortcomings of his fellow citizens than is the historical Jefferson; whether such ignorance is a "non-essential fact" that the poet may justifiably "tamper" with depends upon whether we read the poem as an inquiry into questions of ethics and the human psyche or as an argument on the role of Jeffersonian idealism in American history.

Notes

1. Randall Jarrell, "On the Underside of the Stone," in *Critical Essays on Robert Penn Warren*, ed. William Bedford Clark (Baton Rouge: Louisiana State University Press, 1999), 43.

2. Harold Bloom, ed., *Robert Penn Warren* (New York: Chelsea House, 1986), 145-47.

3. Warren, *Brother*, xii.

4. Warren, "The Way *Brother to Dragons* Was Written," in *Robert Penn Warren: Critical Perspectives*, ed. Neil Nakadate (Lexington: University Press of Kentucky, 1981), 212.

5. Warren, *Brother*, xi–xii.

6. C. Hugh Holman, "Original Sin on the Dark and Bloody Ground," in *Robert Penn Warren's "Brother to Dragons": A Discussion*, ed. James Grimshaw, Jr. (Baton Rouge: Louisiana State University Press, 1983), 195.

7. Richard G. Law, "*Brother to Dragons*: The Fact of Violence vs. the Possibility of Love," in *Critical Essays*, ed. Clark, 199.

8. Warren, *Brother*, xii.

9. Quoted in Holman, "Original Sin," 194.

10. Warren, *Brother*, xii.

11. Warren, *Brother*, 130.

12. Quoted in Grimshaw, *Warren's*, 285.

13. Irvin Ehrenpreis, *Poetries of America: Essays on the Relation of Character to Style* (Charlottesville: University Press of Virginia, 1989), 101.

14. Warren, *Brother*, 14.

15. Warren, *Brother*, 77.

16. Holman, "Original Sin," 196, 198, 199.

17. Richard G. Law makes a point similar to Holman's in two separate essays, arguing first that the poem is "as much an inquiry into the nature of love as a reconstruction of an ax murder" ("Violence," 194) and later that Warren's "aim is not simply to show how it *really* was (*wie es eigentlich gewesen*) at Rocky Hill the night of Sunday, December 15, 1811" ("Notes on the Revised Version of *Brother to Dragons*," in *Critical Essays*, ed. Clark, 214). Similarly, Margaret Mills Harper argues that the poem is concerned with "the permanent values and significances of history, rather than the specific events" ("Versions of History in *Brother to Dragons*," in *Warren's*, ed. Grimshaw, 242), and John Burt writes that "*Brother to Dragons* is a poem not about its events but about how those events are to be evaluated" (*Robert Penn Warren and American Idealism*, (New

Haven: Yale University Press, 1988), 201).

18. Quoted in Grimshaw, *Warren's*, 296.

19. Warren, *Brother*, xiii.

20. Warren, *Brother*, xv.

21. Warren, *Brother*, 8, 10.

22. Warren, *Brother*, 27, 29, 30.

23. Warren, *Brother*, 5, 85.

24. Warren, *Brother*, 33.

25. Warren, *Brother*, 19.

26. Jarrell, "Underside," 44.

27. James Justus, *The Achievement of Robert Penn Warren* (Baton Rouge: Louisiana State University Press, 1981), 65. See also William Bedford Clark, "'Canaan's Grander Counterfeit': Jefferson and America in *Brother to Dragons*," in *Warren's*, ed. Grimshaw, 147; Justus, *Achievement*, 64–65; Law, "Violence," 195; and Burt, *Idealism*, 202.

28. Justus, *Achievement*, 64, 65.

29. Hugh Ruppersburg, *Robert Penn Warren and the American Imagination* (Athens: University of Georgia Press, 1990), 45.

30. Bloom, *Warren*, 145, 147.

31. Lesa Carnes Corrigan, *Poems of Pure Imagination: Robert Penn Warren and the Romantic Tradition* (Baton Rouge: Louisiana State University Press, 1999), 73, 74.

32. Clark, "Canaan's," 145, 146.

33. Holman, "Original Sin," 198.

34. Quoted in Grimshaw, ed., *Warren's*, 179-80.

35. Burt, *Idealism*, 200.

36. Warren, *Brother*, 18.

37. Warren, *Brother*, 47, 52, 58.

38. Warren, *Brother*, 105, 116.

39. Warren, *Brother*, xiii.

40. Quoted in Nakadate, ed., *Warren*, 213.

41. Warren, *Brother*, 114.

42. Ehrenpreis, *Poetries*, 103-04.

43. Quoted in Grimshaw, ed., *Warren's*, 202.

44. Warren, *Brother*, 42, 116, 117.

45. Burt, *Idealism*, 216.

46. Law, "Violence," 194.

47. Ruppersburg, *Imagination*, 62, 63.

48. Law, "Violence," 197.

49. Warren, *Brother*, 118, 120.

50. Warren, *Brother*, 118.

51. Ruppersburg, *Imagination*, 66, 75.

52. Warren, *Brother*, 120.

53. Delmore Schwartz, "The Dragon of Guilt," in *Critical*, ed. Clark, 45.

54. Burt, *Idealism*, 217.

55. Quoted in R. R. Purdy, ed., *Fugitive's Reunion: Conversations at Vanderbilt, May 2-5, 1956* (Nashville: Vanderbilt University Press, 1959), 210.

56. Robert Penn Warren, "The Use of the Past," in *New and Selected Essays* (New York: Random House, 1989), 40.

57. Quoted in Ruppersburg, *Imagination*, 4.

58. Warren, "Use," 37.

59. Warren, "Use," 48.

60. Warren, "Use," 49.

61. Warren, "Use," 51.

62. Ruppersburg, *Imagination*, 44, 45.

63. John C. Calhoun, "Selection from *A Disquisition on Government (c. late 1840s)*," in *American Intellectual*, ed. Hollinger and Capper, vol. 1, 465.

64. Warren, *Brother*, 77.

65. Ruppersburg, *Imagination*, 46.

66. Reinhold Niebuhr's *The Irony of American History* (1952, Chicago: University of Chicago Press, 2008) adopts an attitude toward American history that is deeply consonant with Warren's: "Our modern liberal culture, of which American civilization is such an unalloyed exemplar, is involved in many ironic refutations of its original pretensions of virtue, wisdom, and power" (xxiv).

67. Lewis Simpson, "The Poet and the Father: Robert Penn Warren and Thomas Jefferson," in *The Legacy of Robert Penn Warren*, ed. David Madden (Baton Rouge: Louisiana State University Press, 2000): 139, 140–41, 153.

68. Warren, *Brother*, 85.

69. Thomas Jefferson, "Notes on the State of Virginia," in *Writings*, ed. Merrill D. Peterson (New York: Library of America, 1984), 268.

70. Jefferson, *Writings*, 287.

71. Ruppersburg, *Imagination*, 59, 63.

72. Jefferson, *Writings*, 288, 289.

Chapter 5
T. S. Eliot:
Awaking from the Nightmare of History

In an early episode of James Joyce's *Ulysses*, Stephen Dedalus is teaching ancient history: Pyrrhus's victory over the Romans at Asculum, 279 BC. His students cannot answer a question, and Stephen's mind wanders, imagining the event first as fable, then as historical event, and finally as a general, almost archetypal form: "Fabled by the daughters of memory. And yet it was in some way if not as memory fabled it. . . . From a hill above a corpsestrewn plain a general speaking to his officers, leaned upon a spear. Any general to any officers. They lend ear." Stephen knows that for his students "history was a tale like any other too often heard," but for himself, a teacher of history? He returns to Aristotle's distinction in the *Poetics* between what *did* happen and what *might* happen: "Had Pyrrhus not fallen by a beldam's hand in Argos and Julius Caesar not been knifed to death? They are not to be thought away. Time has branded them and fettered they are lodged in the room of the infinite possibilities they have ousted. But can those have been possible seeing that they never were? Or was that only possible which came to pass? Weave, weaver of the wind." And how significant, finally, are the weavings of the wind? Stephen recalls another line from Aristotle—"The soul is in a manner all that is: the soul is the form of forms"—and with that line at the back of his mind, he moves on to the famous conversation with Mr. Deasy in which he announces that "History . . . is a nightmare from which I am trying to awake."[1]

That High Modernist dream of awaking from the nightmare of history into the reality of the soul recalls Mircea Eliade's account of the psychology of archaic man, who separates reality very sharply into the sacred and the profane. Archaic man's rejection of profane history, writes Eliade, "testifies to his thirst for the real [that is, the spiritually transcendent] and his terror of 'losing' himself by letting himself be overwhelmed by the meaninglessness of profane existence."[2] Like Stephen Dedalus, T. S. Eliot shares this same terror of losing himself amid the chaos of profane history, and this same thirst for the real: an intense desire to believe that something somewhere must be more real than the brutal spectacle of history, and to believe that the self or soul is rooted not in

79

historicity, but rather in the supernatural or divine, which lies somewhere outside history, although as we shall see, later in his career Eliot will acknowledge that it is history that paradoxically affords us access to the extra-historical divine.

Unlike Benét, who aligns himself with the new, non-partisan Civil War historiographers, or MacLeish, who contrasts his own approach to the Conquest of Mexico with the "false as bloody hell" approach of Prescott, or Warren, who challenges the standard reading of Jeffersonian idealism, Eliot does not focus his thinking about history on a particular person or event, nor does he engage the work of particular historians. Instead, Eliot's thinking about history is broadly philosophical and grows out of his graduate work in philosophy at Harvard. In his Ph.D. dissertation on F. H. Bradley, Eliot worked on the epistemological problem of the relationship between "appearance"—which includes the varieties of our experience of the world, ourselves, and others—and "reality," which is the permanent and the Absolute. Eliot was finally unpersuaded by Bradley's account of the Absolute, but he never lost his conviction that the Absolute must in some sense exist, and all of his thinking about history is colored by that conviction. Here, for example, is a letter from November 12, 1927, to Bonamy Dobrée:

> I would not wish to make truth a function of the will. . . . [I]f there is no fixed truth, there is no fixed object for the will to tend to. If truth is always changing, then there is nothing to do but to sit down and watch the pictures. . . . [T]here can be no permanent reality if there is no permanent truth. I am of course quite ready to admit that human apprehension of truth varies changes and perhaps develops, but that is a property of human imperfection rather than of truth. You cannot conceive of truth at all, the word has no meaning, except by conceiving of it as something permanent.[3]

This conviction that truth must adhere to the permanent appears as early as "Tradition and the Individual Talent" (1919), where Eliot writes:

> Tradition . . . involves, in the first place, the historical sense, which we may call nearly indispensable to anyone who would continue to be a poet beyond his twenty-fifth year; and the historical sense involves a perception, not only of the pastness of the past, but of its presence; the historical sense compels a man to write not merely with his own generation in his bones, but with a feeling that the whole of the literature of Europe from Homer and within it the whole of the literature of his own country has a simultaneous existence and composes a simultaneous order. This historical sense, which is a sense of the timeless as well as of the temporal and of the timeless and of the temporal together, is what makes a writer traditional.[4]

So "the historical sense" embraces past and present in a single whole and perceives history as existing within a "simultaneous" order; moreover, the historical sense is cognizant of the relationship between the timeless and the temporal. Certain things belong only to the order of the temporal, or "appearance." But other things belong to the order of the permanent or the absolute, and to the extent that a work of literature embodies such things, it forms a part of what Eliot calls the "tradition." The ability to recognize what is of permanent value is central to the poet, for "he is not likely to know what is to be done unless he lives in what is not merely the present, but the present moment of the past, unless he is conscious, not of what is dead, but of what is already living."[5] The "present moment of the past" exists outside the order of mere appearance or mere temporality; it participates in the permanent and the absolute.

For Eliot the Absolute is ontologically prior to appearance or historical reality, just as in Plato's *Phaedrus* man is supposed to have fallen from the world of forms into the temporal world, and his intellectual task is to try to remember his true (original) nature and the true (original) nature of things. Tradition for Eliot is "an ideal order" outside of time, and this order is always already "complete before the new work arrives."[6] The unified whole of the Tradition reflects what Eliot calls "the mind of Europe,"[7] and the literature of the past participates in the Tradition insofar as it reflects the permanent and absolute values and truths of that mind. This is not to say that the mind of Europe exists entirely outside history, for of course literature is created from within history, and the Tradition itself may be modified by the creation of new literature: "the mind of Europe—the mind of his own country—a mind which he learns in time to be much more important than his own private mind—is a mind which changes . . . this change is a development which abandons nothing *en route*, which does not superannuate either Shakespeare, or Homer, or the rock drawings of the Magdalenian draughtsmen."[8] So history is real, and historical products compose the Tradition, but most historical change belongs to the order of appearance, not to the order of the permanent and absolute, and no historical change can ever dislodge Shakespeare or Homer, whose work participates so fully in the permanent, from the Tradition.

Eliot's "historical sense" is not concerned with what we typically understand as the historian's work, for much of history in and of itself belongs to mere "appearance." Eliot's historical sense is a mode of knowledge that claims the power to apprehend those aspects of the "permanent" that are manifest within the flux of history. Perhaps the closest that Eliot ever comes to thinking like an historian—and it is not particularly close—is his famous claim in the essay "The Metaphysical Poets" that "In the seventeenth century a dissociation of sensibility set in, from which we have never recovered."[9] This dissociated sensibility is not only symptomatic of literature; in a later essay Eliot writes, "The trouble of the modern age is not merely the inability to believe certain things about God and men which our forefathers believed, but the inability to *feel* towards God and men as they did."[10] Eliot links the dissociation of thought from feeling to the rise of Puritanism, the English Civil War, and a burgeoning emphasis on the accumulation of wealth that will feed into the Enlightenment's rational self-interest as well as the hyper-individualism of Romanticism, liberalism, and the psychic alienation characteristic of modernity. These heterodox, materialist attitudes and values have come to dominate the modern world, or what Eliot calls "the immense panorama of futility and anarchy which is contemporary history."[11]

For Eliot, the dissociation of sensibility marks the beginning of the West's decline into secularism and the suppression of those political, religious, and aesthetic values and beliefs that are central to "tradition" in that broader sense which Eliot summed up in the famous phrase from *For Lancelot Andrewes* (1928): "classicist in literature, royalist in politics, and anglo-catholic in religion." For Eliot that broader tradition is manifested most clearly in the hierarchical social organization and Latin-Catholic orthodoxy of medieval Europe, a society that produced such coherent intellectual and aesthetic wholes as the Great Chain of Being, Aquinas's *Summa*, and Dante's *Divine Comedy*. Within the flux of history, something like the dissociation of sensibility can pull political, social, religious, and aesthetic life away from the permanent, but even amid the "futility and anarchy" of contemporary history, the "tradition" nevertheless persists, more or less evident, and always available to an elite who are sensitive enough to recognize its truth and value.

In *T. S. Eliot and Ideology*, Kenneth Asher demonstrates the important role played by Joseph de Maistre, Charles Maurras, and T. E. Hulme in Eliot's understanding of the driving agents of history. For these thinkers "original sin" names the fundamental truth about human beings. We are creatures of powerful lusts and desires, and unless these are disciplined and held in check by some sort of hierarchical, authoritative order, we live amid the "futility and anarchy" that Eliot finds in "contemporary history." That hierarchical order can be legitimized only by its grounding in the truths and values of the "tradition"—genuine order cannot be the arbitrary imposition of one strongman or another, shifting with the vagaries of history. For Eliot the truths and values of the "tradition" are not invented out of whole cloth by human beings; they are objective, and independent of any subjective will or desire. Early in his career, Eliot seems unsure whether the root of the permanent and the absolute is aesthetic, political, or religious—or perhaps somehow all three—but as his thinking develops he comes finally to ground everything in Christianity: "Either everything in man can be traced as a development from below, or something must come from above. There is no avoiding that dilemma: you must be either a naturalist or a supernaturalist."[12]

Before he reaches that point, however, we find him wrestling with the question of history's significance in a world in which man's development does not clearly come "from above." Eliot composed "Gerontion" in London in May-June 1919, in the aftermath of the First World War. The poem's epigraph comes from *Measure for Measure*: Claudio has been sentenced to death, and the Duke tells him that it's not so bad to die: "Thou hast nor youth nor age / But as it were an after dinner sleep / Dreaming of both." In other words, life is no more substantial than a dream; its significance is ephemeral, epiphenomenal. The poem's speaker, Gerontion ("little old man" in Greek), begins: "Here I am, an old man in a dry month, / Being read to by a boy, waiting for rain." The "dry month" and "waiting for rain" prefigure one of the dominant themes of *The Waste Land*, for which Eliot considered using "Gerontion" as a prelude. What the boy reads to the old man sounds like history, which for Gerontion seems to be little more than a kind of spectacle that he has never experienced: "I was neither at the hot gates / Nor fought in the warm rain / Nor knee deep in the salt marsh, heaving a cutlass, / Bitten by flies, fought." The "hot gates" would be Thermopylae, where Leonidas and the Three Hundred Spartans held off the Persian Army during the Greco-Persian War of 480 BC. Gerontion was *not* there, nor was he an active participant in anything like the military engagements he hears of in the boy's reading. Later in the poem he says, "I have lost my sight, smell, hearing, taste and touch"—his is an empirical consciousness that grows more limited with the reduction of his sensory impressions, and his self-description is similarly reductive: "A dull head among windy spaces."

Because Gerontion's consciousness is defined by empirical data, he does not know how to interpret something like the birth of Christ; the infant is supposed to be "The word within a word," but because he is "unable to speak a word" and "Swaddled with darkness," Gerontion does not know what he signifies. He might be the kind of history-overturning force that Yeats imagines in "The Second Coming," and Gerontion briefly imagines him as "Christ the tiger" who "springs in the new year. Us he devours." But Christ has not sprung, and Gerontion is not devoured: he is simply "An old man in a draughty house / Under a windy knob," and in an image that forecasts Stephen Dedalus's "Weave, weaver of the wind," Gerontion remarks, "Vacant shuttles / Weave the wind." If the shuttles are truly vacant, however, whose hand manipulates the weaving? Is the wind woven into any purposeful or meaningful pattern?

In the poem's most well-known passage on the meaning of history, Gerontion asks:

> After such knowledge, what forgiveness? Think now
> History has many cunning passages, contrived corridors
> And issues, deceives with whispering ambitions,
> Guides us by vanities. Think now
> She gives when our attention is distracted
> And what she gives, gives with such supple confusions
> That the giving famishes the craving. Gives too late
> What's not believed in, or if still believed,
> In memory only, reconsidered passion. Gives too soon
> Into weak hands, what's thought can be dispensed with
> Till the refusal propagates a fear. Think
> Neither fear nor courage saves us. Unnatural vices
> Are fathered by our heroism. Virtues
> Are forced upon us by our impudent crimes.

Historical knowledge, the speaker implies, affords us no forgiveness. We may wish to believe that history is driven, as Hegel suggests, by the "cunning of reason" in a manner that continues the progressive unfolding of the *Weltgeist*, or in some other purposive, meaningful manner, but more often history seems like a seductive woman who promises the fulfillment of our desires and intentions, but instead merely plays on our ambitions, passions, cravings, fears, and vanities. In the unpredictable and finally unknowable world of history, crimes are as likely to produce virtues as vices, and virtues more likely to produce vices than salvation.

The poem's strongest recurrent image is that of a directionless, purposeless wind, and in its final section various characters are

> . . . whirled
> Beyond the circuit of the shuddering Bear [the pole star]
> In fractured atoms. Gull against the wind, in the windy straits
> Of Belle Isle, or running on the Horn,
> White feathers in the snow, the Gulf claims,
> And an old man driven by the Trades
> To a sleepy corner.[13]

This image of time as constant flux, of ceaseless becoming without permanence or transcendence, leads only to old age and death: Gerontion's life and his idea of history are finally empty and futile, without direction or purpose.

Whether one finds that same sense of the purposelessness of history in Eliot's best-known poem, *The Waste Land* (1922), is a matter of some contention. In *Modernist Poetics of History*, which is among the most influential studies of Eliot's thinking about the past, James Longenbach calls *The Waste Land* "the poem that offers the richest expression of the modernist sense of the past."[14] For Longenbach, Eliot's idea of history is very close to the "existential historicism" of Wilhelm Dilthey, according to which history is best understood *not* as a sequence of events that occurred in the past, but as simply the individual historian's effort, in the present, to understand the past. In his dissertation Eliot describes F. H. Bradley's claim that ideas about the past "do not qualify a real past . . . for there is no real past . . . for them to qualify. . . . Ideas of the past are true, not by correspondence with a real past, but by their coherence with each other and ultimately with the present moment."[15] In other words, for Dilthey and for Bradley history exists *only* in the present, as a construction of the historian. But for both Bradley and Eliot, the historian's task is not simply to produce his own interpretation of the past, which may be set in competition with other interpretations, but somehow to transcend the relativism of his particular situatedness and to construct a coherent, systematic whole that enfolds the past within the present.

Objective historiography cannot accomplish this task because, as Bradley puts it, no "objective" past exists, yet Longenbach argues that for Eliot, "the critic with the most *whole* and *ordered* system can assay interpretations that approach the absolute."[16] This may seem an extreme claim, but Longenbach is insistent: "Eliot believes that if we can 'somehow' expand our point of view into a 'system' wide and coherent enough to encompass the whole truth, then our interpretations would be absolutely true."[17] One wonders what possible measuring stick a reader might use to determine which historian's "system" is the widest or the most whole, and whether internal coherence and order, by themselves, can help one to distinguish good history from propaganda or fiction. Ernst Breisach points to this difficulty when he describes Dilthey's approach to history as a dead end: "In practice, an unhappy Dilthey ended up with a view of history as a sequence of Weltanschauungen (world views), each of which could be plausibly true, leaving the hermeneutical circle wide open."[18]

At times, Longenbach seems to be aware of concerns like Breisach's, as for example when he concedes that "Eliot had little faith in the individual's ability to achieve this kind of transcendent vision of 'the whole truth' on his own." History and historians in and of themselves, it would seem, leave us in the position of Gerontion. Nevertheless, Longenbach seems to accept Eliot's belief that a visionary grasp of the absolute truth of history remains possible:

> Only the inspired interpreter (such as Dante or Tiresias) can attain a vision of "the whole truth" and escape the inevitable "trap of interpretation." While Eliot recognized that any statement about the world is necessarily an imperfect interpretation, he nevertheless confessed in less guarded moments that he felt himself able to transcend those limitations and feel the presence of the past with visionary intensity.[19]

For Longenbach *The Waste Land* enacts just such a process of transcendence, or the unification of separate points of view, building from individual consciousness to a universal mind that encompasses the whole truth ("And of course," writes Eliot in his Ph.D. dissertation, "the only real truth is the whole truth"[20]). The poem's allusions, its palimpsest of historical references to places like Carthage, persons like Cleopatra, tales like "Tristan and Isolde," and myths like those surrounding the Grail Quest signify the synthesizing of this comprehensive point of view. "In *The Waste Land*," writes Longenbach, "so many individual consciousnesses are unified that the voice intoning the poem often *seems* to be the voice of history itself, an expression of the 'entire past' woven into the texture of the present. The voices in *The Waste Land* are thus both past and present, both personal and universal, both autobiographical and historical—distinctions that Eliot . . . collapses."[21]

Longenbach admits that such apprehension of the "whole truth," such transcendence of a time-bound, individual point of view, is rationally inexplicable, or in other words mystical, and he reads *The Waste Land* as a poem that "vacillates between the assurance of transcendental vision and a skepticism that threatens to obliterate the possibility of knowledge altogether."[22] If he is right, then the poem presents its readers with a dilemma: either we accept its divinely inspired vision of the Whole Truth, or we accept the kind of radical skepticism that renders historical knowledge impossible. Yet Longenbach ends his discussion by asserting that "*The Waste Land* remains the ultimate 'poem including history' produced in the twentieth century."[23]

But what kind of history, after all, does Eliot's poem "include"? Apart from three cryptic fragments—"the ships at Mylae" in Part One, "Elizabeth and Leicester" in Part Three, and the implicit history of the cities ("Jerusalem Athens Alexandria / Vienna London") listed in Part Five—all of the historical references in the poem are to literary or religious texts or to mythology. A commonplace of critical commentary on the poem asserts that its theme involves not only what Eliot calls in one of his endnotes "the present decay of eastern Europe," but in fact the decay of Western civilization.[24] This is an arguable point, but even if we grant its validity, we must admit that the point is supported with minimal reference to historical events or evidence. As Michael Bernstein puts it, "the Waste Land is a spiritual and psychological, not a geographic or political, demarcation. For all its seeming specificity of detail, Eliot's poem presents a vision of a world which the reader accepts for aesthetic, moral, and psychological reasons. There is no attempt at either a logical or historical argument."[25] If Longenbach's claim that *The Waste Land* "offers the richest expression of the modernist sense of the past" is valid, then we might conclude that modernism's sense of the past, its understanding of history, is indeed quite thin.[26]

It is more accurate to say that one of the themes of *The Waste Land* is not the *present* decay of Europe; Eliot is not echoing Spengler and tracing a predictable pattern of historical decline, nor is he showing us that before the dissociation of sensibility set in, things were much happier. Quite the contrary: his point is the *permanent* decay of European civilization, the horror of *all* history. Think about the literary allusions in the poem: the Cumaean sibyl, condemned to literal life imprisonment because she refuses the sexual advances of a god; Tristan, who betrays his King and dies believing his beloved Isolde has betrayed him; the distraught mother in Webster's *The White Devil*, who sings while her son buries the brother he killed; Philomel, raped by her sister's husband, who then cuts out her tongue; the banquet Dido gives for Aeneas, shortly before he deserts her and she burns herself alive; Ophelia's mad scene, just after she learns that her lover has murdered her father, and just before she drowns herself; the song from *The Vicar of Wakefield* about a "lovely woman who stoops to folly" and then has no honorable choice but suicide; the betrayals of Coriolanus.

The essential attitude toward history in this poem might be summed up by Shakespeare's Thersites, who announces, "still wars and lechery; nothing else holds fashion" (*Troilus and Cressida* 5.2). Disgust with history is the poem's dominant emotion, disgust so intense that it crosses the line into horror. Nancy Gish writes:

The mood of horror [in *The Waste Land*] is intensified by Eliot's distortion of time. In the early poems time provides a deceptive façade of order. . . . The significance of time in *The Waste Land* is just its disappearance as a pretense of order. Time is coexistent and, being eternally present, it is unredeemable. All times are juxtaposed and similar events occur in the context of different centuries. . . . The horror is thus a combination of daily misery in personal life, similar to that in earlier poems, with a changelessness precluding salvation or renewal. . . . What creates the mood of horror . . . is precisely the changlessness of this world, its incapacity for redemption.[27]

Calvin Bedient makes a similar point:

What is the good of rising, and sinking, and rising again, going up the hill and down, in a mad, libidinous, profitless cycle? The protagonist has already been alive for so long, so many times: "You who were with me in the ships at Mylae!" As it was in the beginning: . . . . repetition has a stranglehold on the speaker . . . For the protagonist, as for Stephen Dedalus in *Ulysses*, history is a nightmare from which he is . . . trying to wake: in his case, into the true present of the Absolute.[28]

Bedient is exactly right. The attitude toward history in *The Waste Land* is reminiscent of the medieval Christian *contemptus mundi* trope, developed by twelfth-century writers like Peter Abelard and Bernard of Cluny, which stresses the implacable opposition between the "things of this world" and the "things of Christ."[29] Eliot pushes this opposition to a point at which "the world" becomes a *theatrum mundi*, an arena of carnal lusts and appetites for money, power, and blood, a vulgar, violent spectacle that is endlessly and pointlessly repeated, like the awful cycle of "birth, copulation, and death" to which the meaninglessness of existence is reduced in *Sweeney Agonistes*. The Buddha preaches in his "Fire Sermon" that in this world "all things are on fire," i.e., all of our sensory impressions are aflame with the fires of envy, anger, and lust, which are in turn the motivating agents of much of what passes as history, and that such fires must be extinguished if one is to escape this essentially ephemeral plane of existence. The myth of "What the Thunder Said" repeats the same message: envy, anger, and lust are the weaknesses for which the Lord Prajapathi prescribes his spiritual cure: give, sympathize, control. In *The Waste Land*, however, although the protagonist is intellectually cognizant of these spiritual texts, he does not experience them as truths or as articles of faith. He may be marginally ahead of Gerontion, but only marginally.

Bedient suggests that Eliot "will at length turn his back on the abject realm of history," but that he is nevertheless drawn to it, perhaps as Gerontion is seduced by it.

His attraction to it . . . is almost never less than guilty and self-berating—a

willed masochism of conscious meanness. What had fallen off from transcendence [that is, the world of history] . . . at once seduced and horrified Eliot: the
smell of steaks in passageways, yellow soles of feet clasped in the palms of
soiled hands, the physical, the female, the vegetal, the mechanical. A high
dream of purest coherence, living and ungraspable, swift and eternal, terrorized
everything below it, everything of flesh and time and even everything lingual,
even art, though the whole aim of Eliot's career was to perfect art to the point
where it would be forgiven, maybe even graced, by the Absolute.[30]

In *The Waste Land*, the existence of that kind of saving grace is only hinted at,
only suggested, and then only at the very end of the poem. Madame Sosostris
cannot find the hanged man, and the travelers on the road to Emmaus cannot
recognize the third who walks beside them. Eliot's protagonist may long for the
transcendence of history and the attainment of a consciousness affording access
to an order of reality beyond "the immense panorama of futility and anarchy
which is contemporary history," but at the end of the poem all he feels is its absence.

After *The Waste Land*, we get the even more desolate world-views of *The
Hollow Men* (1925) and *Sweeney Agonistes* (1926, 1927), and then in 1927 Eliot
formally joins the Anglican communion, and his thinking about history is utterly
transformed. In *Ash-Wednesday* (1930), Eliot returns to the contrast between the
"things of Christ" and the "things of this world" as he writes, "Against the Word
the unstilled world still whirled / About the centre of the silent Word." His
speaker asks, "Where shall the word be found [?]" and answers himself: "Not
here."[31] The speaker's desire is to "sit still" and "not to be separated,"[32] but he
knows that his desire cannot be satisfied within the whirling world of history.
Eliot's designation of the "centre" as the locus of the Word parallels Mircea
Eliade's account of archaic man, for whom the center is "the zone of the sacred,
of absolute reality."[33] *Ash-Wednesday* picks up the diction and imagery of the
end of "Gerontion," but in the later poem the speaker is clearly oriented in time
and space; he has a focus and a direction. Eliot develops his distinction between
a secular, materialist history and a Christocentric history in his "Choruses" from
The Rock (1934), contrasting the kind of pointless "information" that secular
history provides, with the "wisdom" that Christian revelation affords:

> The endless cycle of idea and action,
> Endless invention, endless experiment,
> Brings knowledge of motion, but not of stillness;
> Knowledge of speech, but not of silence;
> Knowledge of words, and ignorance of the Word.
> . . .
> Where is the wisdom we have lost in knowledge?
> Where is the knowledge we have lost in information?[34]

Any merely secular history becomes a catalog of "perpetual revolution" and "perpetual recurrence," like the wind-blown thoughts of Gerontion, the shattered fragments of *The Waste Land*, or the meaningless, recurrent cycles of birth, copulation, and death to which all human existence is reduced in *Sweeney Agonistes*. For Eliot, such a history is necessarily truncated or incomplete unless and until it apprehends the significance of Christ's incarnation and His subsequent redemption of, and infusion of meaning into, human history:

> Then came, at a predetermined moment, and moment in time
> and of time,
> A moment not out of time, but in time, in what we call history:
> transecting, bisecting the world of time, a moment in time
> but not like a moment of time,
> A moment in time but time was made through that moment:
> for without the meaning there is no time, and that moment
> of time gave the meaning.[35]

Because the Word becomes flesh *in history*, and not in some pre-historical time when the gods roamed the earth (what Eliade calls *in illo tempore*, the time of the origins), historical time can be redeemed, i.e., it can have absolute meaning. History is *centered* around the Incarnation, is given *telos* and absolute significance by means of Jesus Christ.

Eliot is perfectly clear about the fundamental significance of Christian revelation in his world-view: "[T]he division between those who accept and those who deny, Christian revelation, I take to be the most profound division between human beings. It does not merely go deeper than divisions of class or race; it is different in kind and cannot be measured by the same scale."[36] In other words: "There are only two finally tenable hypotheses about life: the Catholic and the materialistic."[37] Our religious sensibility lies at the very center of our humanity: "Man is man because he can recognize supernatural realities, not because he can invent them."[38]

In *Four Quartets*, Eliot articulates his Christocentric idea of history's significance more fully than anywhere else. Some readers dislike what they perceive as a kind of hierophantic posturing on Eliot's part in these poems, and for most readers they lack the vitality of "Prufrock" or *The Waste Land*. They are essential, however, to an understanding of Eliot's resolution to the problem of historical consciousness that he lays out in "Gerontion" and *The Waste Land*. The first of the *Quartets*, "Burnt Norton" (1935), takes its title from a manor house and garden in Gloucestershire built on the site of the Norton House that a drunken Sir William Keyt set afire in 1741, killing himself in the blaze, and known by the locals as "Burnt Norton" ever since. Eliot visited the garden, apparently as an uninvited trespasser and possibly in the company of his American friend Emily Hale, in the summer of 1934. The poem begins with the speaker's speculating on "What might have been" as opposed to "what has been," and on whether past, present, and future are somehow "contained" in one another. "If all time is eternally present," the speaker asserts, "All time is unredeemable."[39] This gnomic utterance seems to suggest that a strictly secular temporality is always and only itself, i.e., a fully materialist historicity cannot transcend itself or point beyond itself to another order of reality. Given such a temporality, no "redemption" from our wholly material condition would be possible.

Later in the poem, though, the speaker compares the figures of the "dance along the artery" with "the drift of stars," suggesting that the natural world consists of "patterns" that are repeated in time and space. These abstract patterns or laws in some sense transcend the particulars of mere temporality, and they may point to what the poem's speaker insists is a far greater, genuine transcendence that he locates "[a]t the still point of the turning world." This "still point" lies beyond the reality construed by our empirical or rational understanding, for it is neither physical nor spiritual ("flesh nor fleshless"), and although it is "still," it is not "fixity."[40] This is the paradoxical language of mysticism, and *Four Quartets* presents a mystical Christian vision of history. The poem's speaker states, from his privileged, mystical position, that "human kind / Cannot bear very much reality," for we are "enchain[ed]" in bodies that perceive temporality as linear, and afford us only "a little consciousness."[41] Yet our limited, time-bound consciousness can sometimes open into "moments" of revelation, figured in this poem as "the moment in the rose-garden,"[42] when the scales drop from our eyes. Such moments link us to the genuinely transcendent, which Nancy Gish describes as "supremely real and opposed to ordinary temporal experience."[43] In such moments, time is redeemed, yet we can experience such moments only in time, as the speaker concedes: "Only through time is time conquered."[44] Nancy Gish argues that in this poem, history or "time has value only as it 'points to' that transcendent moment," and that Eliot implies that "transcendent experience" is the only human experience of any real value, an implication that Gish finds "extreme."[45] This is a fair point, but it is also true that we do not find in "Burnt Norton" the kind of disgust with history that we find in *The Waste Land*, and that the transcendent moment occurs *in* history even as it carries its participant outside history.

"East Coker" (1940), the second of the *Quartets*, takes its title from the Somerset village from which Andrew Eliot (a direct ancestor) emigrated to Massachusetts in the late seventeenth century. Eliot visited East Coker in 1937, and his ashes are interred there. Like "Burnt Norton," "East Coker" begins with a meditation on a strictly secular temporality: "Houses rise and fall," and they may be restored or replaced by open fields or factories. The earth itself enacts a cyclic process of "flesh, fur and faeces, / Bone of man and beast, cornstalk and leaf."[46] The speaker imagines an earlier time, a summer midnight of peasants dancing to pipe and drum around a fire, the rhythm of their dancing reflecting

> The time of the seasons and the constellations
> The time of milking and the time of harvest
> The time of the coupling of man and woman

And that of beasts. Feet rising and falling.
Eating and drinking. Dung and death. [47]

The poem begins, "In my beginning is my end," and if we imagine time as a series of natural cycles, including that of birth, copulation, and death, as *Sweeney Agonistes* has it, then one's end is certainly contained in one's beginning. The regularity of these cyclic patterns may induce feelings of comfort and nostalgia, but finally these patterns carry no significance beyond themselves; in the language of "Burnt Norton," the time of such patterns is unredeemable.

Similarly, the speaker in "East Coker" decides that the "wisdom of age" is deceptive and useless, and like the speaker of "Burnt Norton," he finds "only a limited value / In the knowledge derived from experience."[48] Again as in "Burnt Norton," the limits of empirical knowledge are contrasted with a revelatory or mystical knowledge: "In order to arrive at what you do not know / You must go by a way which is the way of ignorance."[49] The transcendent "moments" of "Burnt Norton" are recalled, but in "East Coker" they seem somehow insufficient, and the speaker seeks a greater access to the transcendent: "Not the intense moment / Isolated, with no before and after, / But a lifetime burning in every moment." Pulling away from the temporal and the material, the speaker declares, "Love is most nearly itself / When here and now cease to matter," and he enjoins his listener: "We must be still and still moving / Into another intensity / For a further union, a deeper communion."[50] Of the four *Quartets*, "East Coker" is the most insistent in its rejection of history and its desire to attain a fully transcendent consciousness.

Like each of the *Quartets*, "The Dry Salvages" (1941) takes its title from a place: a small group of rocks off the coast of Gloucester, Massachusetts; Eliot's father built a house on Gloucester's Eastern Point in 1896, and the family spent many summers there. The poem opens with two distinct images of time: the river, with its recurrent "seasons" or "rhythm" of rise and fall, and its unpredictable floods, and the sea, which represents "not our time," but "a time / Older than the time of chronometers," i.e., the time of "the ground swell, that is and was from the beginning."[51] Like the wind imagery in "Gerontion," the water imagery here suggests an endless, purposeless round of life and death in which "There is no end, but addition,"[52] i.e., meaningless accretion.

Time can be redeemed, however, by the historical fact of "the one Annunciation,"[53] by virtue of which we can discern that

> [. . .] the past has another pattern, and ceases to be a mere sequence—
> Or even development: the latter a partial fallacy
> Encouraged by superficial notions of evolution,
> Which becomes, in the popular mind, a means of disowning the past.[54]

Linear, progressive ideas of history "disown" the past because they are so often teleological: the past exists only as a means of bringing about the present, and it matters only to the extent that it can explain the present state of things. But for Eliot all such Whiggish ideas of history are at least partial fallacies because they neglect the fundamental ways in which the past is no different from the present: by itself, history is the nightmare that it seems to Stephen Dedalus, the horror show that we find in *The Waste Land.* With selective attention, we may persuade ourselves that we are evolving or developing in positive ways, but for Eliot all such arguments are superficial: none of them can redeem time from its ultimate meaninglessness.

And if we are honest, we will admit that we sometimes take a "backward look behind the assurance / Of recorded history," a look "towards the primitive terror."[55] Recorded history, with its calm assurance that things happened as they did for discernible reasons, and its tracing of broad patterns of organic rise and fall, or dialectical progress, pretends to a meaningfulness that Mircea Eliade, like Eliot, suggests is paper-thin, open to doubt, and susceptible to a kind of existential dread that Eliade calls "the terror of history." This terror of losing oneself amid the meaninglessness of profane history can be assuaged only, Eliade claims, by a belief in God or some notion of a transcendent, sacred reality,[56] which is essentially Eliot's claim in the *Quartets*—except that for Eliot, only orthodox Christianity affords access to the *true* Absolute. Even at its most fully developed, our empirical, rational knowledge of history is always insufficient, but if we open ourselves to divine grace and we are fortunate enough to experience one of the "moments" described earlier in the *Quartets*, then we may "apprehend / The point of intersection of the timeless / With time," and in the eternal present of that moment know that "Here the past and future / Are conquered, and reconciled."[57]

The last of the *Quartets*, "Little Gidding," was published in late 1942. The manor at Little Gidding was established and named shortly after the Norman invasion, but its population gradually dwindled. In 1625, Nicholas Ferrar and his family purchased the land, rebuilt the house and church, and established an Anglican community which lasted until 1657. Charles I visited the community twice, in 1642 and again in 1646, after his final defeat at the Battle of Naseby in the Civil War. In 1936, Eliot visited the church, which had been rebuilt in 1848–53. The first three *Quartets* juxtapose images of the profane with images of the sacred: the unredeemed, secular time of nature's seasons, the sea's rhythms, and human history are set sharply against images of "timeless moments." "Little Gidding" is different: here the timeless moment is not so much contrasted with historical time, as it is imagined as concurrent with historical time. As Nancy Gish puts it, in this poem Eliot imagines "not an eternal present but eternity within the present."[58]

Unlike "Gerontion" or *The Waste Land*, in which historical time is imagined as an unredeemed and ultimately meaningless repetition of desire and suffering, a nightmare from which we struggle to awake, "Little Gidding" imagines what Nancy Gish calls an historical "place where a balance of eternal and transient was once achieved."⁵⁹ It is not so much that "Gerontion" and *The Waste Land* are wrong about history, but rather that they tell only part of the truth. In "Little Gidding" Eliot asserts the existence of a more complete truth that he can articulate only in the rhetoric of mystical paradox: "Here, the intersection of the timeless moment / Is England and nowhere. Never and always."⁶⁰ From one point of view, the timeless moment occurs nowhere and never—the pointless violence and suffering of *The Waste Land* lie all around us—but from another point of view that timeless moment occurs right here, in England, right now, always. Moreover, as Gish points out, Eliot's thinking in "Little Gidding" moves beyond the abstract speculation of "Burnt Norton" and here depicts "a timeless moment occurring in a particular time and place and affecting a particular human life."⁶¹

That particular time and place would be the seventeenth-century Anglican community at Little Gidding, in which the work of daily living was woven into a life of Christian worship, and Christ's incarnation, death, and resurrection were at once discrete historical facts and timeless events that informed and structured the lives of the community's members. Eliot recalls the language of 1 John 2:15 and its distinction between love for the things of this world and the love of God when he defines "the use of memory" or history to be "liberation—not less of love but expanding / Of love beyond desire, and so liberation / From the future as well as the past." If we see only as the speakers of "Gerontion" and *The Waste Land* see, if we remain bound to and defined by the desires of our material existence, then "History may be servitude." But for Eliot Christ can redeem us from such bondage, so it is equally true that "History may be freedom. See, now they vanish, / The faces and places, with the self which, as it could, loved them, / To become renewed, transfigured, in another pattern."⁶² To recognize that other pattern is to recognize the timeless in time, i.e., to recognize history—such as the history of the community at Little Gidding—as the site or the field in which human beings experience the sacred. It is to recognize that

> [. . .] A people without history
> Is not redeemed from time, for history is a pattern
> Of timeless moments. So, while the light falls
> On a winter's afternoon, in a secluded chapel
> History is now and England.⁶³

Readers' responses to the idea of history that Eliot lays out in the *Quartets* have been quite diverse. Nancy Gish's *Time in the Poetry of T. S. Eliot* remains the most perceptive and cogent, and is generally sympathetic, but we have other provocative readings as well. Writing in the heyday of Deconstruction's influence, Joseph Kronick suggests that Eliot uses his Christocentric history as a means of escaping actual history, and that for Eliot, "history is the return to the origin, a rediscovery of the beginning that is our end. This 'origin' is the fold wherein the timeless intersects with time; it is, in other words, history constituted as the Logos."[64] For deconstructive critics, a logocentric history is inevitably oppressive and false, but for Eliot, who used a fragment on the logos from Heraclitus as one of the epigraphs to *Four Quartets*, escaping secular history, returning to the origin, and understanding history as a logocentric pattern are entirely positive achievements.

In *T. S. Eliot and American Poetry*, Lee Oser offers a very different reading:

> In the past, critics have understood Eliot's poetics of history along the lines of what Northrop Frye called a 'mythology of decline.' Populating this mythology were, more or less, the dissociation of sensibility, the English Civil War, Donne rising, Milton sinking, and the fact that in some moods Dante was about the only author that Eliot would prescribe for his public. Throughout his oeuvre, though, and with culminating clarity in *Four Quartets*, an American sense of providential history impels Eliot's writing. . . [and makes clear] Eliot's commitment to a future good, his belief in a future good, and not his nostalgia for lost origins or a golden age.[65]

Oser is persuasive when he argues against the "mythology-of-decline" understanding of Eliot's idea of history, but he is less persuasive when he argues for Eliot's commitment to a providential history. The idea of a providential history in America, from the Puritans of seventeenth-century Massachusetts to the nineteenth-century proponents of manifest destiny and up to those today who embrace the idea of America as a nation chosen by God for a particular role in His plan, has almost always operated politically and practically, shaping specific strategies, goals, and actions. In that tradition, we *can* create a city upon a hill, right now, as John Winthrop so famously put it. But if we read *Four Quartets* alongside *The Idea of a Christian Society* (1939) and *Notes Towards the Definition of Culture* (1948), we find in Eliot far more political pessimism toward the foreseeable future than we ever find among American exponents of providential history.[66] For Eliot we are a very long way from the Second Coming.

Among readers on the left, Kenneth Asher's response is representative. In his very fine book *T. S. Eliot and Ideology*, he describes "the *Quartets*' view of time as following cyclical patterns organized around moments of rose-inspired transfiguration" as "a rebuttal to the liberal position of linear progress."[67] Asher is right about Eliot's opposition to a liberal, linear idea of history, but the cyclical images of history laid out in the *Quartets*, such as the peasants' dance in "East Coker" or the river's natural rhythms in "The Dry Salvages," are by themselves equally unredeemed. Perhaps because he is most interested in the political implications of Eliot's thinking, Asher over-emphasizes the centrality of "the cyclical view of history" in the *Quartets*. He finds such a view to be "completely in harmony with Eliot's class-bound view of the ideal society . . . the same sort of people doing the same thing in the same place from generation to generation,"[68] but in the *Quartets* Eliot is not writing about the ideal society, and when he writes about the ideal society elsewhere, he certainly never suggests that history, cyclical or otherwise, has ever brought it about, or is likely to bring it about any time soon.

Four Quartets is important because in these poems Eliot re-thinks the meaning of history within a traditional Christian context. He declares that redemption from the directionless, whirling temporality of "Gerontion" is possible because of Christ, whose incarnation *in* history epitomizes the intersection of time and the timeless. The deep pessimism—one might say the despair—of "Gerontion," *The Waste Land*, "The Hollow Men," and *Sweeney Agonistes* is replaced by the faith and knowledge that God's work is done in *this* world, that salvation is a live possibility in *this* world. The almost beatific conclusion of the *Quartets*, however, is not reflected in Eliot's prose of that same period. In *The Idea of a Christian Society*, *Notes towards the Definition of Culture*, and most notoriously *After Strange Gods*, which to his credit Eliot would not allow to be reprinted, his stance toward the modern world, and particularly toward secular liberalism, is far more hostile than that of, say, Reinhold Niebuhr or many other mainstream Christian intellectuals of the time. Eliot's literary reputation, and the seriousness with which his poems and plays were received, persisted well into the late twentieth century, but the reactionary obduracy of his comments on contemporary politics and society won over almost no one to his point of view. If our thinking about history is diminished by our refusal to take seriously the spiritual dimensions of our lives, the argument for taking that dimension more seriously might be laid out in a poetry less insistently dogmatic and more open to uncertainty than Eliot's.

Notes

1. James Joyce, *Ulysses* (New York: Random House, 1961), 24, 25, 34.

2. Mircea Eliade, *Cosmos and History: The Myth of the Eternal Return*, trans. Willard Trask (New York: Harper & Row, 1954), 91–92.

3. Quoted. in Nancy Gish, *Time in the Poetry of T. S. Eliot* (Totowa, NJ: Barnes & Noble, 1981), 23.

4. T. S. Eliot, *Selected Essays* (New York: Harcourt Brace, 1960), 4.

5. Eliot, *Essays*, 11.

6. Eliot, *Essays*, 5.

7. Eliot, *Essays*, 6. What Eliot means by "the mind of Europe" may be clarified by these remarks: "We suppose a mind which is not only the English mind of one period with its prejudices of politics and fashions of taste, but which is a greater, finer, more positive, more comprehensive mind than the mind of any period. And we suppose to each writer an importance which is not only individual, but due to his place as a constituent of this mind" ("Was There a Scottish Literature?" *Athenaeum*, August 1, 1919, 680). This "mind" is "greater, finer, . . . more comprehensive" to the extent that it participates in the permanent and absolute, just as the individual writer is "important" to the extent that his or her work participates in the permanent and absolute.

8. Eliot, *Essays*, 6.

9. Eliot, *Essays*, 247.

10. T. S. Eliot, "The Social Function of Poetry," *On Poetry and Poets* (New York: Farrar, Straus & Giroux (Noonday Press), 1961), 15.

11. T. S. Eliot, "*Ulysses*, Order and Myth," *Selected Prose*, ed. Frank Kermode (New York: Harcourt Brace, 1975), 177.

12. Eliot, *Essays*, 433.

13. T. S. Eliot, *Collected Poems 1909–1962* (New York: Harcourt Brace, 1970), 29–31.

14. James Longenbach, *Modernist Poetics of History: Pound, Eliot, and the Sense of the Past* (Princeton: Princeton University Press, 1987), x. Longenbach's valuable book offers many insights, but in certain basic ways its argument is unpersuasive. For Longenbach, Eliot shares the kind of skepticism toward positivist, linear understandings of history that was evident among philosophers of history like Nietzsche, Wilhelm Dilthey, F. H. Bradley, and Benedetto Croce. For these thinkers, "Once the methodology of positivist historiography was found to produce fictions, the historian could either languish in his realization of the impossibility of historical knowledge or redefine historical knowledge as something gleaned from artistic intuition rather than scientific categorization" (26). Longenbach writes as if this skepticism of history's objectivity were entirely novel, and as if practicing historians immediately embraced it: "In the late nineteenth and early twentieth centuries, historians began to borrow the tools of the artist and discard the tools of the scientist in their attempts to recapture the past" (18). This is, to put it mildly, an exaggeration; most practicing historians, especially those in the U.S. and the U.K., never read Dilthey, and would dismiss the notion that historical knowledge was either impossible or the product of artistic intuition.

15. Quoted in Longenbach, *Modernist*, 185.

16. Longenbach, *Modernist*, 165–66.

17. Longenbach, *Modernist*, 172.

18. Breisach, *On the Future of History*, 92.

19. Longenbach, *Modernist*, 217.

20. Quoted in Longenbach, *Modernist*, 200.

21. Longenbach, *Modernist*, 208.

22. Longenbach, *Modernist*, 237.

23. Longenbach, *Modernist*, 237.

24. As one example among many, David Craig describes the poem as "groundlessly idealizing about the old and warped in its revulsion from the modern" ("The Defeatism of *The Waste Land*," 1960, reprinted in *T. S. Eliot: The Waste Land*, ed. Nick Selby (New York: Columbia University Press, 2001), 95).

25. Michael Bernstein, *The Tale of the Tribe: Ezra Pound and the Modern Verse Epic* (Princeton: Princeton University Press, 1980), 31.

26. Hannah Arendt makes a similar point about Augustine's idea of history in his *City of God*: "His lack of interest in what we call history was so great that he devoted only one book of the *Civitas Dei* to secular events [. . . and] in commissioning his friend and pupil Orosius to write a 'world history' he had no more in mind than a 'true compilation of the evils of the world'" ("The Concept of History: Ancient and Modern," reprinted in *Between Past and Future*, (1961; repr., New York: Penguin, 1977), 66).

27. Gish, *Time*, 55, 57.

28. Calvin Bedient, *He Do the Police in Different Voices: The Waste Land and Its*

Protagonist (Chicago: University of Chicago Press, 1986), 66.

29. This attitude is expressed succinctly in 1 John 2:15: "Behold, do not love the world, nor the things that are in the world. If anyone loves the world, there is no love for the Father in his heart. For all that is in the world is lust of the flesh, desire of the eyes and pride in life—things that come not from the Father but from the world."

30. Bedient, *Police*, 5.

31. Eliot, *Poems*, 92.

32. Eliot, *Poems*, 95.

33. Eliade, *Cosmos*, 17.

34. Eliot, *Poems*, 147.

35. Eliot, *Poems*, 163

36. Quoted in Paul Morrison, *The Poetics of Fascism: Ezra Pound, T. S. Eliot, Paul de Man* (New York: Oxford University Press, 1996), 65. The quotation is from Eliot's contribution to the anthology *Revelation*, ed. John Baille and Hugh Martin (London, 1937).

37. Eliot, *Essays*, 458.

38. Eliot, "Donne in Our Time," quoted in Morrison, *Poetics*, 65.

39. Eliot, *Poems*, 175.

40. Eliot, *Poems*, 177.

41. Eliot, *Poems*, 176, 178.

42. Eliot, *Poems*, 178.

43. Gish, *Time*, 102.

44. Eliot, *Poems*, 178.

45. Gish, *Time*, 99, 103.

46. Eliot, *Poems*, 182.

47. Eliot, *Poems*, 183.

48. Eliot, *Poems*, 184, 185.

49. Eliot, *Poems*, 187.

50. Eliot, *Poems*, 189–90.

51. Eliot, *Poems*, 192.

52. Eliot, *Poems*, 193.

53. Eliot, *Poems*, 194.

54. Eliot, *Poems*, 194.

55. Eliot, *Poems*, 195.

56. Eliade, *Cosmos*, 151.

57. Eliot, *Poems*, 198, 199.

58. Gish, *Time*, 96.

59. Gish, *Time*, 113.

60. Eliot, *Poems*, 201.

61. Gish, *Time*, 114.

62. Eliot, *Poems*, 205.

63. Eliot, *Poems*, 208.

64. Joseph Kronick, *American Poetics of History* (Baton Rouge: Louisiana State University Press, 1984), 248.

65. Lee Oser, *T. S. Eliot and American Poetry* (Columbia: University of Missouri Press, 1998), 146.

66. In *The Idea of a Christian Society*, for example, Eliot writes, "Britain has been

highly industrialised longer than any other country. And the tendency of unlimited indus-trialism is to create bodies of men and women—of all classes—detached from tradition, alienated from religion and susceptible to mass suggestion; in other words, a mob. And a mob will be no less a mob if it is well fed, well clothed, well housed, and well disci-plined" (17). He continues, "My thesis has been, simply, that a liberalised or negative condition of society must either proceed into a gradual decline of which we can see no end, or (whether as a result of catastrophe or not) reform itself into a positive shape which is likely to be effectively secular" (20). In *Notes towards the Definition of Culture*, he writes, "We can assert with some confidence that our own period is one of decline; that the standards of culture are lower than they were fifty years ago; and that the evi-dences of this decline are visible in every department of human activity. I see no reason why the decay of culture should not proceed much further, and why we may not even anticipate a period, of some duration, of which it is possible to say that it will have *no* culture" (91). See T. S. Eliot, *Christianity and Culture* (New York: Harcourt Brace, 1967).

67. Kenneth Asher, *T. S. Eliot and Ideology* (New York: Cambridge University Press, 1995), 100.

68. Asher, *Ideology*, 101.

Chapter 6
The Varieties of History in
Hart Crane's *The Bridge*

For some readers, Hart Crane is the American poet who takes the spiritual dimension of history as seriously as Eliot, without succumbing to Eliot's dogmatic certainty. But although *The Bridge* is often labeled an "epic" in line with Ezra Pound's glib definition, the critical response to its "inclusion" of history has varied widely. Some readers take the poem as a serious statement on American history, while others insist that it is not about history at all. More recent critics have taken the poem as a "queering" of American history. In what follows, I will argue that, while history does not matter for Crane in the ways that some of Crane's more enthusiastic readers have claimed that it matters, *The Bridge* embodies a deep awareness of the mysterious connection between the secular material of history and the spiritual, aesthetic consciousness toward which Crane aspires.

Crane on "The Bridge"

We ought, first, to consider what Crane himself had to say on the subject. He began thinking about *The Bridge* as early as 1923 (the poem was published in 1930), and the role of history in his imagined poem is sketched in a letter of February 18, 1923, to Gorham Munson:

> Very roughly, it concerns a mystical synthesis of "America". History and fact, location, etc. all have to be transfigured into abstract form that would almost function independently of its subject matter. The initial impulses of "our people" will have to be gathered up toward the climax of the bridge, symbol of our constructive future, our unique identity, in which is included also our scientific hopes and achievements of the future.[1]

The role of history in this "synthesis" is not entirely clear, but in his essay "General Aims and Theories" (1925), Crane describes the contemporary world as "in

transition from a decayed culture toward a reorganization of human evalua-
tions," and he continues: "I am concerned with the future of America, but not
because I think that America has any so-called par value as a state. . . . It is only
because I feel persuaded that here are destined to be discovered certain as yet
undefined spiritual qualities . . . not to be developed so completely elsewhere."[2]
He never explains why these spiritual qualities will be developed in America as
opposed to another country, nor why our present "decayed culture" will give rise
to such qualities, but he clarifies his use of history when he quotes Blake—"We
are led to believe in a lie / When we see *with* not *through* the eye"—and continues: "It is my hope to go *through* the combined materials of the poem, using our
'real' world somewhat as a spring-board . . . toward a state of consciousness, an
'innocence' (Blake) or absolute beauty. In this condition there may be discover-
able under new forms certain spiritual illuminations."[3] To see merely *with* the
eye is to miss the aesthetic and spiritual dimensions of the world, but interestingly, for Crane, those dimensions are implicated in the "real" world of history, i.e.,
one does not attain spiritual or aesthetic illumination by escaping or avoiding
history, but by going *through* it.

As his poem takes shape, Crane offers this outline in a March 18, 1926, letter to Otto Kahn:

> I Columbus—Conquest of space, chaos
> II Pokahantus—The natural body of America-fertility, etc.
> III Whitman—The Spiritual body of America (a dialogue between Whitman
> and a dying soldier in a Washington hospital; the infraction of physical death,
> disunity, on the concept of immortality)
> IV John Brown (Negro porter on Calgary Express making up berths and sing-
> ing to himself (a jazz form for this) of his sweetheart and the death of John
> Brown, alternately)
> V Subway—The encroachment of machinery on humanity; a kind of purgatory
> in relation to the open sky of last section
> VI The Bridge—A sweeping dithyramb in which the Bridge becomes the sym-
> bol of consciousness spanning time and space[4]

Edward Brunner makes the astonishing claim that "This ambitious scheme is no
less than the history of America"—quite a truncated history, most readers would
think—but he quickly adds that the breadth of Crane's topic leads to "a copybook version of American history which is a creative dead end."[5] In some ways,
Crane seems to have agreed, for he found his long poem difficult to write, and in
the following letter to Waldo Frank, written on June 20, 1926, we see him losing
faith in the "mystical synthesis" and "constructive future" with which he began
his project:

> The form of my poem rises out of a past that so overwhelms the present with its
> worth and vision that I'm at a loss to explain my delusion that there exist any
> real links between that past and a future destiny worthy of it. The "destiny" is
> long since completed, perhaps the little last section of my poem is a hangover

echo of it—but it hangs suspended somewhere in ether like an Absalom by his hair. . . . If only America were half as worthy today to be spoken of as Whitman spoke of it fifty years ago there might be something for one to say—not that Whitman received or required any tangible proof of his intimations, but that time has shown how increasingly lonely and ineffectual his confidence stands.[6]

He continues to work at it, however, perhaps because he continues to believe that the "destiny" he imagined still "hangs suspended somewhere" and that such a destiny need not require "tangible proof." In fact, in a burst of sustained creativity that summer, he writes the bulk of the poem, and in an August 19, 1926, letter we see that Crane's optimism could be as extreme as his pessimism: "To handle the beautiful skeins of this myth of America—to realize suddenly, as I seem to, how much of the past is living under only slightly altered forms, even in machinery and such-like, is extremely exciting."[7] One year later, he writes to Otto Kahn (September 12, 1927): ". . . in more than one sense I feel justified in comparing the historic and cultural scope of *The Bridge* to this great work [*The Aeneid*]."[8] But that optimism doesn't last. On July 13, 1930, in response to Allen Tate's review of *The Bridge* in *Hound and Horn*, he writes to Tate somewhat defensively: ". . . perhaps it [*The Bridge*] can serve as at least the function of a link connecting certain chains of the past to certain chains and tendencies of the future . . . I can't help thinking that my mistakes may warn others who may later be tempted to an interest in similar subject matter."[9] Finally, in the year before his suicide, he writes to Waldo Frank (February 19, 1931): "Present-day America seems a long way off from the destiny I fancied when I wrote that poem. In some ways Spengler must have been right."[10] And if Spengler was right, then *The Bridge* is wrong.[11]

Some of Crane's Critics

The critical response to *The Bridge* is extensive, and in what follows I will look only at the more significant responses to the poem's engagement with history. One group of critics simply accepts the poem's "inclusion" of American history. John Unterecker, for instance, finds that "America's various pasts are recapitulated, each of the first four major sections investigating one of them: the European heritage in 'Ave Maria,' the primitive past of the continent in 'Powhatan's Daughters [sic],' the past of whaling days and exploration in 'Cutty Sark,' and the nineteenth-century democratic past of Whitman's Open Road in 'Cape Hatteras.'"[12] For David Perkins, "The poem packs in an enormous amount of American . . . history."[13] Jeffrey Westover tells us that, like a good cultural historian, "Crane evokes colonial and national history in order to describe, diagnose, and judge American culture."[14] These responses are difficult to take seriously, for as we shall see, *The Bridge* "investigates" very little actual history.

Another group is more skeptical, and among these, Edward Brunner is typical: "Apart from the passage on Columbus, the historical references were fragmentary and negligible: clipper ships, an Indian myth (which had been invented), and snippets from a schoolboy's textbook."[15] Jeffrey Walker agrees: ". . . the American history upon which Crane has tried to force a Whitmanesque affirmation really consists of the most obvious of figures—Columbus, Indians, pioneers, clipper ships, and technological modernity. This is the stuff of grade-school primers."[16] Yet it was precisely the "primer" approach to history that Crane believed he was avoiding:

> It seemed altogether ineffective, from the poetic standpoint, to approach this material from the purely chronological historic angle—beginning with, say the landing of *The Mayflower*, continuing with a resumé of the Revolution through the conquest of the West, etc. One can get that viewpoint in any history primer. What I am after is an assimilation of this experience, a more organic panorama, showing the continuous and living evidence of the past in the inmost vital substance of the present. Consequently I jump from the monologue of Columbus in "Ave Maria"—right across the four intervening centuries—into the harbor of 20th-century Manhattan. And from that point in time and place I begin to work backward through the pioneer period, always in terms of the present—finally to the very core of the nature-world of the Indian. What I am really handling, you see, is the Myth of America.[17]

The question is whether the materials of American history, when organized according to Crane's "organic panaorama," lend themselves to the kind of idealistic "Whitmanesque affirmation" that Walker claims he seeks to elicit from them. Or whether "the Myth of America" can bear a serious connection to the history of America.

For Allen Tate, the answer is no:

> If we subtract from Crane's idea its periphery of sensation, we have left only the dead abstraction, the Greatness of America. . . . America stands for a passage into new truths. Is this the meaning of American history? The poet has every right to answer yes, and this he has done. But just what in America or about America stands for this? Which American history? The historical plot of the poem, which is the groundwork on which the symbolic bridge stands, is arbitrary and broken. . . .

Tate claims that Crane "never acquired an objective mastery . . . of the history of his country—a defect of considerable interest in a poet whose most ambitious work is an American epic."[18]

For other readers, however, Crane's "epic" aims did not require an objective mastery of American history. Alan Trachtenberg makes this case when he argues that in *The Bridge*, "history is not chronological nor economic nor political," but that Crane attempts "to perceive the unity and wholeness of history" and "to re-create American history according to a pattern he derived from its and "to re-create American history according to a pattern he derived from its facts."[19] That pattern is mythic, and "*The Bridge* is a sophisticated and well-wrought version of the archaic myth of return."[20] In order for Trachtenberg to save the poem's depiction of history, however, it becomes necessary to destroy it: "Thus in no sense of the word is *The Bridge* a historical poem. Its mode is myth. Its aim is to overcome history, to abolish time and the autonomy of events, and to show that all meaningful events partake of an archetype: the quest for a new world." For Trachtenberg, Crane constructs his Bridge in order "to rise above the wreckage of history."[21]

Echoing Trachtenberg, Joseph Kronick agrees that "it is Crane's insistence on the poet as seer that makes him so averse to history," and so eager to transform history into myth. "Despite the appearances of Columbus, Pocahontas, and the pioneer, Crane really has little interest in the historical figures of America's past. He wishes to move beyond them to some vision of eternity"; but unlike Trachtenberg, Kronick does not find Crane's mythic attempt to rise above history very compelling: "Crane's poem repeats . . . the failure to escape history."[22] Joseph Riddel essentially agrees with Kronick and Trachtenberg regarding history and myth, but his language is a bit stronger: because the vision that Crane seeks can be corrupted by history, "the enemy is history." As Riddel reads the poem, "*The Bridge* . . . reduces history to a primary mythical pattern, thereby bespeaking the poet's distrust of history. . . He is not interested in history as such at all, except in that it offers evidence of the recurrent and universal pattern that obsessed him."[23] These are the strongest critical responses to Crane's use of history, and I will return to them later in this essay.

Another critical approach to the use of history in the poem is to claim that Crane subsumes history to autobiography. Trachtenberg suggests that Crane's poem, in its earliest stages, centered on "his own personal struggles for transcendence," but that the poem's quest for "the conversion of the ordinary, through vision, into the spiritual" gradually broadened from the autobiographical "to include the historical and the cultural [development of] America as a whole." "How else," asks Trachtenberg, "are we to understand the epic proportions of *The Bridge* except as the poet's quest to find himself in American history—to discover and disclose the poetic self as the center, the redemptive consciousness of the history as a totality?"[24] L. S. Dembo makes a similar point—"[*The Bridge*] tries to present American history as an enlarged or collective version of the romantic poet's biography"—and bolsters it with an appeal to Emerson's essay "History": "all public facts are to be individualized, all private facts are to be generalized. Then at once History becomes fluid and true, and Biography deep and sublime."[25]

Jared Gardner disagrees with critics who argue "that the poem has no interest in history at all" and puts a contemporary spin on the autobiographical reading: *The Bridge* should be understood as Crane's "project of remaking Americans in his own [queer] image." In the section of the poem titled "The Dance," Crane "attempts to claim a historical place for the homosexual by inventing a nativist history purified through a marriage between white man and Indian."[26] One problem with Gardner's reading is that it is difficult to understand how "inventing" a counter-history can establish a "historical place for the homosexual" in American history.

Crane's poem has elicited such disparate critical responses in part because it fails to meet some readers' expectations of the epic genre—an epic ought to tell its readers something important about the history of the nation—and in part because the poem engages history in what seem to be inconsistent ways.

History as Legend and Memory: "Van Winkle"

The "Van Winkle" section of *The Bridge* might seem the least serious in its engagement with history. Crane's speaker recalls his childhood, when "You walked with Pizarro in a copybook, / And Cortes rode up, reining tautly in— / . . . / There was Priscilla's cheek close in the wind, / And Captain Smith, all beard and certainty, / And Rip Van Winkle bowing by the way."[27] It is difficult to agree with Jeffrey Westover's claim that "Crane shows how these disparate characters are yoked together to produce a unifying national myth,"[28] particularly when no such myth is ever described in "Van Winkle." These are figures of romance and adventure, lifted from history into the more fictive territory of legend, appropriate to the imagination of a schoolboy. The conjunction that links the historical John Smith with the fictional Rip Van Winkle establishes their equivalence—both are literary characters. Crane drops the historical figures quickly, but he uses Rip Van Winkle for the rest of the poem, partly to suggest the ways in which remembering and forgetting shape our grasp of the past: Rip "*forgot the office hours, / and he forgot the pay*"; he inhabits a space that is neither wholly present nor past: "*And Rip was slowly made aware / that he, Van Winkle, was not here / nor there . . . .*" Much of the rest of the poem recounts particular childhood memories. Such early memories are often inaccurate, like the schoolboy's notions of Pizarro or Priscilla Alden, yet like popularizations of history, such memories can strongly shape the way we think about the past. There is a playfulness in Crane's piling up of references to the past— "Remember, remember," "Recall—recall," "memory, that strikes a rhyme out of a box,"—ending with these lines addressed to Rip: "Have you got your '*Times*'—? / And hurry along, Van Winkle—it's getting late!"[29] That playfulness is Crane's dig at the Rankean historiographer who insists on his ability to record the past *wie es eigentlich gewesen*, uncontaminated by the vagaries of memory or the biases of desire. Such putatively objective history is for Crane a dead end, and he avoids it.

History as Loss: "The River," "Indiana," "Cutty Sark," "Quaker Hill"

Part of the difficulty in interpreting Crane's use of history lies in the letters in which he explains *The Bridge* in sometimes extravagant ways. For instance, can he be wholly serious when he tells his patron Otto Kahn, regarding "The River," that "They [the tramps] are the leftovers of the pioneers in at least this respect—that their wanderings carry the reader through an experience parallel to that of Boone and others. I think [I] have caught some of the essential spirit of the Great Valley here, and in the process have approached the primal world of the Indian. . ."?[30] Plainly, the experience of twentieth-century hobos parallels that of Daniel Boone in only the most superficial ways. Crane's hobos are sentimental rather than historical, "ancient men" who possess a knowledge of the land that more genteel citizens have lost: "humpty-dumpty clods / Yet they touch something like a key perhaps." That *perhaps* suggests that Crane himself recognizes the audacity of his claim, and he finally acknowledges that, unlike Boone, the hobos "win no frontier by their wayward plight."[31] But if the hobo/Boone parallel is specious, there are other more interesting ways in which "The River" depicts the experience of historicity.

"The River" opens with a train, the 20th Century Limited, speeding westward amid a blur of advertising slogans, and that sense of time as a rushing torrent yields a sense of history as a kind of hyper-mutability or instability amid which we struggle to maintain balance, all too conscious of "Time's rendings, time's blendings." Here, history is a force within which we are inexorably displaced and buffeted, and Crane depicts that force first as a speeding train and then as the Mississippi River: "its one will—flow!" History is not something that we create, but rather something that we suffer or endure—we are the acted upon, not the actors—and what we suffer is loss. The Mississippi moves "Over De Soto's bones" (their location long forgotten) in an "alluvial march of days," finally flowing "past the City storied of three thrones"[32] (the Spanish and French "thrones" ruled New Orleans, but is the third "throne" the American, or is it a sign of Crane's shaky grasp of American history?). As should be clear by now, the specifics of history are less important to Crane than is "history" as a signifier for the quotidian, the material, the temporary. History names what vanishes. The great river is "Tortured with history" as it slides and spreads its way to the Gulf, as it flows through particular days, months, and years, but finally it moves out of history and onto a plane that can only be described as ecstatic and spiritual: "—The Passion spreads in wide tongues, choked and slow, / Meeting the Gulf, hosannas silently below."[33]

That sense of history as an external force that drives us before it and tortures us with loss is repeated in "Indiana," the sentimental monologue of an Indiana farmer's wife who has lost her husband in a failed attempt to find gold in Colorado in 1859. Similarly, "Cutty Sark" ends with the speaker walking across

Brooklyn Bridge after drinking and talking with an old sailor, and imagining or hallucinating the great clipper ships of the nineteenth-century tea trade in the waters below: *Cutty Sark, Thermopylae, Taeping, Ariel,* and others. But these beautiful ships are gone, displaced by steam power, and here they figure as one more element in the poem's catalogue of historical loss and decline, along with "The last bear, shot drinking in the Dakotas / [that] Loped under wires that span the mountain stream," as telegraph wires displace the world of nature. The Quaker Meeting House is replaced by the "New Avalon Hotel," a commodity for real estate speculators ("This was the Promised Land," writes Crane), and Pocahontas as a *"wanton yong girle"* is displaced by the striptease dancer in "National Winter Garden," who dances to a "tom-tom scrimmage" and wears snake jewelry recalling the "serpent down her [Pocahontas's] shoulder."[34]

This bleak and bitter sense of history as a force that rends and blends, that tortures with suffering and loss, that moves with an inexorable, "alluvial" linear motion leaving us conscious of nothing so much as what we have lost yields a line in "Quaker Hill"—"What cunning neighbors history has in fine!"[35]—that echoes Eliot's "History has many cunning passages" from "Gerontion," a poem that presents a similarly ironic attitude toward the past. But irony is only one of Crane's attitudes toward history, and certainly not the most important.

History as Seasonal Time: "Powhatan's Daughter"

If in "The River" history is imagined as an inexorable linear forward movement, whether alluvially slow or express-train fast, in "Powhatan's Daughter" Crane imagines time as cyclical, a matter of day-and-night or the passing of the seasons. Instead of loss, the theme here is return—this is the part of the poem to which Trachtenberg's claim about Eliade's myth of eternal return most clearly applies. Crane opens with an epigraph from William Strachey's *History of Travaile into Virginia Britannica* (1615), which he may have found in William Carlos Williams's *In the American Grain*: "—*Pocahuntus, a well-featured but wanton yong girle . . . of the age of eleven or twelve years, get the boyes forth with her into the market place, and make them wheele, falling on their hands, turning their heels upwards, whom she would followe, and wheele so herself, naked as she was, all the fort over.*"[36] The epigraph's focus on the body plays perfectly into Crane's intention; he tells Kahn,

> Powhatan's daughter, or Pocahontas, is the mythological nature-symbol chosen to represent the physical body of the continent, or the soil. She here takes on much the same role as the traditional Hertha of ancient Teutonic mythology. The five sub-sections of Part II are mainly concerned with a gradual exploration of this 'body' whose first possessor was the Indian. . . . I begin to work backward through the pioneer period, always in terms of the present—finally to the very core of the nature-world of the Indian.[37]

Later in the same letter, Crane explains the section of "Powhatan's Daughter" titled "The Dance":

> Here one is on the pure mythical and smoky soil at last! Not only do I describe the conflict between the two races in this dance—I also become identified with the Indian and his world before it is over, which is the only method possible of ever really possessing the Indian and his world as a cultural factor. I think I really succeed in getting under the skin of this glorious and dying animal, and in terms of expression, in symbols, which he himself would comprehend. Pocahontas (the continent) is the common basis of our meeting, she survives the extinction of the Indian, who finally, after being assumed into the elements of nature (as he understood them) persists only as a kind of "eye" in the sky, or as a star that hangs between day and night—"the twilight's dim perpetual throne."[38]

Once again, his claims seem extravagant: only in Crane's fevered imagination does he reach "the very core of the nature-world of the Indian" or "[possess] the Indian and his world as a cultural factor." His mythical Pocahontas bears almost no relation to the historical woman, whose mediation of the conflict between the two races, apart from John Smith's celebrated account of her saving his life, is terribly one-sided: she was captured by the English and effectively Anglicized. She learned their language, accepted their religion and manner of dress, adopted the name "Rebecca," married an Englishman, and finally traveled to England, where she was treated as a celebrity and a sign of the natives' willingness to be civilized. Ironically for Crane's mythic appropriation of her body, she died and was buried in England, so her actual body lies on the other side of the Atlantic.

But Crane's more generous readers take him at his word. For Helga Nilsen, "Pocahontas . . . bridges the gap between the races,"[39] and it's as simple as that. R.W.B. Lewis explains the shift from naked young wanton to earth goddess as Crane's "poetic conversion of unwashed fact into beautiful archetype."[40] For the Native Americans, Crane suggests, the land itself was full of gods, and their relationship to the land involved a higher spiritual consciousness. "Powhatan's Daughter" suggests that the conquest of the Native Americans has driven that consciousness underground, but that it is still possible for contemporary Americans to come into contact with it, as the poem's protagonist does in "The Dance," in which he travels by canoe to a village of "Grey tepees" in the Appalachians and witnesses the ritual dance and sacrifice of the chieftan Maquokeeta. That the Native Americans of the Appalachians never lived in tepees, and that the ritual and Maquokeeta are imaginary and not historical,[41] is of no importance, argues Lewis: "Crane is not, of course, possessing the Indian and his world 'as a cultural factor,' and historical familiarity with the actual American Indian will only divert the reader's understanding. Crane is, quite legitimately, deploying a phenomenon of American cultural history as an element in a purely poetic and visionary structure." Whether the mythic sensibility that Crane describes in "The Dance" was actually "a quality of the Indian age" is, argues Lewis, "beside the point."[42] If Lewis is right, then "The Dance" has nothing to say about history. But many readers disagree.

Jeffrey Walker argues that for Crane, Maquokeeta represents "a native ethos in right relation with the spiritual essence of America," but he points out that this "right ethos, somewhat disturbingly for Crane's American mythology, is embodied in the vanished or vanishing Indian," i.e., that "Maquokeeta, the one definite index of a possible society in *The Bridge*, exists beyond the bounds of Western civilization and history."[43] Whereas for Lewis, the aesthetic image of the myth is itself sufficient, for Walker, the myth implies the solution to a problem—contemporary Americans lack a spiritual consciousness of the land— but the solution is untenable: one may wish that civilized Westerners would embrace the vision of the native people they have displaced, but such a wish is just that. Crane seems to acknowledge as much when he writes, "Medicine man, relent, restore— / Lie to us,— dance us back the tribal morn!"[44] But the medicine man can dance back, or restore, the tribal morn only for Crane and his most sympathetic readers, and even Crane acknowledges that such a restoration is purely imaginary, a "lie" in the world of history and politics.

"The Dance" has occasioned particular interest among contemporary critics because Crane's speaker identifies so intimately with Maquokeeta's suffering, and for some readers the imagery is homoerotic, and that homoeroticism has historical implications. Peter Lurie, for example, suggests that "Maquokeeta's sacrificial burning in 'The Dance' appears in the section of *The Bridge* that evokes not only John Smith's fabled marriage to Pocahontas[45] but the role played by white settlement in Native American genocide." For Lurie, Crane's "historical awareness" is evident in "the traces of a queer sexuality that evokes a shared suffering with his historical subject."[46] Lurie is uncomfortable with some aspects of Crane's treatment of Native Americans, but the queering of history outweighs the discomfort: "While it is true that Crane's rendering of this scene partakes of the same nostalgic, guilt-laden tropes of 'celebrating' the Native American that have motivated white writers since Cooper, I am struck by the mutuality of suffering that Crane effects for both his presumably white speaker and his Native American subject." Struggling to square what he takes as the poem's post-colonial infelicities with its celebration of a queer sensibility, Lurie insists that "Crane accomplishes more than a romantic re-colonizing of an Other for the purposes of modernist aestheticizing or myth-production. . . Crane shows the extent of his desire to supplant a white, male, heterosexual presence in American history with that of a marginalized subject."[47] One may wish that many things in history had occurred otherwise than they did, but such wishing does little to deepen one's historical understanding. Lurie wants Crane to be far more political than he is: "Crane's treatment of the Indian in 'The Dance' involves his own self-conscious use of a deviant masculinity, one that deliberately undermines 'the existing social formation' and thus mounts a stubborn resistance—a resounding 'no'—to formations of power that are manifest in the social order and, significantly, in history"[48] For Lurie, the counter-historical fantasy seems far more significant than the actual history— imagining a history that *should* have happened, in the service of our contemporary political desires, seems to be what matters most.

Jared Gardner goes so far as to read these lines from "The Dance"—"We danced, O Brave, we danced beyond their farms, / In cobalt desert closures made our vows . . ."[49]—as indicating that "Maquokeeta transfer[s] his identity to the poet through a bond of marriage," as if the word "vows" could refer only to a wedding. For Gardner, Crane rewrites "the miscegenist [Pocahontas] story into a homosexual myth. Instead of offering herself to the white man, Pocahontas here acts as mediator between white and red man. It is in this union, through the bridge of the female body of Pocahontas, that our America is born." The point of Maquokeeta's sacrifice is simple: "the red man dies that the homosexual poet can be reborn as the true American."[50] Gardner never explains why the red man must die in order for this to happen, or how such a death could effect such a rebirth, and one wonders precisely when, or where, "our America" was "born" from the fantasized sexual union of a white man and an Indian, but again, what ought to have happened seems more significant than what did happen.

Lurie and Gardner build their readings by attending to a very narrow selection of the poem's images. In "The Dance" Pocahontas is plainly a fertility symbol—"she rose with maize—to die"—as is Maquokeeta, who is compared to the "snake that lives before, / That casts his pelt, and lives beyond!" In this poem, the cyclical temporality of the seasons emerges as a timeless pattern: Maquokeeta gazes through "infinite seasons" and Pocahontas is both the bride "whose brown lap *was* virgin May" (my italics) and simultaneously "virgin to the last of men."[51] This is not to deny that certain lines may be read as homoerotic, but rather to suggest that the homoeroticism is not as central to the poem's theme as Lurie and Gardner suggest, and that such homoeroticism has very little to add to Crane's thinking about history. In terms of history, "The Dance" offers a cyclic image of temporality depicted in the fertility figures of Pocahontas and Maquokeeta, an image that complements the linear images of the express train and the Mississippi in "The River." That neither model is finally adequate for Crane is made clear in the ecstatic, visionary conclusion of each poem: history points beyond itself to another order of reality.

History as Prophecy and Ecstatic Vision: "Ave Maria"

The section of the poem in which Crane makes his only use of primary and secondary historical sources is "Ave Maria," which focuses on Columbus in the mid-Atlantic, returning to Spain after his first voyage to the West Indies. His largest ship, the *Santa Maria*, has struck a reef off the coast of Hispaniola, so Columbus returns to Spain on the *Niña*. He encounters violent storms near the Azores, and in his journal entry of February 14, 1493, Columbus describes the storm, his crew's fear, and his leading the crew in prayer and vows to the Virgin Mary. Crane had read Columbus's *Journal* of the first voyage, as well as Waldo Frank's *Virgin Spain* and Prescott's *Ferdinand and Isabella*, and "Ave Maria" is the most detailed treatment of actual history in *The Bridge*.

The poem is a dramatic monologue spoken by Columbus that begins with his fear that the two ships will founder and he will never be able to report his great discovery at the Spanish court. He invokes two Franciscan priors, both of whom were important advocates for his cause —"Luis de San Angel" (Luis de Santángel), who was keeper of the privy purse to King Ferdinand and raised much of the money for Columbus's voyage, and Juan Perez, who was Queen Isabella's confessor—and implores them: "Be with me . . ." and "Witness . . ."[52] Brunner sees Columbus as an unattractive character early in the poem; his primary desire seems to be to return in triumph to the Spanish court so that he can gloat at those who had argued against his journey.[53] "I bring you back Cathay!" he imagines himself crying, and boasts of "our Indian emperies" that will be carved from "The Chan's great continent." But as the poem continues, his attentions seem to shift. He turns the focus of his speech from his partisans at the Spanish court to "Madre Maria," and finally to God, "Thou who sleepest on Thyself," and he imagines warning King Ferdinand against avarice: "—Yet no delirium of jewels! O Fernando, / Take of that eastern shore, this western sea, / Yet yield thy God's, thy Virgin's charity!" The poem ends in an ecstatic vision of God in which Columbus claims to see in the night sky "in one sapphire wheel: / The orbic wake of thy once whirling feet," and to hear, although presumably the "*once* whirling feet" (emphasis added) are now still, the tread of God: "Elohim, still I hear thy sounding heel!" In this ecstatic vision, Columbus sees himself as an instrument of God's will, and suggests that despite the initial success of his voyage, that will has not yet been fulfilled: "Thy purpose—still one shore beyond desire!"[54] The poem's epigraph, from Seneca's *Medea*, prophesies a time when Tiphys (the *Argo*'s helmsman) or his equivalent will discover new worlds beyond *Ultima Thule*. Here we have another model of history: it is the fulfillment of what is already ordained to happen. This idea of history recalls the letter quoted earlier, in which Crane writes, "I feel persuaded that here [in America] are destined to be discovered certain as yet undefined spiritual qualities."

Unlike Brunner, some critics read Crane's Columbus as a wholly positive figure. James Miller, for example, writes that Columbus's prayerful encounter with God is meant to contrast with the faithlessness of contemporary America, and that the wonder of Columbus's original view of America is similarly meant to contrast with the bleaker, more vulgar contemporary views depicted in "Quaker Hill" and "The Tunnel."[55] Helge Nilsen reads Crane's Columbus as "a religious visionary who carried out his exploits in answer to the call of a higher purpose," a man who "embodies the original, supreme aspirations of the white man in America, the quest for a new, perfect world."[56] And here is John Carlos Rowe: "Columbus' warning [to Ferdinand] anticipates Crane's general critique of modern American history, which finds its 'civilized' origin in Fernando's impulse toward exploitation."[57]

Jeffrey Walker is more hesitant; although Columbus seems to grasp "the divine meaning of America . . . [he] cannot clearly fathom or articulate what that destiny is." More importantly, Columbus is simply wrong:

> [He] has misidentified his discovery. Even if he is the instrument of an inscrutable deific intent, he has misinterpreted the nature of his role, and he is heading toward a future of wangles and betrayals that will leave him ruined. Moreover, and as Crane's reader well knows . . . Columbus' actual main purpose was personal enrichment, not redemption. If Columbus' 'heralding' of the New World is an analogue for Crane's action in The Bridge, the gap between idealist perception and reality bodes ill.[58]

Is "Ave Maria" as garbled as Walker's reading suggests? We know that Columbus believed he was guided by God, and that he was deeply religious, but what is Crane doing when he ignores the less admirable facets of the historical Columbus? Why does Crane have Columbus warn Ferdinand against avarice, when in fact Columbus himself left men behind after his first voyage with orders to search for gold, and went on to search obsessively for evidence of gold on his next three voyages? Why ignore Columbus's cruelty toward the Native Americans, such as his "repartimiento" system in Hispaniola, under which all of the natives were divided among the Spanish settlers for use as workers? Why ignore his obsession with fame and honor? On his return to Spain after his first voyage, he worries incessantly that the captain of the Pinta, Martín Pinzón, will sail ahead and claim the glory of discovery for himself, but Crane never mentions this. Why "include" history in the poem if one's purpose is not to tell the truth about history?

Perhaps because telling the truth about history is not as simple as it sounds. In fairness to Crane, he is focusing on one particular moment in Columbus's life—he never suggests that he wants to provide the whole truth about Columbus. More importantly, he uses that moment as an image of the broader concerns of The Bridge. "Ave Maria" moves from historiography to ecstatic vision: as the poem opens, Columbus is at once deeply frightened that the storms may destroy both his ships and the knowledge of what he has found, and intensely proud of an accomplishment that vindicates him against all of his doubters. At first he asks the two Franciscans to "witness" what he has done; then he asks the Virgin Mary to intercede and assure his ships' return (though he places a document detailing his discoveries in a watertight "casque," just in case). And finally he sees in the night sky a vision of God: "The orbic wake of thy once whirling feet, / Elohim . . ." For Crane the most important thing about Columbus is his vision. He has a vision of Cathay, and he has a vision of Elohim, and the two are conflated in interesting ways. Crane tells Waldo Frank that "Cathay" means more than China: "Cathay being an attitude of spirit, rather than material conquest throughout, of course."[59] In bringing back Cathay, then, Columbus is bringing back a vision. However, in believing that he had sailed to an archipelago off the coast of Asia, that he had reached "the Chan's Great continent," he was plainly wrong (although what he had actually found is arguably far more important than what he thought he had). He may be equally wrong about hearing the heel of Elohim. Such consciousness is always open to doubt and misinterpretation. What seems to be a genuine vision may be something else entirely, and even if it is genuine, it may be impossible to convey to others or to find again. Crane uses Columbus to embody the kind of spiritual visionary whose consciousness and quest are dramatized in his poem. Columbus seeks, finds, and tries to bring back a spiritual higher consciousness. And curiously, as *The Bridge* will make clear, such consciousness always requires a ground in history.

Sacred Time and Ecstatic Vision

Throughout *The Bridge*, Crane depicts the past in terms of memory and legend, the time-line of progress and its attendant losses, the cyclical time of nature's seasons and the eternal return, the reconstruction afforded by primary and secondary historical sources, and the fulfillment of prophecy. This last depiction, however, moves from history into fiction as the poet imagines Columbus in an ecstatic vision of God. Such a vision will return in the final poem of *The Bridge*, "Atlantis," which Crane describes as "the mystic consummation toward which all the other sections of the poem converge."[60] Crane's alcoholism and sexual promiscuity can deflect attention from his spirituality, but his most recent biographer, Clive Fisher, describes Crane as "avid always for epiphany" and notes "the enormous influence [P. D. Ouspensky's *Tertium Organum*] was to have on the poet's thinking."[61] Ouspensky's book matters to Crane because it confirmed his belief in the existence of another reality beyond that of our senses, and it played to Crane's idea that an elite group of cutting-edge artists might form the vanguard of an incipient higher consciousness toward which the entire species was evolving. In 1923, Crane writes to Tate, "I have also enjoyed reading Ouspensky's *Tertium Organum* lately. Its corroboration of several experiences in consciousness that I have had gave it particular interest,"[62] and later that year he writes to Alfred Stieglitz, the great photographer of the Brooklyn Bridge, in language drawn from Ouspensky: "I feel our identities so much alike in spiritual direction . . . we center in common devotions, in a kind of timeless vision . . . I feel you as entering very strongly into certain developements [sic] in *The Bridge*. May I say it, and not seem absurd, that you are the first, or rather the purest living indice of a new order of consciousness that I have met?"[63] To other correspondents, Crane is more general in discussing his spiritual interests, but they clearly persist throughout the composition of *The Bridge*. For instance, he tells Yvor Winters, "I have a more or less religious attitude toward creation and expression. I respond more to revelation—or what seems revelation to me—than I do to what seems to me 'repetitious'—however classic and noble,"[64] and he thanks Herbert Weinstock for his positive review of *The Bridge* by complimenting his "amazing insight into . . . the essential religious motive throughout my work."[65]

In "Atlantis," Crane's bridge collapses time, turning "Tomorrows into yesteryear" and "translating Time / Into what multitudinous Verb." Here we are "at time's end" or even "beyond time," and the speaker says of God, "Thou leadest from time's realm" and asks "Thy pardon for this history."[66] This is strong, clear language that makes it easy to see why Trachtenberg, Riddel, Kronick and others have argued that *The Bridge* is not a poem including history. But "Atlantis" recalls "Ave Maria" not only in its ecstatic vision, but also in its skepticism. In "Atlantis" the Bridge is called "Psalm of Cathay," as if to equate the speaker's vision with that of Columbus in the earlier poem. But that equation introduces doubt—"Is it Cathay[?]"[67] asks the speaker in the poem's final stanza. We know that in Columbus's case the answer is "no," and in this case the vision is also liable to falsification. There is a very strong likelihood that Atlantis never existed, but the myth of Atlantis is like most ecstatic or religious experience: after it passes, its significance may be doubted, but faith holds that the experience will recur. Like Arthur, who is *rex quondam rexque futurus*, the myth promises that Atlantis will rise again.

For Crane's sympathetic readers, this kind of skepticism is nowhere to be found. Helge Nilsen, for example, finds that "the 'myth of America' emerges as a mystical, supralogical synthesis of several historical and modern episodes, images and scenes that combine into the grand unity of the finale of the poem," and reads the entire poem as "an act of religious faith." The project of *The Bridge* is the "illumination of the quotidian" by a higher consciousness, and that illumination "relates itself to American history as the possible growth of an awareness in the minds of men."[68]

Alan Trachtenberg sees in the image of the bridge "a rhetorical figure, signifying a crossing-over from one state to another. Like the priestly function of bridges preserved in the word 'pontiff,' 'bridge' represented for Crane an active mediation between here and there, now and then . . . an act of fusion, healing, transcendence."[69] In another essay, Trachtenberg describes the poem's "neo-Platonic conception of a 'reality' beyond the evidence of the senses," and reads the image of the bridge as an "emblem of the eternal, providing a passage between the Ideal and the transitory sensations of history, a way to unify them."[70]

Similarly, Brian Reed finds "a mythic-ecstatic point of view" in "Atlantis" that seeks to open readers' eyes to "the transhistorical real." But Reed notices that Columbus's dilemma recurs in "Atlantis": "How can a human (as opposed to divine) reader be offered reliable access to the myth when there is no assurance that the gateway that enables someone to perceive it at one moment will still be working at another?" Reed suggests that because the myth appears in different forms in each of the poem's various section, it is somehow able "to remain valid and available in the mortal realm of mutability, where all is subject to change."[71] but not all of Crane's readers agree.[72]

Jeffrey Walker offers the most sustained critique of Crane's ecstatic vision of history. Walker reads the first part of the poem as a depiction of "U.S. history as an agon between a truly American vitalistic individualism and the infidelistic powers of industrial capitalism." The poem's various sections present "a neo-Romantic version of the modernist antithesis between mythic ideality and fallen, historical actuality."[73] For Walker, the fallen actuality of American history clearly betrays the poet's mythic ideal, with the result that Crane can offer nothing but

> a declaration of faith. Although the present in itself is unredeemable, he now [in "Atlantis"] seems to say, it leads to a redeeming future . . . outside time and history. Here the present, or modernity, or history itself, is something to be endured, because history leads, despite appearances, toward some incognizable apocalypse in which the urge toward Love may be fulfilled. This, ultimately, is the basic perorative stance in "Atlantis": the bridge . . . leads us "from time's realm."[74]

But in leading us away from history, where does Crane bring us? Not to any end that Walker finds compelling: "All he can do, in the end, is gesture toward a generalized but probably Bergsonian (or Buckean and Ouspenskian) notion of self-effacing universal Love as the essential act of vital and ethically enlightened will, and therefore as the destined terminus of history."[75] The "myth of America" that Crane so grandly announces as his subject is finally, Walker concludes, nothing but "the myth of untransacted destiny worked out in terms of Burke's and Ouspensky's ideas of evolution toward a sacred brotherhood of the higher consciousness."[76]

For Walker, "Crane's argument . . . reveals itself as indefensible. It develops no evidence that gives his modernist reader reason to believe that Crane's (and Whitman's) faith in a providential and evolutionary progress toward apocalyptic Love is justified. Nor is there evidence that those who believe in that progress are engaged in anything but wishful or deluded thinking."[77] As I will argue below, Crane himself was not immune to such skepticism.

Faith and Doubt: "Cape Hatteras"

In "Cape Hatteras," Crane's speaker imagines Walt Whitman in the New York of the 1920s, looking at the "prison crypt / Of canyoned traffic" in contemporary Manhattan, "Confronting the Exchange, / Surviving in a world of stocks," but ranging also "Across the hills where second timber strays / Back over Connecticut farms, abandoned pastures." Can Whitman's vision be translated into the idiom of 1920s America? Can the present give rise to a vision like

Whitman's? The speaker wants to believe that it can, but he isn't sure. The poem celebrates the Wright Brothers' first flight at Kitty Hawk, but acknowledges that this marvelous invention is used in warfare to make killing more efficient: "The soul . . . / Already knows the closer clasp of Mars."[78] The Civil War deaths mourned by Whitman are echoed and amplified in the even greater carnage of World War I, yet one more addition to the "Ghoul-mound of man's perversity," and Crane's speaker confronts "all that sum / That then from Appomattox stretched to Somme!"[79]

But despite the horror of modern war and the "prison crypt" into which Wall Street may transform the nation, "Cape Hatteras" affirms Whitman's vision and links it to Crane's: Whitman "flung the span on even wing / Of that great Bridge, our Myth, whereof I sing!" Crane's speaker asserts that Whitman's "vision is reclaimed!" and discerns a "rainbow's arch"[80] above the "Ghoul-mound" of the war dead. Crane's affirmation of Whitman parallels his affirmation of the visionary optimism of his friend Waldo Frank's *Our America* and Ouspensky's *Tertium Organum*, and it marks his response to T. S. Eliot, about whom he tells Gorham Munson in 1923:

> [M]y work for the past two years (those meagre drops!) has been more influenced by Eliot than any other modern. . . . There is no one writing in English who can command so much respect, to my mind, as Eliot. However, I take Eliot as a point of departure toward an almost complete reverse of direction. His pessimism is amply justified, in his own case. But I would apply as much of his erudition and technique as I can absorb and assemble toward a more positive, or (if [I] must put it so in a skeptical age) ecstatic goal. . . I feel that Eliot ignores certain spiritual events and possibilities as real and powerful now as say in the time of Blake. Certainly the man has dug the ground and buried hope as deep and direfully as it can ever be done.[81]

Crane takes as his task the restoration of that hope; he tells Waldo Frank in that same year that "it is vision, and a vision alone that not only America needs, but the whole world," in order to answer "the complete renunciation symbolised in *The Wasteland*."[82] And in 1926, he writes to Yvor Winters: ". . . in it [The Bridge] I shall incidentally try to answer all my friends who have for three years, now, sat down and complacently joined the monotonous choruses of *The Waste Land*."[83]

So Crane imagined *The Bridge* as a response to what he perceived as the cultural and historical pessimism of Eliot's *The Waste Land* and Spengler's *The Decline of the West*. Like Whitman, Ouspensky, and Waldo Frank, Crane was an idealist who believed that human consciousness was evolving spiritually, yet he was also enough of a skeptic to be shaken by the arguments and observations of writers like Eliot and Spengler, and to be shaken as well by the evidence of his own experience of early twentieth-century America. The "spiritual events and possibilities" that Crane mentions in his letter to Munson may be "real," as he claims they are, but such events by their very nature do not last, and their significance is always open to doubt or misinterpretation, especially as one tries to convey such an experience to one who has not had it. As the ecstatic experience recedes into the past, it may come to seem less real than quotidian experience, or, if its reality remains vivid, then quotidian experience may come to seem a kind of unreal prison that cannot live up to that higher reality.

What does this have to do with Crane's use of history? Should we conclude with Trachtenberg that "in no sense of the word is *The Bridge* a historical poem," or with Kronick that Crane is "averse to history," or with Riddel that for Crane, "the enemy is history"? Is history simply the antagonist to, or an impediment toward, that ecstatic consciousness Crane seeks? If so, why does Crane need history at all? Why introduce Columbus, Pocahontas, De Soto, the 1859 gold rush, the tea trade of the great clipper ships, Appomattox, the Somme? Why not simply present the myth, the vision, the ecstatic consciousness?

Clearly for Crane, history in and of itself is not the whole truth. Nor is history particularly useful, despite what some readers have argued, as an allegory of the poet's life, or as raw material to be subsumed into myth, or as raw material to be re-written in order to celebrate one's queer identity. In *The Bridge*, Crane presents different ways of imagining history: memory and legend in "Van Winkle," linear time in "The River," cyclic time in "The Dance," historiography and prophecy in "Ave Maria." But none of these by itself is especially illuminating; none is an end in itself. So why does Crane include them? In all its materiality and decadence and intractability, history may seem an enormous obstacle to the kind of spiritual vision that Crane is seeking, calling into question the seriousness or even the actuality of such vision. But in *The Bridge*, history is not merely an obstacle; Crane recognizes that such visions are inextricably entangled in the detritus of history, perhaps analogous to the way in which the visceral sensations of alcohol and loud phonograph music were for Crane so often entangled in the production of the poetry that limns that visionary consciousness.

In *The Waste Land*, history is a kind of nightmare from which the poem's speaker(s) struggle(s) desperately to awake, but at that point in his life, Eliot is unable to believe in a spiritual reality apart from history. When he does finally come to believe in that reality, its existence transforms history into the site of the Incarnation, i.e., history's significance became wholly Christocentric. Like Eliot, Crane seeks a higher reality, but unlike Eliot, he cannot find it in any available orthodoxy. Crane comes to believe that history is somehow implicated in spirit, indeed that only through and in history are we afforded access to spirit, but the nature of that implication remains mysterious.[84] One may say that in *The Bridge* history functions as an antagonist, but it is an antagonist like the mysterious "man" with whom Jacob wrestles one night in *Genesis*: they wrestle "until the breaking of the day," and the fight is so violent that Jacob's hip is dislocated; nevertheless, the man is unable to prevail over Jacob, and Jacob refuses to release him unless the man blesses him. The man does so, and announces that Jacob's name shall now be "Israel," and he tells Jacob, "as a prince hast thou power with God." The man's identity is never made clear—some readers identify is clear is that for Jacob, this wrestling match in which his hip is wrenched from its socket has generated a powerful spiritual experience. For Hart Crane history, i.e., the world in all its rank, unstable, violent, visceral materiality, is the "man," or the dark angel, with whom his speaker wrestles throughout the poem. Jacob attains his vision at the cost of a dislocated hip, just as the River in Crane's poem attains the Gulf only as it is "Tortured with history." For Crane at his most spiritually ecstatic in "Atlantis," the "call" of the Bridge and its "One arc synoptic of all tides below" is always already answered by the mysterious and beautiful "reply" of the "labyrinthine mouths of history."

Notes

1. Hart Crane, *Complete Poems and Selected Letters*, ed. Langdon Hammer (New York: The Library of America, 2006), 321.
2. Crane, *Poems*, 161.
3. Crane, *Poems*, 163.
4. Crane, *Poems*, 440–41.
5. Edward Brunner, *Splendid Failure: Hart Crane and the Making of* The Bridge (Urbana: University of Illinois Press, 1985), 116, 117.
6. Crane, *Poems*, 467.
7. Crane, *Poems*, 484.
8. Crane, *Poems*, 558–59.
9. Crane, *Poems*, 646.
10. Crane, *Poems*, 664.
11. Crane writes to Kenneth Burke (September 28, 1926): "I was most happily surprised at your review of Spengler in the recent Dial. It's hard to find a man, these days, or any, that doesn't swallow the whole hook and sinker in favor of his private predilections . . . . Your analysis of that book (and the psyche behind it) was amazing. One of the most magnificent and formidable books I ever read, but falsely led and falsely leading" (Crane, *Poems*, 490). He also thanks Waldo Frank (January 28, 1927) for Frank's review of Spengler and his "magnificent rebuttal of the man's psychology" (Crane, *Poems*, 519). Spengler reads *with* the evidence of world history and finds an inevitable "decline of the West"; history is like nature, governed by predictable, inexorable, and discernible laws. Crane, on the other hand, wants to read *through* the evidence of American history to an ecstatic vision of love, beauty, and hope.
12. John Unterecker, "The Architecture of *The Bridge*," in *Hart Crane: A Collection of Critical Essays*, ed. Alan Trachtenberg (Englewood Cliffs, NJ: Prentice Hall, 1982), 94.
13. David Perkins, *A History of Modern Poetry: Modernism and After* (Cambridge: Harvard University Press, 1987), 71.
14. Jeffrey Westover, *The Colonial Moment: Discoveries and Settlements in Modern American Poetry* (DeKalb: Northern Illinois University Press, 2004), 129.
15. Brunner, *Splendid*, 190. William Pritchard claims that its treatment of American history is "the least attractive and corniest aspect of *The Bridge*." See *Lives of the Modern Poets* (New York: Oxford University Press, 1980), 253. Robert Rehder seems to hold both views; at one point he writes: "Crane has no particular interest in American history,

Poets (New York: Oxford University Press, 1980), 253. Robert Rehder seems to hold both views; at one point he writes: "Crane has no particular interest in American history, even in *The Bridge* where he is concerned that the poem span the American past. ... He is interested, not in what actually happened, but in what the past feels like in the present." See *Stevens, Williams, Crane and the Motive for Metaphor* (New York: Palgrave Macmillan, 2005), 133. But twenty pages later we find: "Yet again he asserts his connection to the past. This is . . . why *The Bridge* is a historical poem, why in *The Bridge* he goes back to before Columbus and why the Indians have such an important place in the poem. The autochthonous inhabitants offer the most primitive, fundamental and authentic experience. The past holds the origins of all things. He uses the past to get to the bottom of the present, but the present must speak in its own voice" (153). John Carlos Rowe reads *The Bridge* in the light of Nietzsche's *The Use and Abuse of History*: "*The Bridge* is 'unhistorical' in its effort to 'forget' the historical burden that compels man to hate his own existence; *The Bridge* is 'super-historical' in its effort to affirm human and natural transience as that radical becoming 'which gives existence an eternal and stable character.'" See "The 'Super-Historical' Sense of Hart Crane's *The Bridge*," *Genre* 11 (1970): 623.

16. Jeffrey Walker, *Bardic Ethos and the American Epic Poem* (Baton Rouge: Louisiana State University Press, 1989), 144.

17. Crane, *Poems*, 554.

18. Allen Tate, "Hart Crane," *Essays of Four Decades* (Chicago: Swallow Press, 1968), 316, 311.

19. Alan Trachtenberg, "The Shadow of a Myth," in Alan Trachtenberg, ed., *Brooklyn Bridge: Fact and Symbol*, 2nd ed. (Chicago: University of Chicago Press, 1979), 146.

20. Trachtenberg, "Shadow," 147. R. W. B. Lewis also tries to salvage Crane's treatment of history by arguing that the poem is engaged in "a search for a mythic apprehension of history." See *The Poetry of Hart Crane: A Critical Study* (Princeton: Princeton University Press, 1967), 240; such an apprehension would transfigure historical actuality into the reality of myth. History and myth, however, as Mircea Eliade has argued, are antithetical means of understanding the past. More recently, Brian Reed has suggested that "*The Bridge* . . . sought to be a definitive statement on the United States, an epic that . . . would lucidly sum up a people's past and launch a grand future." However, the poem finally "devalues history in favor of transcendental bliss . . . . A nation is imagined so that it can then be superseded in the name of *joussaince*." See *Hart Crane: After His Lights* (Tuscaloosa: University of Alabama Press, 2006), 164.

21. Trachtenberg, "Shadow," 148, 165.

22. Joseph Kronick, *American Poetics of History: From Emerson to the Moderns* (Baton Rouge: Louisiana State University Press, 1984), 236, 238, 251.

23. Joseph Riddel, "Hart Crane's Poetics of Failure," in *Modern American Poetry*, ed., Jerome Mazzaro (New York: David McKay Co., 1970), 276, 280.

24. Alan Trachtenberg, "Introduction: Hart Crane's Legend," in Alan Trachtenberg, ed., *Hart Crane: A Collection of Critical Essays* (Englewood Cliffs, NJ: Prentice-Hall, 1982), 10, 11.

25. L. S. Dembo, *Hart Crane's Sanskrit Charge: A Study of* The Bridge (Ithaca: Cornell University Press, 1960), 131. Ralph Waldo Emerson, *Selected Writings*, ed. Donald McQuade (New York: Modern Library, 1981), 117. Emerson's essay "History" offers further support for the autobiographical reading put forth by Trachtenberg and

Dembo: "The instinct of the mind, the purpose of nature, betrays itself in the use we make of the signal narrations of history. Time dissipates to shining ether the solid angularity of facts. No anchor, no cable, no fences avail to keep a fact a fact. . . . Who cares what the fact was, when we have made a constellation of it to hang in heaven an immortal sign?" (110). And again: "there is properly no history, only biography" (111). For a very fine psychoanalytic reading of *The Bridge*, see Eric Sundquist's "Bringing Home the Word: Magic, Lies, and Silence in Hart Crane," *ELH* 44, no. 2 (Summer 1977): 376–99.

26. Jared Gardner, "Our Native Clay: Racial and Sexual Identity and the Making of Americans in *The Bridge*," *American Quarterly* 44, no. 1 (March 1992): 35, 27.

27. Crane, *Poems*, 39–40.

28. Westover, *Colonial*, 145.

29. Crane, *Poems*, 39–41.

30. Crane, *Poems*, 556.

31. Crane, *Poems*, 42–43, 44.

32. Crane, *Poems*, 42, 45, 44, 45.

33. Crane, *Poems*, 45.

34. Crane, *Poems*, 41, 65, 38, 62.

35. Crane, *Poems*, 65.

36. Crane, *Poems*, 38.

37. Crane, *Poems*, 554.

38. Crane, *Poems*, 556.

39. Helge Nilsen, *Hart Crane's Divided Vision: An Analsysis of* The Bridge (Oslo: Universitetsforlaget, 1980), 62.

40. Lewis, *Hart Crane*, 289.

41. Crane writes to Yvor Winters: ". . . I'm anxious to know if there is an Indian philology or symbolism concerned in the name 'Maquokeeta'. I chose the name at random, merely from the hearsay of a NY taxi driver who was obviously of Indian extraction (and a splendid fire-drinker by the way) who said that his Indian name was 'Maquokeeta'. I think he came from Missouri, or thereabouts. You know much more about Indian fable, symbolism, etc. than I do. Will you let me know if the name is 'sufficient' to the role it plays in the poem?" (Crane, *Poems*, 512–13).

42. Lewis, *Hart Crane*, 312–13.

43. Walker, *Bardic Ethos*, 19, 132.

44. Crane, *Poems*, 47.

45. Pocahontas married John Rolfe, not John Smith.

46. Peter Lurie, "Querying the Modernist Canon: Historical Consciousness and the Sexuality of Suffering in Faulkner and Hart Crane," *The Faulkner Journal* 20, no. 1–2 (2005): 150, 151.

47. Lurie, "Querying," 163.

48. Lurie, "Querying," 160.

49. Crane, *Poems*, 48.

50. Gardner, "Native Clay," 41, 26, 41.

51. Crane, *Poems*, 45, 47, 45, 48.

52. Crane, *Poems*, 35.

53. Brunner, *Splendid*, 135–36.

54. Crane, *Poems*, 35, 36, 37.

55. James E. Miller, Jr., *The American Quest for a Supreme Fiction: Whitman's*

Legacy in the Personal Epic (Chicago: University of Chicago Press, 1979), 179.

56. Nilsen, *Divided Vision*, 42.

57. Rowe, "Super-Historical," 600.

58. Walker, *Bardic Ethos*, 129–30.

59. Crane, *Poems*, 431.

60. Crane, *Poems*, 440.

61. Clive Fisher, *Hart Crane: A Life* (New Haven: Yale University Press, 2002), 129.

62. Crane, *Poems*, 321.

63. Crane, *Poems*, 341.

64. Crane, *Poems*, 531.

65. Crane, *Poems*, 640.

66. Crane, *Poems*, 72, 73, 74.

67. Crane, *Poems*, 73, 74.

68. Nilsen, *Divided Vision*, 18, 33, 176

69. Trachtenberg, "Legend," 9.

70. Trachtenberg, "Shadow," 144, 145. David Perkins labels "Atlantis" a poem of "religious ecstasy" (*Modern Poetry*, 70) in which "everything is present in timeless ecstatic being" (73), and sees the Bridge as a "symbol of that which expresses and aspires to the divine" (73).

71. Reed, 154, 156.

72. William Pritchard is among the more skeptical readers of "Atlantis": "In a very real sense he had nothing to 'say' beyond reiterated appeals for moving onward and upward. . . ." See *Lives of the Modern Poets* (New York: Oxford University Press, 1980): 254.

73. Walker, *Bardic Ethos*, 49, 136.

74. Walker, *Bardic Ethos*, 136–37.

75. Walker, *Bardic Ethos*, 132.

76. Walker, *Bardic Ethos*, 51.

77. Walker, *Bardic Ethos*, 137.

78. Crane, *Poems*, 55, 56.

79. Crane, *Poems*, 58.

80. Crane, *Poems*, 59, 60.

81. Crane, *Poems*, 308.

82. Crane, *Poems*, 326.

83. Crane, *Poems*, 491–92.

84. Yeats imagines the mysterious connection between matter and spirit in terms of each desiring the other, a condition he depicts in his whirling gyres of antithetical and primary forces. In a playful mood, he offers the following image of spirit's need for matter: "the people of Faery cannot even play at hurley unless they have on either side some mortal. . . . Without mortal help they are shadowy and cannot even strike at the balls." See *Mythologies* (New York: Collier Macmillan, 1969), 9. In a more serious mood, he writes of that same desire: "The love of God for every human soul is infinite, for every human soul is unique; no other can satisfy the same *need* in God" (*Mythologies*, 347–48, my italics. What God loves is soul embodied in human form).

Chapter 7
Carolyn Forché: History and Theophany

If He ever did come back, if he ever *dared* to show His face . . . if after all this destruction, if after all the terrible days of this terrible century He returned to see . . . how much suffering His abandonment had created, if He did come back you should sue the bastard . . . Sue the bastard for walking out. How dare he.
—Tony Kushner, *Angels in America*

. . . we must be not forgetful / for some have entertained angels unawares.
—H.D., *Tribute to the Angels*

Carolyn Forché is best known as a political poet—for her poems on the Civil War in El Salvador, her war correspondence from Lebanon for National Public Radio, her work for Amnesty International, her editing of the monumental anthology *Against Forgetting*, and her translations of such poets as the Salvadoran exile Claribel Alegría and the French Resistance fighter Robert Desnos. With such a reputation, it is not surprising that response to *The Angel of History* has focused on its treatment of politics. Calvin Bedient calls it "the most humanitarian and aesthetically 'inevitable' response to a half-century of atrocities that has yet been written in English,"[1] and many readers have responded similarly. Sue Russell, for example, reads *The Angel of History* as continuing in the vein of Forché's earlier "socially conscious poetry,"[2] and Thomas Fink describes the poem as a "representation and contestation of the erasure of aspects of twentieth-century history."[3] To read the poem in terms of politics is entirely legitimate—Bedient and Fink, in particular, offer perceptive, insightful readings.

However, this focus on the political has also led to reductive misreadings.[4] One such misreading takes *The Angel of History* not as a political poem, but as an echo of Eliot's *The Waste Land*. An unsigned review in *Publisher's Weekly*, for example, claims that Forché's poem "invokes the horror of contemporary times in a mode reminiscent of Eliot's *The Waste Land*." Fredric Koeppel makes a similar observation, claiming that Forché's poem "takes up where T. S. Eliot's [*The Waste Land*] ended," and noting that Forché, like Eliot, "shores fragments against the ruins." This is meant as high praise, but by reading *The Angel of History* as a kind of sequel to *The Waste Land*, Koeppel seriously misreads the poem.[5]

Forché's catalog of history's cruelty easily equals Eliot's, but in *The Waste Land* April is cruel because it stirs up memory, and the poem as a whole enacts a disgust with history that borders on horror, as well as a longing to transcend that horror. Like Eliot, Forché raises the issue of remembering or forgetting the past: one speaker mentions children who were "forbidden to ask about the years before they were born," and another says, "*They didn't want you to know the past. They were hoping in this way you could escape it.*" But whereas for Eliot such "escape" is recast as the kind of spiritual transcendence of history he attains in *Four Quartets*, for Forché such escape is not only impossible, it is not desirable. In Part I, Ellie, a holocaust survivor, tells the narrator, "you must not forget anything." And near the end of the poem a voice remarks, "And so we revolt against silence with a bit of speaking. / The page is a charred field where the dead would have written / *We went on*. And it was like living through something again one could not live through again."[6] *The Waste Land* is a register of horror at the return of April, at having to live through it again; but *The Angel of History* takes listening and remembering as ethical imperatives.

However, those ethical imperatives, instead of leading to the kind of political action that some of Forché's readers demand, lead instead to the question of God in the aftermath of Hiroshima and the Holocaust. One way of interpreting Adorno's dictum, "To write poetry after Auschwitz is barbaric,"[7] is that it is barbaric to continue to write poetry, or to think about history or politics or human psychology, as if Auschwitz had never occurred. Is it also barbaric, we might ask ourselves, to imagine God after Auschwitz as loving, omnipotent, and omniscient? Is it barbaric, after Auschwitz and the historical wreckage of that bloodiest of all centuries, the twentieth, to take seriously a religious or spiritual view of the human condition? Forché raises these questions in *The Angel of History*, but few of her critics have paid attention.

Kevin Stein is one of those few, mentioning "the ethical questions these incidents [the historical atrocities Forché depicts] must, implicitly, pose of God." Stein goes on to note that "the terrible irony of this presence [i.e., the possibility of God's presence], given God's immutable silence, is what puts into doubt meaning of any kind—aesthetic, moral, or ethical."[8] But he fails to develop this important line of questioning, focusing instead on the "public" or "worldly," i.e., the political and ethical issues that Forché engages. And indeed, in a poem that takes as its subjects the Nazi Holocaust, the bombing of Hiroshima, and other historical atrocities, we might expect an author as tough-minded and clear-headed as Forché to conclude that religious questions, if not irrelevant, escapist, or reactionary, are clearly subordinate to questions of political engagement. But that is not the case, and the question of God's presence in the midst of the devastation that this poem recounts is so unexpected as perhaps to account for so many of the poem's readers not attending to it.

One of the chief concerns of *The Angel of History* is the possibility of theophany amid the historical cataclysm of the twentieth century. In her exploration of this possibility, Forché is not as direct as Elie Wiesel or Martin Buber, nor as assertive as someone like Hans Jonas, a German Jewish philosopher whose mother perished in the holocaust. If *The Angel of History* has been misread as a political poem, or as a poem that echoes *The Waste Land*, it would be just as misleading to read it as a Christian or Jewish poem, or as a poem that comes to any conclusions about religious concerns. Eileen Gregory correctly points out that *The Angel of History* completely lacks the kind of "totality" of spiritual vision to which H.D. aspires in her syncretic *Trilogy*.[9] Yet Forché's poem is deeply informed by her reading of H.D., and in its emphasis on the interconnectedness of past and present, of self and other—an interconnectedness so profound that it becomes translucence—this is a deeply religious poem, a poem that raises the question of what Forché calls our "responsibility . . . our ability to respond" not only to the history that we have made, but to the uncertain religious dimension of that history. Finally, the poem suggests that we are fundamentally implicated not only with other human beings, but also and equally fundamentally with the divine. In her most recent collection of poems, Forché imagines God as "not a being but a force, and humans, / the probative tip of that becoming."[10] In *The Angel of History*, Forché probes the possibility of a theophany framed by God's absence and silence amid the violence and suffering of the twentieth century—a theophany in which God appears from within that violence and suffering.

   The Angel of History is made up of five sections, most of which were published initially as separate poems: Part III ("The Recording Angel"), Part V ("Book Codes"), and earlier versions of Part I ("The Angel of History") and Part II ("The Notebook of Uprising") appeared first in different publications.[11] Each of the sections can stand alone, as can, for instance, individual *Cantos* by Ezra Pound or the poems that make up Eliot's *Four Quartets*. But like those poems, the five sections of *The Angel of History* gain in depth and resonance when they are read as parts of a whole. For example, a description of the Terezinstadt camp in Part II is colored by a holocaust survivor's memories in Part I, and both of these add depth to a Hiroshima survivor's memories in Part IV.

   The Angel of History differs from Forché's earlier work most dramatically because in this poem the lyric "I," the central subject's sensibility, is not the center of the poem. Many different voices speak—one voice seems to be Forché's own; some of the voices belong to her grandmother and her relatives living in the former Czechoslovakia; one voice belongs to an elderly Jewish holocaust survivor named Ellie, with whom Forché spends a week in a Paris hospital; another is an unnamed survivor of Hiroshima; some of the voices belong to authors whom Forché quotes, such as Walter Benjamin, Paul Valéry, or René Char. And other voices are nameless. So we get this polyphonic collage effect, and we get a catalog of horrors from twentieth-century history.

   The first section of the poem focuses on Ellie, an elderly Jewish woman with whom Forché shares a hospital room in Paris. Ellie survived the Holocaust by hiding in various locations, but lost her two sons, her aunts and uncles, her friends, and her parents during the war. Her husband fought with the French

Resistance and survived the war, but died of cholera shortly afterward. Ellie tells Forché about forty-four Jewish children hidden in a farmhouse in the French village of Izieu for an entire year, then discovered and sent to Auschwitz. Ellie's vision of the world has been irreparably marked by all that she has endured: *"And the world is worse now than it was then,"* she tells Forché, who asks, "Worse?" And Ellie replies, *"Mais oui."* Her conversation with Ellie on the horrors of the Holocaust leads Forché to remember vultures *"belching and vomiting flesh, / as you saw them at Puerto Diablo and El Playon,"* body dumps that she saw in El Salvador during the civil war, as well as helicopters, aircraft carriers, and white phosphorus bombs ("So beautiful, ma'am, from here, the sailor said, if you don't stop to think"[12]) that she witnessed during the Lebanese Civil War.

The poem's second section focuses on Forché's trip to Czechoslovakia before the fall of the Berlin Wall, where she meets some of her relatives for the first time. There she visits the remains of the Nazi camp at Terezinstadt, where the poet Robert Desnos was imprisoned and died. She walks amid the detritus of history: "a child's leather prayer book from Terezin," an empty box labeled *"Important,"* "a diary open to the words *cannot remain here.*"[13] She visits the street in Prague where Jan Palach, a young college student, set himself on fire and burned to death in protest of the Soviet invasion of Czechoslovakia in 1968. In the third section, we are confronted with more atrocities: "The dead girl was thought to be with child / Until it was discovered that her belly had already been cut open / And a man's head placed where the child would have been / . . . / In every war someone puts a cigarette in the corpse's mouth." Part IV returns to the Holocaust with references to the film *Shoah,* and then shifts to an ornamental garden in Hiroshima which has been restored to look just as it did before the bomb was dropped. Forché tours the garden with a survivor of the bombing: "She has always been afraid to come here. / It is the river she most / remembers, the living / and the dead both crying for help. / . . . / I was weak and my skin hung from my fingertips like cloth."[14]

How does one write the history of such events? What significance does one ascribe to such events? Eliot turns in revulsion from the repeated horrors of history and seeks solace in the transcendent, spiritual reality of orthodox Christianity. Hart Crane imagines poetry as a bridge to a zone of the aesthetic imaginary, on the other side of history. But Forché refuses to turn away; she keeps her gaze steadily on history and its victims.

And where is God amid all this? His name appears quite often: in the poem's first section Ellie, the Holocaust survivor, says, *"Le Dieu est un feu.* [God is a fire.] *A psychopath. Le Dieu est feu* [God is fire]"—and then four pages later: *"Hôtel-Dieu?* [the name of the hospital where Ellie and Forché meet] *Some people say so. I say this God is insane."* Another voice in that section describes God's name as *"a boneless string of vowels,"*[15] which is a curious but powerful image—no consonants, no bones, just this shapeless, amorphous thing.

In Part II, in Czechoslovakia, Forché speaks of her grandmother Anna, who lived with Forché's family in Michigan but maintained a close correspondence with relatives in Czechoslovakia before and during the Second World War. Addressing her grandmother, Forché tells her, "You loved the shabbiness of the world: countries invaded, cities bombed, houses whose roofs have fallen in, / women who have lost their men, orphans, amputees, the war wounded"—all of this the old woman has known, and all of this she can love. But "What you did not love any longer was a world that had lost its soul." Forché herself describes Czechoslovakia as "a world emptying of human belief,"[16] which I take as a kind of gloss on a world that has lost or is losing its soul. In this soulless world without belief, meaning drains away and we hear another voice speak of "the sovereignty of the accidental," and someone else comments, "It is playing chess with us"[17]—and who or what is "It"? God? The laws of history? The laws of biology or physics? Zuzana Borovská, the daughter of Anna's sister, whom Forché meets in Brno in 1990, advises her to ". . . put into question God. / Whatever can be taken away is taken / to allow suffering to remain." From Czechoslovakia Forché travels to East Berlin, where she comes across what seems to be graffiti: "*Wie im himmel so auf erden* as in heaven so on earth. / *Wer ist unser gott*? who is our god?"[18] The first line is from the Lord's Prayer—on earth as it is in heaven—but in the context of the poem it takes on a bitter irony, and the potential answers to the question "who is our god?" include the insane psychopath described by Ellie, the "it" that plays chess with us, and Zuzana Borovská's questionable God who takes away everything but allows suffering to remain.

Part III includes almost no personal names or place names, focusing instead on the general or universal: the dead woman with the man's head in her belly, the corpse with the cigarette in its mouth. But God appears in this line from the poet Georg Trakl: "*Where an angry God, spilled blood itself, lives.*"[19] Pulled from its context, the line is enigmatic, and "God" seems to be apposite with "spilled blood." However, this spilled blood seems in no way redemptive, and the image is stark and violent.

In Part IV, at a garden in Hiroshima meticulously reconstructed to look just as it did before August 1945, Forché listens to a Japanese survivor of the bombing:

> We have not, all these years, felt what you call happiness.
> But at times, with good fortune, we experience something close.
> As our life resembles life, and this garden the garden.
> And in the silence surrounding what happened to us
>
> it is the bell to awaken God that we've heard ringing.[20]

It's a startling image, suggesting that God has fallen asleep and needs to be awakened; and while he's been asleep, Hiroshima and the Holocaust and all sorts of horrible things occurred. The image is picked up on the next page, in a quotation from Peter Schwenger's *Letter Bomb: Nuclear Holocaust and the Exploding Word*: "*For if Hiroshima in the morning, after the bomb has fallen, / is like a dream, one must ask whose dream it is.*"[21] This god is perhaps less night-marish than Ellie's psychopath or the "it" that plays chess with us—this god has simply fallen asleep during the twentieth century, and needs to be woken up, and then perhaps everything will be all right. But is God really only sleeping, and if so, is it within our power to awaken him? Will he answer the bell?

And if he does, what then? In Part III, just before the quotation from Trakl about the "*angry God*" and "*spilled blood,*" we read: "And always he thought: this is it, the end of the world. God is coming."[22] This line carries two kinds of force: one is the force of an imagined or implied threat, the angry God of the Old Testament who intervenes in history, the God of "The Battle Hymn of the Republic" who will "loose the fearful lightning of his terrible swift sword"; the other kind of force is ironic: we may imagine a climactic end of the world, at-tended by God's coming, but in fact no such thing happens. Perhaps God is asleep, or perhaps, as in *Angels in America*, he has abandoned us. As in Beck-ett's great play *Waiting for Godot*, we wait, but things simply continue in their impoverished, painful, wretched way, and God never comes, and the world nev-er ends. We can't go on, but we go on, in our steadily diminishing condition.

Up to this point, I've been describing one set of references to God in the poem, references that suggest a bitterness toward God, a disappointment in God, a fear of God, a doubt of God. God has apparently stood by and watched during the Holocaust and Hiroshima; he has permitted the myriad atrocities of the twen-tieth century, perhaps because he is insane or psychopathic or angry, perhaps in a kind of heartless chess game, or perhaps because he is asleep. Eileen Gregory, in a perceptive and sensitive reading of this poem, writes that "'God' is a recur-rent sign in Forché's poem, but it signifies something inexplicable and dark. . . . Here the spiritual is manifest as tragic questioning within bitterness and ab-sence." For Gregory, God is less a presence than an absence in Forché's poem, a signifier of our desperate desire to make sense of extreme suffering: "'God'—however problematic or displaced—signifies a need to imagine human life, both individual and collective, in terms of assent: purposefulness, justice, intelligibil-ity, and love."[23]

Gregory's somewhat Feuerbachian concept of God is provocative, but it re-duces God to a dimension of the human psyche, and in *The Angel of History* God is something other than that. We may conclude that God in the twentieth century is a *deus absconditus*, in Aquinas's beautiful Latin phrase—God has absconded, has fled the scene of the crime. But that would be to misread the Latin: *abscondere* means "to hide," not "to flee," and *deus absconditus* is a hid-den god, not necessarily a god who has fled or abandoned his children, but a god who is not readily knowable. In her early poem "Message," Forché writes that our history has arrived at "the hour farthest from God,"[24] but *The Angel of His-tory* suggests that such distance, such alienation, can be the occasion for a mys-terious and unexpected theophany.

There is another set of references to God in the poem, less frequent than those mentioned already, and somewhat ambiguous, but nonetheless disturbing and richly suggestive. The first is a quotation from Elie Wiesel that occurs alongside Ellie's description of the forty-four Jewish children who had been hidden in the farmhouse and then discovered and sent off to Auschwitz. Wiesel writes, "*le silence de Dieu est Dieu*," or "*the silence of God is God*" and Forché repeats the line, once in French and twice in English, as Ellie tells that horrible story. In Part III of the poem, in a long stanza beginning "The child asks about earth," we find the line "God returns to the world from within. . ."[25] The poem's opening line, "There are times when the child seems delicate, as if he had not yet crossed into the world," is echoed much later: "There are times when the child seems not yet to have crossed into the world / Despite having entered a body."[26] These lines suggest a space from which one crosses into the world—a space of nothingness or non-being, perhaps, or something else? But "God returns to the world" not from that other space, but "from within" this world. Later in Part III is a quotation from René Char: "*Comment vivre sans inconnu devant soi?*" How can we live without the unknown before us? And a few pages farther on we read: "In the worst of centuries, a merely difficult week, nothing, nothing, then from nothing, something." Char's "unknown" and the "something" that emerges from "nothing" may of course have nothing to do with God. But in Part IV Forché asks, "To what and to whom does one say *yes*?" and then she quotes Paul Valéry: "If God were the uncertain, would you cling to him?"[27]

This second set of references may limn a God who is silent, unknown, uncertain, a "something" that emerges from "nothing" (or who calls "something" out of "nothing"), a God who "returns to the world from within." This last phrase suggests that God, *deus absconditus*, is not hidden in some transcendent otherworld, but within this world, and that our experience of theophany occurs always from within human history—in fact, in this poem, God returns from within the Holocaust and Hiroshima, from within our most extreme experiences of suffering and loss. Forché never draws the connection, but such a God might be similar to the one described by Dietrich Bonhoeffer who, in his *Letters and Papers from Prison*, writes of "the powerlessness of God in the world" and "the suffering of God in the life of the world."[28]

But that experience of theophany—if that is what it is—is far more rare than the kind of anger toward God that Ellie expresses, or the bitterness and absence that Eileen Gregory summarizes. How does God return from within? In one of the poem's most beautiful images, Forché's grandmother, Anna Bassarová, burns old newspapers in an outdoor trash container at night:

Anna stands in a ring of thawed snow, stirring a trash fire in an iron drum until her face
        flares, shriveled and intent, and sparks rise in the night along with pages of
burning
        ash from the week's papers,
        one peeling away from the rest,
an ashen page framed in brilliance.

For a moment, the words are visible, even though fire has destroyed them, so
transparent has the page become.[29]

"For a moment the words are visible" against the transparency of the burnt
pages, just as for a moment Ellie's stories, or the empty box labeled "Important," or the "cold, swept-clean barracks" through which Forché walks at
Terezin bring back, in fragments, the past. When Forché finds the apartment
house where her grandmother's niece lives, in Czechoslovakia, she approaches
the call box and identifies herself: "This is the granddaughter of Anna Bassarová
and the daughter of Michal." And her grandmother's niece, Zuzana Borovská,
comes downstairs in amazement: "She stood on the landing of disbelief in Brno
as if the war were translucent behind us"[30]—as if the war were translucent behind us, as if the present were not separated from the past by an opaque and impermeable wall, but as if the translucent past were constitutive of the historical
present. In her essay "H.D. after H.D.," Forché describes what she calls the in-
tensification of H.D.'s "palimpsestic vision" in her poem *Trilogy*: "past and future are fused in a 'poignant and ethereal present' that is not stasis." In *Trilogy*,
H.D. shows us "that we are not living sequentially or 'after' events in time but
rather in their aftermath . . . the past is never behind but rather within us."[31] *The
Angel of History* lacks the hortatory, prophetic confidence of *Trilogy* and its
insistence that history is an epiphenomenon of the sacred, but both poems dis-
rupt and discard the idea of history as sequentiality. What happened to Ellie,
what happened in Czechoslovakia, or in Hiroshima, or in El Salvador, did not
merely happen in the past; all of these things continue in some sense to "happen" in the present.

The translucence between past and present points toward another, more important translucence between self and other. In *The Waste Land*, the self is isolated and opaque—its experience is finally inaccessible to anyone else: "I have
heard the key / Turn in the door once and turn once only / We think of the key,
each in his prison / Thinking of the key, each confirms a prison."[32] In *The Angel
of History*, however, the lyric "I" is translucent, its borders permeable: "In the
windows of my earlier life, it is often winter, a glass white with my own breath,
/ and in rubbing it clear I see only my own reflection. / It was years before my
face would become hers, yours, and hers, the other's, facing / each other through
days, pain, the prisoner's visiting window."[33]

Kevin Stein notes perceptively that the "fulcrum" of *The Angel of History* is
"the folly of regarding oneself as safely and protectively apart from others,"[34]
and in an interview with David Wright, Forché speaks of the "mode of wakeful
listening" in which this poem is written, "of recording rather than . . . pro-
nouncement or confession or establishment of lyric identity or selfhood."[35] Moments of intense historical consciousness occur always, in this poem, with another—with Ellie in the Paris hospital, or with Anna, or with Zuzana Borovská
in Czechoslovakia, or with the nameless survivor of the Hiroshima bombing in
the restored Garden Shukkei-en. These are moments of almost visionary or ec-

static consciousness—one speaker describes "the ecstasy of standing outside oneself,"[36] alluding to the word's etymology from the Greek *ex histanai*, to cause to stand outside—and Calvin Bedient must have this ecstatic quality in mind when he describes "a blessed fatality of [Forché's] nature, her liability to lose herself to others,"[37] i.e., her liability to efface her own subjectivity, a liability which is nowhere more evident in her work than it is in this poem.

Anita Helle observes that Forché never indulges in "false attempts at unification" between self and other, or "easy identification between survivors and witnesses," but she also claims to detect "a kind of maternal rememoration which is disturbing, if not potentially fatal in its implication—at least if what is to be avoided is a reabsorption of the grieving body, into an archaic representation of maternal presence—the mother who reconciles all."[38] I would argue that, while some of the poem's speakers may express a desire for such reconciliation or redemption, the poem finally is deeply suspicious of such closure. While past and present, like self and other, are not opaque or impermeable for Forché, neither are they ever transparent or wholly permeable. When she asks Ellie "in what sense the world was worse," Ellie answers, *"Pardon, est-ce que je vous dérange? / Je ne sais pas trés bien m'éxpliquer en français"* [Excuse me, am I disturbing you? I cannot explain myself very well in French].[39] Clearly it is not simply French, but rather the human condition, that prevents Ellie from fully explaining herself.

Nonetheless the interconnectedness of past and present, and of self and other, imperfect as it is, provides the ground for the possibility of the unexpected theophany of *deus absconditus*. Martin Buber writes of the dialectical interplay between God's absence and presence, or between our affirmation and denial of the spiritual:

> Doom becomes more oppressive in every new eon, and the return [of the divine] more explosive. And the theophany comes ever *closer*, it comes ever closer to the sphere *between beings*—comes closer to the realm that hides in our midst, in the between. History is a mysterious approach to closeness. Every spiral of its path leads us into deeper corruption and at the same time into more fundamental return.[40]

If Forché is not as hortatory or didactic as H.D., neither is she as authoritative as Buber. *The Angel of History* makes clear that in the face of the horrors of the twentieth century, it makes perfect sense to "put into question God," as Zuzana Borovská suggests, or to conclude as Ellie does that God must be insane, or to suspect that he is asleep, or playing chess. Yet the poem suggests that other conclusions are possible as well. If God is connected, at least metonymically, with "silence," "the unknown," "the uncertain," and if God "returns from within" the horrors of the twentieth century, what would such a theophany entail? Forché quotes Elie Wiesel on "the silence of God," and in his memoir *Night*, Wiesel recounts an unexpected theophany: three Jewish concentration-camp prisoners are being hanged, and one of them, a small boy, is so lightweight that he won't strangle properly, and as he twitches and convulses, struggling between life and death, the other prisoners watch, and one cries out, "Where is God? Where is He? . . . . Where is God now?" And Wiesel writes, "And I heard a voice within me answer him: 'Where is he? Here he is—He is hanging here on this gallows.'"[41]

Wiesel's theophany is bitter bread for those who seek a theodicy, i.e., a justification of human suffering, or some kind of redemption from our historical condition. A god who is silence, the unknown, and the uncertain is a difficult god, "a God that cannot be talked about,"[42] as Walter Kaufmann says of God in Martin Buber's *I and Thou*. In many ways, God's return "from within" is as fraught with questions as are the two angels who open and close the poem. The first comes from Walter Benjamin's "Theses on the Philosophy of History," a passage from which stands as the book's preface:

> This is how one pictures the angel of history. His face is turned toward the past. Where we perceive a chain of events, he sees one single catastrophe which keeps piling wreckage and hurls it in front of his feet. The angel would like to stay, awaken the dead, and make whole what has been smashed. But a storm is blowing in from Paradise; it has got caught in his wings with such a violence that the angel can no longer close them. The storm irresistibly propels him into the future to which his back is turned, while the pile of debris before him grows skyward.

Our word *angel* derives from the Greek *angelos*, which means simply "messenger," and is applied in classical Greek most often to human beings. Its related verb, *angellein*, means "to announce," and is interestingly close in meaning to the verb *kleiein*, "to proclaim," which is the root from which the Muse of History, Clio, derives her name.

Eileen Gregory reads the poem's angel as she reads the poem's God, as a figure for a dimension of the human psyche: "the trope of the angel functions . . . . as a displaced sign of an absent or dark God, as a figuration of the human desire to comprehend the incomprehensible and to minister to the human world." For Gregory, human psychology gives the image its force: "the governing trope of Forché's poem, Benjamin's angel, is powerful because it figures a human desire for a 'messianic' or 'redemptive' sense of history and for an angelic intervention or care for the human, 'to awaken the dead, and make whole what was [sic] smashed.'" "The angels in these poems," she concludes, "are finally images of 'watchers,' figures for human vision, endurance, and guardianship."[43] Gregory's reading here is instructive, but the poem's angels, like its God, seem to be more than figures for human desire.

Benjamin's angel is important, first, because his vision of history is not the "chain of events" that most of us see, but rather the palimpsestic present that Forché describes in her comments on H.D.'s *Trilogy*, i.e., that vision of inter-

connectedness of past and present, of self and other, that the poem bodies forth
in repeated instances. Second, the angel is important because, although he
"would *like* to . . . awaken the dead, and make whole what has been smashed"
(my italics), he cannot—he cannot close his wings, he cannot prevent his irre-
sistible propulsion into the future. The angel's inability to act in history gets
picked up in the title of Part III, "The Recording Angel," which Forché says
"refers to the Metatron, the prince of the Seraphim."[44] Angelology is an inexact
discipline, but according to some traditions, the Metatron is the angelic scribe
who records everything that happens, a kind of divine historiographer whose
text includes, literally, all of history. Forché connects the figure of this angel to
her rejection of the lyric "I" in this poem: in *The Angel of History*, the central
consciousness takes on "the role of passive recorder: the angel Metatron who
listened but could not intervene, like the *deus abscondi* [sic] of the Holocaust."[45]
Gregory is correct that the angel is a figure of witness, one who watches and
remembers the pain and suffering and destruction that we endure and inflict upon one another over the course of our history. But in his capacity to see history
only as "one single catastrophe," and never as "a chain of events," his is always
that intense, ecstatic consciousness that most of us attain only in scattered moments, if at all. The message that this divine *angelos* bears is that such moments
reveal the truth about us—he is an emissary of those historical "others" with
whose experience and suffering each of us is fundamentally implicated.

The angel imagery is continued in the section on Prague, where we learn
that "The wind has eaten the faces from the angels of Charles Bridge," and later
in the section on Hiroshima, where in the restored garden we see "the stone angel holding paper cranes."[46] Another angel closes the book, this one from Paul
Valéry. Valéry's speaker has a vision in which an angel appears to him:

> The angel handed me a book, saying, "It contains everything
> that you could possibly wish to know." And he disappeared.
>   So I opened the book, which was not particularly fat.
>   It was written in an unknown character.
>   Scholars translated it, but they produced altogether
> different versions.
>   They differed even about the sense of their own
> readings, agreeing upon neither the tops nor the bottoms of
> them, nor upon the beginnings of them nor the ends.
>   Toward the end of this vision it seemed to me that
> the book melted, until it could no longer be distinguished from
> this world that is about us.[47]

Eileen Gregory reads this angel, too, as a figure of human attitudes and behavior: "Valéry's parable suggests that the angelic book of the knowable is 'indistinguishable from the world that is about us.' Likewise, angelic 'redemption'
and ministry belong to this world among those who remember the dead and who
'watch over life' in conditions of extremity."[48] Again, she is right in part, but I

would add that Valéry's angel's book recalls Metatron's archive of all history which, because it includes everything, is finally indistinguishable from this world, in all its polysemous ambiguity. Gregory wants to argue that in this poem "God" is merely a signifier of the human desire for an absolute, and that "angel" is simply a trope for ethical human behavior. Hers is a coherent reading of the poem, but one feels finally its reductive domestication of the poem's deepest, most radical religious speculations. In *The Angel of History* Forché is much closer in spirit to H.D. in *Trilogy* than Gregory is prepared to admit.

Finally, Gregory notes that *The Angel of History* "refer[s] to traditions of Jewish mysticism in which God is manifest through suffering and absence";[49] I would say that the poem does more than simply "refer" to those traditions—they lie very near the poem's heart. Annie Dillard, in such works as *Holy the Firm* and "For the Time Being," uses many of the same terms that Gregory uses in her bitter or tragic depiction of God in this poem, but Dillard does not conclude that God is essentially a figure for human desire. In "For the Time Being," Dillard takes as her epigraph a question from Nelly Sachs, a German Jewish poet whose work, like Forché's, addresses the religious implications of human suffering: "Who is like you, O Lord, among the silent, remaining silent through the suffering of His children?" For Dillard, this hidden God "does not give as the world gives. His home is absence, and there he finds us. In the coils of absence, we meet him by seeking him. God lifts our souls to their roots in his silence."[50] *The Angel of History* suggests that in the absence and silence that attend our remembering and listening to testimony of the historical cataclysm of the twentieth century, perhaps a space is cleared for a new kind of theophany—a God who emerges from within history's most extreme violence and suffering.

Unlike Eliot in *Four Quartets* or Crane in *The Bridge*, Forché does not lay out a series of alternative ways of imagining historical time, each of which conveys a partial but finally inadequate truth. Her understanding of history and God lacks Eliot's dogmatic, redemptive confidence, and it lacks Crane's final glorious vision of the great Bridge spanning the sacred and profane. In Forché's poem history takes the shape of Benjamin's "one single catastrophe," a palimpsest in which new episodes of suffering are inscribed over older episodes, and the older episodes bleed through the more recent. Here are no signs of progress or the dialectic, no affirmation of a spiritual order that transcends and completes the order of history. Nor is history here anything about which objective or scientific methodologies might yield some sort of complete or adequate knowledge. A *gnosis* is hinted at, but its knowledge can be articulated only in the sometimes obscure, indirect, fragmentary language of poetry. We are admonished to listen, to remember, to empathize, but we are not granted the kind of final truth that Eliot and Crane promise us we can attain.

Notes

1. Calvin Bedient, "Postlyrically Yours," *The Threepenny Review*, Summer 1994, 19.

2. Sue Russell, "The Workings of Chance and Memory," *Women's Review of Books*, July 1994, 31.

3. Thomas Fink, *"A Different Sense of Power": Problems of Community in Late Twentieth-Century U.S. Poetry* (Madison, NJ: Fairleigh Dickinson University Press, 2001), 94.

4. Rochelle Owens calls Forché "always politically correct," and describes the book as an attempt "to define oneself and the rest of humanity through an ideological . . . journey" consisting of "shallow surfaces and fashionable self-examinations." See Rev. of *The Angel of History*, *World Literature Today* 68 (1994): 816. But ideology is nowhere evident in this poem, and self-definition is the least of the poet's concerns. Nora Mitchell and Emily Skoler label Forché "one of our leading writers of political poetry." See "History, Death, Politics, Despair," *New England Review* 17, no. 2 (1995): 75, and describe the book as a reproduction of "historical consciousness" (74). However, they continue, "This consciousness that Forché enacts, with no consideration of the future, cannot provide a basis for a sense of political agency. If we're fixated on the past, we can't envision or plan for where we are going. . . . This is disempowering, disabling" (77). They conclude, "In the context of women's political poetry . . . [Forché does] not seem to write to teach, to mobilize, to give voice, to identify, to console, or to propose a new ethic," and this failure, along with what they call the book's difficulty and relative inaccessibility, they find "remarkable considering that this is political poetry" (79). Like Owens, Mitchell and Skoler misread *The Angel of History* because they confine it to a genre—political poetry—to which it belongs in only a limited sense, and they criticize Forché for failing to meet generic expectations which are too narrow and restrictive.

5. See Rev. of *The Angel of History* in *Publisher's Weekly*, January 31, 1994, 16, and Fredric Koeppel, "Taking the Pain of a Violent History into Poetry's Oblivion," *San Jose Mercury News*, April 24, 1994, E1. And yet it is not hard to see why he, like other reviewers, is reminded of Eliot. *The Angel of History* displays many of the formal elements of High Modernism: multiple voices, a fragmented surface, embedded quotations, disjunctive narratives. On the first page, the word "April" appears five times, as if to echo the opening line of Eliot's great poem, "April is the cruelest month." Similarly, the line "a woman broken into many women" (3) may remind readers of Eliot's Tiresias, "the most important personage in the poem, uniting all the rest." And where Eliot presents a catalog of horrors drawn from literary history—the Cumaean sibyl, condemned to literal life imprisonment; Tristan, who dies believing his beloved Isolde has betrayed him; the distraught mother in Webster's *White Devil* who sings while her son buries the brother he has killed; Philomel, raped by her sister's husband, who then cuts out her tongue; the "lovely woman [who] stoops to folly" in *The Vicar of Wakefield*, and then commits suicide—Forché presents a catalog of horrors drawn from the history of the twentieth century.

6. Carolyn Forché, *The Angel of History* (New York: Harper Collins, 1994), 4, 26, 10, 69.

7. Theodor. Adorno, "Cultural Criticism and Society," in *Prisms*, ed. Samuel and Shierry Weber (Cambridge, MA: The MIT Press, 1981), 34.

8. Kevin Stein, *Private Poets, Worldly Acts: Public and Private History in Contem-*

porary American Poetry (Athens: Ohio University Press, 1996), 158, 161.

9. Eileen Gregory, "Poetry and Survival: H.D. and Carolyn Forché," in *H.D. and Poets After*, ed. Donna Krolik Hollenberg (Iowa City: University of Iowa Press, 2000), 277.

10. Carolyn Forché, *Blue Hour* (New York: Harper Collins, 2003), 40.

11. An early version of Part I, "The Angel of History," appeared in a special issue of *The Graham House Review* dedicated to the memory of Terrence Des Pres (*Graham House Review* 11, Spring 1988). An early version of Part II, "The Notebook of Uprising," appeared in the Twentieth Anniversary Issue of *The American Poetry Review* (22.1, Jan/Feb 1993). Part III, "The Recording Angel," appeared first in *Antaeus* 64–65 (Spring-Autumn 1990) and later in *The Best American Poetry of 1991*. Part V, "Book Codes," appeared in *No Roses Review* (Spring 1993).

12. Forché, *Angel*, 8, 15, 19.

13. Forché, *Angel*, 37, 38, 39.

14. Forché, *Angel*, 63, 70.

15. Forché, *Angel*, 7, 11, 14.

16. Forché, *Angel*, 28, 36.

17. Forché, *Angel*, 43, 36.

18. Forché, *Angel*, 46, 49.

19. Forché, *Angel*, 64.

20. Forché, *Angel*, 71.

21. Forché, *Angel*, 72.

22. Forché, *Angel*, 63.

23. Gregory, "Poetry and Survival," 277.

24. Carolyn Forché, *The Country Between Us* (New York: Harper & Row, 1981), 22.

25. Forché, *Angel*, 5, 58.

26. Forché, *Angel*, 3, 65.

27. Forché, *Angel*, 61, 65, 69.

28. Quoted in John A. T. Robinson, *Honest to God* (Philadelphia, Westminster, 1963), 82, 83.

29. Forché, *Angel*, 26.

30. Forché, *Angel*, 34, 42.

31. Forché, "H.D. after H.D.," 260.

32. T. S. Eliot, *Collected Poems, 1909–1962* (New York: Harcourt, 1970), 69.

33. Forché, *Angel*, 16.

34. Stein, *Private Poets*, 158.

35. David Wright, "Assembling Community: A Conversation with Carolyn Forché," last modified Feb. 20, 2000. <http://www.english.uiuc.edu/maps/poets/a_f/forche/wrightinterview.htm>

36. Forché, *Angel*, 27.

37. Bedient, "Postlyrically," 20.

38. Anita Helle, "Elegy as History: Three Women Poets 'By the Century's Death-bed,'" *South Atlantic Review* 61, no. 2 (1996): 55, 57.

39. Forché, *Angel*, 11.

40. Martin Buber, *I and Thou*, trans. by Walter Kaufmann (New York: Scribner's, 1970), 168.

41. Elie Wiesel, *Night*, trans. Stella Rodway (1958; repr., New York: Bantam, 1982), 62.

42. Buber, *I and Thou*, 26.

43. Gregory, "Poetry and Survival," 278, 279.

44. Quoted in Mark Strand, ed., *The Best American Poetry 1991* (New York: Macmillan Collier, 1991), 280.

45. Forché, "H.D. after H.D," 263–64.

46. Forché, *Angel*, 35, 70.

47. Forché, *Angel*, 78.

48. Gregory, "Poetry and Survival," 279.

49. Gregory, "Poetry and Survival," 278.

50. Annie Dillard, "For the Time Being," in *The Best American Essays, 1999*, ed. Edward Hoagland (Boston: Houghton Mifflin, 1999), 75, 83.

Chapter 8
Ezra Pound and the Problem of History

The famous passage in Joyce's *Ulysses* in which Stephen Dedalus describes history as a nightmare from which he is trying to awake is followed by a scene in which Stephen, as he listens to a soccer game outside, thinks to himself, "What if that nightmare gave you a back kick?" Nightmares belong to the interior world of the mind, but history belongs to the exterior world as well: history can kick back. Mr. Deasy, who is Stephen's interlocutor in this scene, responds to Stephen's "nightmare" remark with his own quasi-Hegelian, quasi-Augustinian assertion—"All history moves towards one great goal, the manifestation of God"—but he precedes this vaguely benign notion with a far darker depiction of contemporary history: "Mark my words, Mr Dedalus . . . . England is in the hands of the jews. In all the highest places: her finance, her press. And they are the signs of a nation's decay. Wherever they gather they eat up the nation's vital strength. I have seen it coming these years. As sure as we are standing here the jew merchants are already at their work of destruction. Old England is dying."[1]

In *Ulysses*, these remarks signal a contrast between Stephen and Deasy that is entirely in Stephen's favor, yet such remarks are disturbingly common in the work of Joyce's great advocate, Ezra Pound. Pound's more sympathetic readers remind us that anti-Semitism was fairly widespread prior to World War II, but rhetoric such as Pound's in the radio broadcasts that he made from Mussolini's fascist Italy beginning in January 1941 has never been widespread. In the transcripts of those broadcasts, we find, for example, this echo of Mr Deasy—"Roosevelt is more in the hands of the Jews than Wilson was in 1919"—and crude references to "Jewspapers" and "Franklin Finkelstein Roosevelt," as well as the rhetoric of racist hygiene: "No Rothschild is English, no Streiker is English, no Roosevelt is English, no Baruch, Morgenthau, Cohen, Lehman, Warburg, Kuhn, Kahn, Schiff, Sieff or Solomon was ever yet born Anglo-Saxon. And it is for this filth that you fight. It is for this filth that you have murdered your Empire. It is this filth that elects, selects, elects your politicians."[2]

These broadcasts led to Pound's being charged with treason and confined for twelve years, on the grounds of his being mentally unfit to stand trial, in St. Elizabeths Hospital for the Criminally Insane in Washington, DC. History was

kicking back at Ezra Pound. On the occasion of Pound's death, Archibald Mac-
Leish, who along with Frost, Hemingway, and Eliot was instrumental in secur-
ing Pound's eventual release from St. Elizabeths, wrote:

> That he was often anti-Semitic is only too clear. That he never protested against
> the nasty little triumphs of Mussolini in Ethiopia and Spain or the monstrous
> behavior of Hitler in Germany or even against the Gestapo terror and torture in
> Paris—that he never protested against any of this (only against the decision of
> his own country to put a stop to it) is sadly true. . . . He adjusted the facts to his
> theories. He read but did not see. Insofar as fascism fitted his preconceptions he
> admired it: What did not fit he merely ignored. By the time of the Roman
> broadcasts he must have been the only intelligent man left in Europe who did
> not understand what a Nazi conquest of the world would mean to art and hu-
> man decency and everything else he loved, including civilization itself. . . . Any
> man who could make a religion of Social Credit in the lifetime of Adolf Hitler,
> and fix his mind on usury as the key to the world's ills at a moment when the
> writers and artists of Paris were being tortured and executed for their addiction
> to human liberty must be written down as childish, to put it as kindly as possi-
> ble. And when that same man goes on in the same lifetime of this same Adolf
> Hitler to equate usury with the Jews—to make the Jews a symbol of the crime
> of usury—the naiveté becomes something else and worse: unspeakably worse.[3]

MacLeish's judgment is clear, yet he worked to secure Pound's release, and
everything he mentions was known to the committee that selected Pound's *Pisan Cantos* for the 1949 Bollingen Prize in Poetry. The Bollingen judges argued
that Pound's poetry was completely separate from the politics and behavior of
its author, and the question of the relationship between the aesthetic and the ideological has been central to literary study for some time now. Lawrence Rainey
correctly notes that "[m]any readers consider *The Cantos* of Ezra Pound the
most important work of Anglo-American literary modernism,"[4] and Alfred
Kazin speaks for many when he writes, "we are astonished by the absolutely
faultless ear that will remain with Pound even in the most discursive sections of
the Cantos . . . [and by t]he ease with which Pound assimilates other poets, other
languages."[5] Pound's brilliance as a poet is in my judgment beyond question,
but his reading of history is eventually entangled in a rigidly simplistic, either/or
world view that leads him to embrace and defend fascism and anti-Semitism, a
position from which he never fully retreated.[6]

Representative of those early readers who were unsympathetic to Pound's
engagement with history in his poetry, Allen Tate wrote that in *A Draft of XXX
Cantos* (1933) Pound's "powerful juxtapositions of the ancient, the Renaissance,
and the modern worlds reduce all three elements to an unhistorical miscellany,
timeless and without origin, and no longer a force in the lives of men."[7] When
Pound was awarded the 1949 Bollingen Prize, Tate's opinion hadn't changed:
"Insofar as the *Cantos* have a subject it is made up of historical materials. But if
there is any poetry of our age which may be said to be totally lacking in the his-

torical sense, the sense of how ideas move in history, it is Pound's *Cantos*. His verse is an anomaly in an age of acute historical awareness."[8] After Pound's death, Alfred Kazin concluded that "as we drift through the *Cantos*, history turns out to be anything that interests Ezra Pound," and that Pound "abolish[es] . . . all sense of historicism."[9]

Tate and Kazin are formidable critics, but Pound has had his sympathetic readers as well. Among the most gifted of these is Hugh Kenner, who defends the poet's rejection of the merely aesthetic and his attempt to understand history and influence the course of public events. Kenner reverses a line from the Gospel of Mark and asks, "What does it profit a man, whispered Mauberley's ghost, if he gain his soul and the whole world be lost? . . . The world, [Pound] was convinced, had once known the order it now lacked, and what has been known should not be difficult to recover, a simple matter of reactivating knowledge."[10] To recover lost knowledge that might save the world sounds laudable, but in Pound's case it led to his defense of Mussolini's invasion of Ethiopia and support of the fascists in the Spanish Civil War, and to a broader embrace of the Axis cause during the Second World War.

Earlier in his career, however, Pound displayed few traces of anti-Semitism and no attraction to totalitarian politics and the kind of history such politics encourages. In chapter five I discussed James Longenbach's claim that T. S. Eliot and Ezra Pound write a type of "existential historicism" that grows out of the thinking of writers like Dilthey and Collingwood. In her *Epic Reinvented*, Mary Ellis Gibson agrees with much of Longenbach's argument regarding the kind of "affective encounter with history" that existential historicism evokes, but she notes that such a stance toward history lends itself to irony or skepticism with regard to our ability to know the past—such "affective encounters" may afford aesthetic pleasure, yet at their best they leave both writer and reader "rapt before the spectacle of the past as he has formed it,"[11] but uncertain of the epistemological status of that imaginative reconstruction.

This approach to the past is typical of Pound's "personae" poems such as "Cino" or "Sestina: Altaforte," dramatic monologues after the manner of Browning in which the poet takes on the persona of an historical figure. In the epigraph to "Sestina: Altaforte" (1909), which takes as its subject the Provençal warrior/poet Bertrans de Born (1140–1209), Pound challenges his reader: "Judge ye! Have I dug him up again?"[12] But the reader's judgment must be largely a matter of the aesthetic vitality of the poem, rather than a historical consideration of evidence, for few of Pound's readers, then or now, would have much knowledge of Bertrans. Pound was aware of the limits of this approach as a means of engaging history, and he dramatizes those limits in "Near Perigord" (1915), another poem which takes Bertrans as its subject; more accurately, the poem takes as its subject the frustrating ambiguity and opacity of history. The poem begins with a challenge: "You'd have men's hearts up from the dust / And tell their secrets . . . / . . . Then read between the lines of Uc St. Circ, / Solve me the riddle, for you know the tale."[13] St. Circ is a Provençal poet who, Pound assumes, is the author of a commentary on Bertrans' canzon "The Borrowed Lady" (which Pound imitates in his poem "Na Audiart"); the canzon recounts Bertrans' rejection by an unnamed woman who is even more beautiful than the imaginary "lady" that he constructs from various body parts—eyes, throat, stature—"borrowed" from the ladies of the castles that surround his. St. Circ claims that the lady who rejected Bertrans is Maent of Montaignac, and Pound's speaker suggests that the canzon may in fact be a veiled attempt at stoking jealousy and rivalry among the "borrowed" ladies and their husbands, who are Bertrans' political rivals. Bertrans' castle Altafort is the "Hub of the wheel" formed by the castles of these rivals, and Bertrans is well known as the "stirrer-up of strife" between Prince Henry and both his brother Richard the Lionhearted and his father, Henry II. For severing brother from brother, Dante sets Bertrans in Hell as a "headless trunk 'that made its head a lamp.'" As Pound's speaker puts it, "What could he do but play the desperate chess, / And stir old grudges?"[14]

Longenbach argues that the question that opens the poem is a false one because Pound knows that attempting to answer it is pointless: the commentary itself is dubious, Maent may be a fiction, and we have no way of knowing the answer. But the question is not "false" simply because it is unanswerable in any final sense. Many of the most intriguing questions of history cannot be answered in any final sense, but we continue to consider the available evidence and pose potential answers. For example, Bertrans was captured by Richard after the death of Prince Henry and brought before Henry II to face a treason charge (Henry II was Bertrans' king), but he is supposed to have expressed such overwhelming grief at the death of the prince that the old king pardoned him. Pound's speaker notes that that "great scene" may be apocryphal ("maybe, never happened!"[15]), but that doesn't make the question of that scene's accuracy a "false" one. Pound's speaker continues with his challenge: "Take the whole man, and ravel out the story," which is what historians attempt to do. Consider the possibilities: "And Maent failed him? Or saw through the scheme?" Given Bertrans' exposed position, both geographically and politically, "how could he do without her?" Isn't it quite likely that "He wrote the catch to pit their jealousies / Against her"? Pound's speaker cites other examples of men who "sing one thing when [their] song means another," but the question persists: "Is it a love poem? Did he sing of war?"[16]

At the opening of Part II, Pound's speaker announces, "End fact. Try fiction,"[17] and imagines Bertrans sending his jongleur to sing the canzon at the neighboring castles, at one of which Arrimon Luc D'Esparo "guesses" at the song's political intent and informs Richard, thus provoking the 1183 attack mentioned above, in which Richard captures Bertrans and delivers him to Henry II. But other narratives are equally plausible: "Or no one sees it, and En Bertrans prospered?"[18] Or another: a conversation between Richard and the poet Arnaut Daniel in which they try to answer the question of the canzon's intention. "You knew the man," says one; "*You* knew the man," replies the other. Yet neither can solve the riddle. Part II ends with images of what we know, or don't know—

Richard's death in 1199, "a quarrel-bolt shot through his vizard"; Arnaut's death in a monastery (but "that's apocryphal!"); Dante's description of Bertrans in Hell, holding his head by the hair as if it were a lantern—and then offers one more possibility: "Or take En Bertrans?" Pound will "take En Bertrans" in Part III, i.e., he reverts to his old "personae" strategy, and imagines Bertrans himself recounting his love affair with Maent and their subsequent estrangement. The poem ends with Bertrans imagining Maent in her castle, a regretful woman "who could never live save through one person" (presumably Bertrans), describing her in the poem's final line as "A broken bundle of mirrors . . . !"[19]

Longenbach claims that this poem enacts a redefinition of historical knowledge rather than the impossibility of such knowledge. Disregarding "quibbles about the truth of the facts," Pound "employs what information he has for an imaginative reconstruction of the past" and shows his readers "that real knowledge *is* aesthetic satisfaction," and "that the only way we know anything about the past is through imaginative reconstruction."[20] But italicizing the "*is*" is not particularly persuasive, for it is plainly true that an aesthetically satisfying text may be historically false. "The image from Dante is Pound's one certainty,"[21] insists Longenbach, but if that is true, then the knowledge that the poem affords is literary or spiritual, not historical.

Apparently agreeing with Longenbach, A. David Moody reads the poem as "a thoroughly Browningesque study in ways of doing history, and one designed to show how the dramatic monologue [Part III] outdoes both 'fact' and 'fiction' [Parts I and II] . . . But then hadn't he already done what he could with that form and method in his early *personae*?"[22] Indeed he had, and far from suggesting that the difference between "fact" and "fiction" is insignificant, as Moody's scare quotes might suggest, "Near Perigord" registers Pound's recognition that the visionary or existential historicist approach to the past cannot yield the knowledge that the poet seeks. The monologue of Part III does not "outdo" the earlier parts of the poem in terms of either poetry or history; the poem's initial question remains unanswered, and the image of the "broken bundle of mirrors" applies to Bertrans and his canzon as it does to Maent: the historian/poet sees his or her own distorted reflection in the fragments of the evidence.

With the publication of "Three Cantos" (the so-called Ur-Cantos) two years later, in 1917, we find Pound turning over these same historiographical questions. The first Canto opens with Pound considering whether to take the "whole bag of tricks" or "rag-bag" structure of Browning's long narrative poem *Sordello*, on the thirteenth-century Italian troubador, as a model for his own long poem. If the "aesthetic satisfaction" of "imaginative reconstruction" had in fact been Pound's central concern, as Longenbach suggests, then it is difficult to understand his focus on *Sordello*'s anachronisms: "The rough men swarm out / In robes that are half Roman, half like the Knave of Hearts." Moreover,

> . . . half your dates are out, you mix your eras;
> For that great font Sordello sat beside—

'Tis an immortal passage, but the font?—
Is some two centuries outside the picture.

"Does it matter?" Pound asks, and at first he answers, "Not in the least.
Ghosts move about me / patched with histories." In purely aesthetic terms the
anachronisms matter "not in the least"; but are these ghosts simply projections
of the poet's imagination? Even if they are, writes Pound, what Browning imagines is nevertheless "more real than any dead Sordello." But in what does their
"reality" consist? Pound concedes that in "setting figures up and breathing life
upon them," he and Browning are merely extending "*our* life, your life, my
life," and that Browning's "trick" is a high-culture form of "the showman's
booth." The claim that the poet knows, in any significant historical sense, the
lives of the figures he purports to breathe life into is, Pound admits, a "Sweet
lie." Hugh Kenner claims that "In those elegiac cadences we read the doom of
the historical novel, that long intolerance with fragmentary knowledge, that urge
to 'imagine' and 'complete' as Scott imagined Louis XI, as Pound's friend Maurice Hewlett imagined Bertran de Born, encouraging Pound to imagine him, not
long before he published this Ur-Canto. . . . So Browning 'imagined' Sordello
and Fra Lippo Lippi."[23] Kenner is right. Pound is rejecting the historical novel's
intolerance with fragmentary knowledge, as well as the *personae* approach to
history that he learned from Browning, the "existential historicist" impulse to
"imagine" and "complete" figures like Bertrans and his canzon. If we look
ahead to Canto 13's praise for Confucius's emphasis on honesty and his lament
for the passing of "A day when the historians left blanks in their writings, / I
mean for things they didn't know," we might expect to see Pound growing more
rigorously empirical in his approach to the past. As *The Cantos* unfold, however,
instead of cultivating a tolerance for fragmentary knowledge, Pound moves toward what Mary Ellis Gibson describes as "a utopian, and eventually an authoritarian, alternative."[24]

As early as Cantos 8-11 we see this authoritarian strain beginning to
emerge. These Cantos take as their subject Sigismondo Malatesta, who ruled
Rimini from 1432-68 and engaged the great Renaissance architect Leon Battista
Alberti to rebuild the church of San Francesco, also known as the Tempio Mala-
testiano. The Malatesta Cantos have occasioned considerable critical disagreement as to their treatment of history. Michael Harper's 1981 essay remains one
of the most cogent defenses of Pound's Malatesta. Harper takes issue with critics like George Dekker, who finds Pound an untrustworthy historian, as well as
those like Daniel Pearlman and Christine Brooke-Rose, who defend him as a
visionary who idealizes or mythicizes historical material, and whose factual errors don't matter. Harper takes Pound seriously as a historian who "believed that
by 'reading' history correctly, by determining its true significance, one could
derive valid general laws that could be put into action to bring order and justice
to society."[25] Harper is right, but Pound's over-confidence in the accuracy of his
reading will lead him into tragic error.

Briefly, the controversy over these Cantos lies in Pound's defense of Mala-testa against the standard historical depiction of him as a murderer, rapist, and traitor who, in his free time, financed the reconstruction of the remarkable Tempio. Burckhardt, for example, describes Malatesta in that way. But Harper shows that the "ultimate source" for these claims about Malatesta is his enemy, Pope Pius II, and argues that we ought to be skeptical of Pius's claims. We cannot know whether Pius's claims were accurate, but Pound quotes from letters from both Pius and Malatesta, and Harper suggests that he intends his reader to take the rhetoric of each man as an index of his character, and that Malatesta emerges clearly on top. As his final piece of evidence, Harper cites an Oxford doctoral thesis of 1954 that concludes that Pius's claims about Malatesta are unreliable. For Harper, Pound is a careful scholar who finds in Malatesta an example of "patron and protégé cooperat[ing] in mutual respect,"[26] an ideal relationship that produces the Tempio, but a type of relationship that becomes increasingly difficult and rare as usury rots the fabric of European social relations.

Peter Makin is typical of those who find these Cantos important because they signal the beginning of the "documentrary method" that will become so common in later Cantos: many of the poems' lines are taken verbatim, or nearly verbatim, from other documents, and the poet sometimes cites his sources. Yet Makin also notes that

> Pound was quite content with romances, college anthologies of documents, and a variety of sources that did not have the historian's sense of 'fact', if he felt they told the truth (a matter more of wholes than of details). And while playing fast and loose with fact in this way, he erected certain fictions. . . . One was the fiction of a greater scholarliness than it really possessed.[27]

Makin cites Pound's challenge to "the critic of his historiography to find any error in his Malatesta Cantos," and admits that "the critic, my experience suggests, could find a great many," but he dismisses those who harp on Pound's errors as fussy pedants who cannot see the forest for the trees. For Makin, Pound's depiction of Malatesta, despite its minor errors of fact, shows a firm grasp of the "total situation."[28]

Longenbach is less sympathetic toward these Cantos because he finds in them the beginning of a turning away from the "existential historicism" that Pound had been practicing in his earlier work, in which the poet's role as vision-ary had been central. In the Malatesta Cantos, for Longenbach, Pound takes on the role of the "historical positivist . . . rather than the inspired historian, breath-ing his life into the past."[29] If Harper is right about Pound's desire to "read" his-tory correctly, then we can understand his turning away from "existential histor-icism" as the surest path to historical truth. But Longenbach dismisses the cut-and-paste, documentary method that Pound begins to use in the Malatesta Can-tos and brings to its fullest development in the Adams Cantos as a "neopositivist method of concatenation of facts."[30] Moreover, "[t]he 'facts' that Pound presents

. . . are preconditioned by Pound's personal notions about the man and his age,"[31] i.e., Pound selects his facts to fit his preconceived idea of what he wants to find. Pound comes close to admitting as much in a letter to John Quinn: "I suppose one has to 'select.' If I find he was TOO bloody quiet and orderly it will ruin the canto. Which needs a certain boisterousness and disorder to contrast with his constructive work."[32]

Longenbach's skepticism of Pound's documentary method may be valid, but it does not follow that the visionary approach of existential historicism offers a clearer path to historical truth. Moreover, the Malatesta Cantos are less concerned with any putatively positivist truth about Malatesta than with making the point that an ideal patron/artist relationship once existed, but is no longer possible in a society like ours. And what else did Pound's reading of the history of Sigismondo teach him? Antonio Beltramelli, whose *Un tempio d'amore* is an important study of the Tempio that Pound had read, described Malatesta as a great man who imagined new forms of cultural life. Beltramelli was also the author of *L'uomo nuovo*, the first biography of Mussolini, in which he cited Sigismondo as a forerunner of "the new man" who would finally be embodied by Mussolini.[33]

Having rejected existential historicism, how did Pound attempt to tell the truth about history? Just as he was certain that the dominant philological approach to the poetry of the Romance languages was utterly wrongheaded, Pound had little use for academic historians. When he returned to Italy in 1958, he called American universities "places where U.S. history and economics are not taught, where imbecilities abound, and the works of John Adams, Van Buren, Alex Del Mar [a late nineteenth-century economist], and Brooks Adams are not included in the curricula" and claimed that "the payola of 'endowments' is given freely to the concealers of truth" at those institutions.[34] For decades, he had been claiming, as he does in *Guide to Kulchur*,

> that whole beams and ropes of real history have been shelved, overclouded and buried. As in more recent times the thought of Van Buren, A. Johnson, A. Jackson and the story of Tuscany under Pietro Leopoldo, have been buried. We know that history as it was written the day before yesterday is unwittingly partial; full of fatal lacunae; and that it tells us next to nothing of causes. We know that these causes were economic and moral.[35]

He devoted the "Nuevo Mundo" Cantos (31–41) to recovering the thought of Van Buren and Jackson, and the Leopoldine Cantos (42–51) to telling the story of Tuscany under Pietro, all the while insisting that most historians are in the pockets of the concealers of truth, those powerful financial interests whom he identifies as the "usorocracy" that controls the governments and financial institutions of the West: "The one history we have NOT on the news-stands is the history of Usura. . . . All this is still blank in our histories."[36]

A major part of Pound's historiography in the *Cantos* and in his prose from the late 1920s onward consists in lifting the historical "blackout" and telling the plain truth about the causes of war and economic injustice, but he never wrote plain cause-and-effect narrative because the notion that history unfolds in linear fashion is simply false. In *The Spirit of Romance*, he announced, "All ages are contemporaneous,"[37] an assertion that authorized the existential historicism of his *personae* poems, but also served as foundation for the world-historical project of the *Cantos*. "We do NOT know the past in chronological sequence," Pound instructed his readers. "It may be convenient to lay it out anesthetized on the table with dates pasted on here and there, but what we know we know by ripples and spirals eddying out from us and from our own time."[38]

But how is one to read those ripples and spirals, or to identify them in the first place? And who is authorized to do so? Pound was convinced of his own intellectual superiority: as an undergraduate he quarreled with the curriculum and the pedagogy at the University of Pennsylvania, and in 1913, he told the assistant editor of the journal *Poetry* that "From his twelve-year 'study of the laws of the art' . . . he knew 'more about poetry of every time and place than any man living.'"[39] On the frontispiece to his *Gaudier/Brzeska* he quoted Machiavelli—"There are few real men and the rest are just sheep"—clearly implying that he and Gaudier-Brzeska were among the former. In 1920, he told William Carlos Williams, "there is no longer any intellectual *life* in England save what centers in this eight by ten pentagonal room [i.e., Pound's apartment]."[40] Pound's intellectual confidence extended far beyond literature; he believed he understood the past better than the historians did, and his goal was to teach his readers how to understand it as accurately as he did. Kenner writes that Pound "assumed . . . the role . . . of amanuensis for the mind of Europe,"[41] an interesting image because it sets Pound in the humble role of a secretary taking dictation or making copies, while at the same time it implies that he has a privileged, and perhaps unique, access to "the mind of Europe."

A more common image for Pound's approach to history is that of the prosecuting attorney. Makin, for example, writes that Canto 66 "has the rhetorical form of a prosecutor's address: it gives the damage inflicted by the economic crime . . . the steps by which the investigator was led to track the crime down, and the documentation as to the time and the place where it was perpetrated."[42] Maud Ellmann suggests that "Pound uses history tendentiously, and the facts that he amasses in *The Cantos* constitute a kind of legal dossier against usury."[43] And Jeffrey Walker claims that, especially in the cantos of the late 1930s, Pound speaks "as a prosecuting attorney, presenting 'evidence' and marshaling his spectral, textual voices as witnesses," but because he knows in advance that his client is guilty, he "has chosen his evidence because it fits what he wants to prove."[44]

In the American justice system, a prosecuting attorney is not so much interested in determining the truth of the case as in attaining a guilty verdict, and the image suggests the deductive cast of Pound's approach to history. Alfred Kazin employs a different metaphor, suggesting that Pound claimed for himself "at-

tributes of the shaman, the medium through which we touch a great mystery,"
and that Pound saw "[h]istory as an excavation made possible only to those who
know . . . where the old wisdom is hidden."[45] Kenner's amanuensis becomes
Kazin's hierophant, the privileged seer who can interpret the baffling hiero-
glyphs of history, detecting in a relative handful of isolated facts the pattern that
remains obscure to lesser, prose historians. Where the early Pound is absolutely
confident in his aesthetic judgments, which form the basis of the existential historicism of his *personae* poems, the later Pound is equally certain of his grasp of
the central truths of history, and that certainty leads to a didactic, ideological
ferocity and to a moral absolutism that dogmatically endorses fascism and anti-
Semitism and closes off all alternative interpretations.

The certainty that we expect from an amanuensis, a prosecutor or a shaman
is evident in Pound's praise of Confucius's commitment to calling things by
their proper names, and his praise of the "high verbal culture" of medieval scho-
lastic thinkers who "cared for (that is took care of) their terminology."[46] We
might find this emphasis on precise diction reminiscent of Orwell's "Politics and
the English Language," but Pound is not just attacking the ambiguity of sloppy
or duplicitous thinking; he is arguing that words exist in a one-to-one correspondence with things. He is that *rara avis*, a poet who is skeptical of polysemy,
and skeptical of the possibility that language, or a historical event, might be susceptible of more than one good interpretation. On this point, as on others, he can
be extreme: "Italy went to rot, destroyed by rhetoric, destroyed by the periodic
sentence and by the flowing paragraph. . . . For when words cease to cling close
to things, kingdoms fall, empires wane and diminish."[47]

The shaman's vision, like the inspired poet's, is different from most people's, and when he looks at history he sees what they cannot. In "I gather the
Limbs of Osiris," Pound sets out his "method of Luminous Detail"[48]:

> Any fact may be "symptomatic", but certain facts give one a sudden insight in-
> to circumjacent conditions, into their causes, their effects, into sequence, and
> law. . . . A few dozen facts of this nature give us intelligence of a period—a
> kind of intelligence not to be gathered from a great array of facts of the other
> sort [the method of multitudinous detail]. . . . The artist seeks out the luminous
> detail and presents it. He does not comment. . . . Each historian will "have ide-
> as"—presumably different from other historians—imperfect inductions, vary-
> ing as the fashions, but the luminous details remain unaltered.[49]

The visionary poet/historian simply presents and does not comment because for
Pound there is only one true way to read the patterns formed by these luminous
details, patterns that Kenner describes as "the coming and going of vortices in
time's river," vortices that form and dissipate, metamorphose and repeat over
the course of history.[50] Kenner calls these recurrent patterns "subject-rhymes,"
and as an example cites the "rhyme" that Pound detects between the "New
Birth[s]" of Renaissance Italy in 1500 and British North America in 1770: "Spe-

cifically, Jefferson and his successors building a nation are rhymed with Malatesta building the Tempio, and a careful structural parallel enforces this
rhyme."[51] Whereas a traditional linear model of history may suggest evolution
or progress (or decline), a vorticist or spiral-shaped history in which subjects
"rhyme" suggests repetition of the same achievements or errors. When Pound
rhymes or juxtaposes particular events or individuals, he wants his reader to
draw the analogy and infer the lesson or moral at work in each. Pound extends
the rhyme that Kenner mentions with the publication of *Jefferson and/or Mussolini* in 1935, and repeats it in 1942: "I insist on the identity of our American
Revolution of 1776 with your Fascist Revolution. Two chapters in the same war
against the usurers."[52] Michael Bernstein points out that this is a static view of
history, devoid of historical process, that "reduce[s] history to a series of vivid
friezes, full of activity within each panel, but immobile in their interrelation-
ship."[53]

Kenner seems to agree, but does not find Pound's approach troubling; for
him, the profusion of historical detail in *The Cantos* reflects Pound's search for
"eternal, archetypal situations" that point toward a "paradigm, beyond time,"
and that this timeless paradigm, once discerned, will afford "absolute moral
judgment" and "clear simple principles in a time of confusion."[54] One may wonder. Mutlu Blasing has noted the similarity between Pound's historiography and
Puritan typology: each posits a suprahistorical design (Kenner's paradigm), a
pattern of historical "repeats" (Kenner's archetypes), and moments of visionary
access to a divine world that gives history its providential order and macrocos-
mic significance. For both the Puritans and Pound, Blasing concludes, this typology "confirms a totalitarian, closed system of meaning that enfolds historical
development."[55] Like an amanuensis who takes dictation from the "mind of Europe," or the shaman who simply reports his divine vision, Pound presents a
vision, or version, of history that is not open to doubt or argument. As Michael
Heller puts it, "Pound has made up his mind about history, and his vigilance
enables him to grasp reinforcing and ramifying 'likenesses' as he goes. There is
no history, as we usually know history, in *The Cantos*."[56]

Pound, of course, would insist that what "we usually know" as history is
simply wrong. So what does Pound's vision of history look like? In *Guide to
Kulchur*, he outlines something like a conspiracy theory of history:

> Shallow minds have been in a measure right in their lust for "secret history".
> I mean they have been dead right to want it, but shallow in their conception
> of what it was. Secret history is at least twofold. One part consists in the se-
> cret corruptions, the personal lusts, avarices etc. that scoundrels keep hidden,
> another part is the "plus", the constructive urges, a *secretum* because it pass-
> es unnoticed or because no human effort can force it on public attention.[57]

The "secret history" tells the true story, and the true story will explain the vortices formed by luminous details, i.e., it will reveal the hidden shape of history.

For Pound that shape is the result of "two forces in history: one that divides, shatters, and kills, and one that contemplates the unity of the mystery."[58] The former of these two forces is the "one enemy, ever-busy obscuring our terms; ever muddling and muddying terminology, ever trotting out minor issues to obscure the main and the basic, ever prattling of short range causation for the sake of, or with the result of, obscuring the vital truth."[59] As Alec Marsh puts it, "from about the mid-1930s till the end of his life [Pound] fought a losing battle against an increasingly powerful belief in the satanic powers of darkness . . . These are most often Jews."[60] The Jews are Pound's metonym for the forces of usury, a compound of malice, insatiable greed, and coarse materialism that drives those in control of international finance, the small group that instigates and profits from wars and all other forms of debt. Theirs are the "interests" that incite and prolong the First World War in Canto 16, and are responsible for "one war after another" in Canto 18. The latter of the two forces is the source of all natural order, beauty, and justice. Over the course of *The Cantos*, Pound will depict archetypal manifestations of that force in people and events as various as Confucius (whom he calls "Kung") and the ancient Greek mystery religion centered at Eleusis (he stakes his ground "Between KUNG and ELEUSIS" in Canto 52[61]), and including quattrocento Italy and the America of Jefferson and Adams. Confucius, Jefferson, and Adams represent his ideals of ethics, justice and social order, while Eleusis and the quattrocento embrace the aesthetic, the erotic, and the spiritual values he finds developed most fully in Dante's *Commedia* and troubadour poetry.

Pound's vorticist history maps the interplay of these two forces as, in various places, first one and then the other is dominant. The usorocracy has given us the useless history peddled in the schools and universities, but the secret history reveals a "conspiracy of intelligence" evident in particular luminous details: "Avicenna, Scotus Erigena in Provence, Grosseteste in Lincoln, the Sorbonne, fat-faced Frankie Petrarch, Gemisto, the splendour of the XVth century, Valla, the over-boomed Pico. . . . The real history went on."[62] In "The Jefferson-Adams Letters as a Shrine and a Monument" Pound describes a "Mediterranean paideuma" or "state of mind" that animates Constantine, Justinian, Charlemagne, St. Ambrose, Duns Scotus, and Dante. This paideuma "developed a system of graduations, an hierarchy of values among which was, perhaps above all other, 'order'. . . . Things neither perfect nor utterly wrong, but arranged in a cosmos, an order, stratified, having relations with one another." However, shortly after the time of the Renaissance this "state of mind" was overwhelmed by "the onslaught of brute disorder of taboo," a competing "state of mind" that Pound links to Semitism and Puritanism, in which "[c]ertain things were 'forbidden'. . . . All sense of fine assay seemed to decline in Europe. A whole table of values was lost, but it wasn't just dropped overboard."[63] The Mediterranean paideuma, pushed to the margins of European civilization, survives in the "conspiracy of intelligence" that persists into the present.

The Cantos in their entirety may be read as an exposition of the persistence of that mythic Eleusinian force and the "conspiracy of intelligence" that recognized and embraced it throughout history, along with that force's periodic dispersal by the agents of usury that have come to dominate the modern world. Imagining history in this way leads Pound to depict it as a catalogue of *exempla*; individuals or events represent either virtue or vice, justice or injustice, eros or sterility, and historical significance consists in the extent to which events manifest one force or the other.

Such an historical imagination has no time for ambiguity or nuance, no patience for complexity (apart from the simple complexity of a "secret history"). Kenner writes that Pound believed it would be "a simple matter" to recover historical knowledge of the order the world once knew,[64] and the word "simple" is apt. In one of his Rome radio broadcasts, Pound says, "Well, that looks simple to me. Things often do look simple to me. . . . The pattern often is simple. . . . My politics seem to me simple,"[65] and the word is also embedded in Wyndham Lewis's description of Pound as "a revolutionary simpleton."[66] Pound found a simple but for him thoroughly persuasive armature for his "two forces" notion of history in the work of Major C. H. Douglas, the promoter of an economic policy he called "social credit," whom Pound met in 1919. Pound saw social credit as the simple key to economic justice. From Douglas, Pound learned that the root problem facing the West's economies was not production—more than enough goods and services could be produced—but rather a fair distribution of those goods and services. The unjust distribution of wealth was the result of the private control of credit by chartered banks, which manipulated the availability of credit to serve their own interests. This problem could be solved by the state reclaiming its right to issue money and establish its value, and by putting purchasing power, i.e., "social credit" or access to money, in the hands of consumers. In other words, Douglas was an underconsumptionist who traced the West's economic woes to an inadequate money supply and an overproduction of goods, which led to cycles of booms and busts. For Pound, Douglas's diagnosis of the problem was so persuasive that he believed that governments that did not embrace Douglas's ideas had to be in the grip of the international usorocracy, the only group that truly benefited from the current system. This included all of the West's liberal democracies, which Pound dismissed as tools of international finance. "USURY," he wrote, "is the cancer of the world which only the surgeon's knife of Fascism can cut out of the life of nations."[67]

Douglas may have been correct on certain points—many complaints can be leveled against the excesses of finance capitalism—but economics is a dismal science, and the relationship between theory and practice, or more precisely the ability of theory to predict what will happen in practice, is not as strong as we might wish. Pound sounds reasonable when he asserts, "History that omits economics will not eternally be accepted as anything but a farce or a fake."[68] But major American historians like Charles Beard and Frederick Jackson Turner were certainly including economics in their historiography; what Pound really meant was that history that omitted the "social credit" version of economics was a farce, and he simply could not grasp why well-informed, intelligent people might be skeptical of Douglas's ideas. Leon Surette writes that Pound "came to believe that the 'good ideas' of Social Credit were blocked by a conspiracy of Jewish bankers who controlled world events. Such a conspiracy theory is not historicism, but paranoia."[69] Usury would come to explain almost everything for Pound, from the political ("The order of the Roman empire, the possibility of organising such an empire is indissolubly bound up with reduction of usury rates"[70]) to the aesthetic: "finer and future critics of art will be able to tell from the quality of a painting the degree of tolerance or intolerance of usury extant in the age and milieu that produced it."[71]

His emphasis on usury leads Pound to posit a three-part model of history: a noble past free from excessive usury, evident in Renaissance Italy, Confucian China, and the America of John Adams; a present and recent past corrupted by usury; and a utopian future that will root out usury (that future has begun with Mussolini's fascism). Here he applies the model to American history:

> 1. American civilisation, 1760 to 1830 [the period of Adams and Jefferson].
> 2. The period of thinning, of mental impoverishment . . . 1830 to 1860 [when Jackson and Van Buren fight the establishment of a national bank].
> 3. The period of despair, civil war as hiatus, 1870 to 1930 [the period of the usorocracy's emergence and dominance] . . .
> 4. The possibilities of revival, starting perhaps with a valorisation of our cultural heritage . . . should we lose or go on losing our own revolution (of 1776–1830) by whoring after exotics, Muscovite or European?[72]

A similar three-part model characterizes anti-Semitic millenarian accounts of history from the Middle Ages to the Third Reich,[73] probably because of the ease with which it can be made to fit ideological agendas. The danger of all such models is their tendency to oversimplify. Reed Dasenbrock has argued that Homer's ethical complexity yields to simpler ideological visions in the epics of Vergil, Spenser, and Tasso, who are "apologists of conquest" and depict the "other" with contempt. Similarly, in *Homage to Sextus Propertius* Pound criticizes Vergil, and in "Hugh Selwyn Mauberley" he satirizes the unthinking patriotism of "dulce et decorum est," but as *The Cantos* unfold and Pound's thinking grows less ethically complex and increasingly ideological, we get the two Italian Cantos, 72 and 73, which Dasenbrock calls "appalling, morally, politically, and aesthetically." These Cantos were written in 1944, after Mussolini's government had been forced from Rome and briefly reorganized in the north. In Canto 72, the Futurist F. T. Marinetti, a committed fascist who had just died, encourages Pound to continue fighting, and in 73 Pound repeats a crude, fabricated propaganda story in which an Italian girl, who has been raped by Allied troops who have taken Rimini and damaged Malatesta's Tempio, leads Canadian soldiers into a minefield in order to avenge the death of her brother. "Gloria!" writes Pound, "gloria / Morir per la patria," totally reversing, as Dasenbrock points out, his satirizing of that sentiment in "Mauberley."[74]

The rigidity of Pound's thinking about history is also evident in the middle Cantos (31–71), where American, Sienese, and Chinese history form his central topics. In Cantos 31–41 (1934), Pound depicts Thomas Jefferson, John Adams, John Quincy Adams, and Martin Van Buren as avatars of the "conspiracy of intelligence" in the tradition of Confucius and Malatesta, leaders who combine civic virtue with resolute action and forge the beginnings of a new nation. They are interested in and knowledgeable of art, literature, philosophy, foreign languages, public works projects, economics, and contemporary politics, and their opponents are their opposites not only in their lack of learning and curiosity, but especially in the narrow self-interest of their politics. Cantos 31–33 are composed largely of excerpts from the letters of Jefferson and Adams. Often so brief that it is difficult for the reader to grasp what is being said, these "luminous details" are meant to provide objective evidence for Pound's reading of American history, in which Jefferson and Adams "rhyme" with Malatesta (whose family motto is quoted at the opening of Canto 31) and Mussolini, whose nation-building rounds out Canto 41. Pound quotes from Jefferson and Adams in ways that make their view of economics sound similar to Douglas's Social Credit, and in Canto 37, he presents Andrew Jackson and Martin Van Buren's successful struggle against the Second Bank of the United States as another "rhyme" with Douglas's economics. Jefferson's agrarian republicanism, however, is displaced by Hamilton's federalism, and after 1830, in Pound's reading, the nation's promising beginnings are betrayed by the same usurocratic interests responsible for the Federal Reserve banking system.

Pound turns to this documentary method in an attempt to establish the objectivity of his claims and to send his readers to his sources, and indeed, the literary and intellectual quality of the Jefferson–Adams correspondence is every bit as good as he says it is. Readers have, however, noted a number of errors in transcription or in the identification of a particular letter's author. As with the Malatesta Cantos, Pound's defenders claim that these Cantos are historically valid "not necessarily in verifiable truth or in accuracy of detail, but in a large-scale pattern of truth."[75] Other readers, however, have suggested that the large-scale pattern also fails the test of truth. Alec Marsh, for example, looks closely at Cantos 34 and 37, which focus on John Quincy Adams, Martin Van Buren, and the Bank War, and concludes that these Cantos "are in part based on disinformation, both on inauthentic, or counterfeit documents that reflect parapolitical interventions into history that Pound has mistaken for genuine historical evidence, and much more troubling, Pound's own willful misreadings of sources to score political points."[76] Marsh argues that Pound's selective quotations misrepresent J. Q. Adams's judgment of Van Buren, whom he saw "as a slick political operator and a sycophantic toady to Jackson,"[77] and ignore Adams's favorable opinion of the Bank of the United States. In Pound's rigid view of history, however, individuals are either on the side of virtue or the side of vice, and because he places Adams and Van Buren on the side of virtue, he represses their many points of difference (including Adams's successful argument before the Supreme Court on behalf of the slaves who seized the *Amistad*; the opposing side was the U. S. government and its President, Martin Van Buren).

Marsh's point could be extended to Pound's conflation of the ideas of Jefferson and John Adams, who despite their mutual respect during their retirements were bitter enemies during their political careers. In Pound's account of history they speak with one voice, but within a decade of the drafting of the Constitution, the drafters had split into two parties: the Federalists led by Hamilton and Adams, and the Republicans led by Jefferson and Madison. Each acccused the other of betraying the Revolution, and the vitriol grew so intense that Adams and the Federalists passed an Alien and Sedition Act aimed at halting criticism of Adams and the war measures associated with his party. Of the twenty-five Republicans arrested under this act, ten stood trial. Like Pound in his Rome radio broadcasts, they had denounced the president as a blockhead and a tyrant, and accused him of preparing for an unnecessary war. Jefferson and Madison persuaded the governments of Virginia and Kentucky to pass resolutions affirming state sovereignty and declaring the Sedition Act unconstitutional, none of which readers of these Cantos would guess.

Pound's most intense and least effective use of the "documentary method" occurs in the Chinese history Cantos (52–61), condensed almost entirely from de Mailla's *Histoire générale de la Chine* (1777–83), and the Adams Cantos (62–71), taken almost entirely from *The Works of John Adams*, both of which were published in 1940. Without some sort of critical gloss, these Cantos are almost unreadable, and even with such a gloss, they aren't much better. The Chinese history Cantos depict good rulers who establish order, tax fairly, and cultivate the arts, and bad rulers who do none of these things. These *exempla* underscore Pound's belief that the character and strength of a great leader can establish a good society, and the Adams Cantos further illustrate that belief by presenting Adams as a leader manifesting Confucian values. Makin suggests that the juxtaposed, fragmented quotations and lack of narrative structure in the Adams Cantos, where Pound brings his cut-and-paste approach to its zenith, were meant "to free the material into intensity and resonance."[78] For many readers the result, however, does not match the intention, and Kazin exaggerates only slightly when he writes that "John Adams becomes absolutely meaningless in the so-called Adams Cantos."[79]

Another cluster of luminous details appears in Cantos 42–44, which focus on Siena under the Medician Grand Dukes, and more specifically on the Monte dei Paschi bank, which Pound presents as a model of economic justice. Unlike most banks, which profit by restricting credit and by the difference between their borrowing and lending rates, the Monte guaranteed its depositors' money by backing it with state-held pasture lands, and in *avant-la-lettre* Social-Credit style, distributed communal dividends based on what Pound calls the "abundance of nature," i.e., the state's stake in the agricultural economy. For Pound the historical detail of this Sienese bank illuminates the meaning of history:

> Without history one is lost in the dark, and the essential data of modern history
> cannot enlighten us unless they are traced back at least to the foundation of the
> Sienese bank, the Monte dei Paschi; in other words, to the perception of the
> true basis of credit, viz., "the abundance of nature and the responsibility of the
> whole people."[80]

In his imagination, Pound sets the Monte alongside the founding of the
Bank of England in 1694, which Pound interprets as a small group of very
wealthy men manipulating the nation's credit and money supply for their own
profit. The Bank of England, then, provides the template for finance capitalism
that the international usorocracy has employed ever since, and Pound rhymes the
founding of the Bank of England with the American Bank Wars pitting Andrew
Jackson and Martin Van Buren against the Bank's corrupt supporters, most no-
tably Nicholas Biddle, Henry Clay, and Daniel Webster. For Pound, Jackson is
entirely right: the Bank is dangerous because Congress grants a special privilege
to a tiny elite who can then corrupt the government by giving favors to con-
gressmen in exchange for special legislation; in short, it concentrates too much
undemocratic power in one place. Jackson succeeded in destroying the Second
Bank of the United States in 1832, but it could be argued that the Bank, far from
enriching a conspiratorial cabal, as Pound believed, in fact contributed significantly to the economic health of the nation by stabilizing the currency and curb-
ing bad banking practices such as the excessive issuing of notes by state banks.
   Pound returns to the Bank question in Cantos 88–89, in which he recounts
Senator Thomas Hart Benton's campaign against the renewal of the Bank's
charter in a somewhat clearer, more accessible narrative than he had used in the
Adams Cantos.[81] Again, however, everything boils down to evil, greedy capital-
ists oppressing farmers and tradesmen who need credit. And again, many of
Pound's criticisms of the injustice of the West's economic system are fair. How-
ever, he is hardly the first to have made them. Alec Marsh correctly places
Pound squarely in the "populist conflict theory of history, which stresses the
decisive effect of the class struggle between debtors and creditors,"[82] and points
out that Pound's endorsement of the economic determinism of Brooks Adams's
Law of Civilization and Decay also complements that populist theory. Adams's
"law" announced the inevitable failure of capitalism, and he and his brother
Henry shared in the anti-Semitism that ascribed Jewish control to international
finance and supported William Jennings Bryan's populist free silver campaign.
American populism was fertile soil for conspiracy theories in which cabals of
creditors corner markets in precious metals, seize control of credit, and foment
wars and poverty, and anti-Semitism was often an element of those conspira-
cies.[83] But Pound went further than the Adams brothers in the ferocity of his
commitment to his vision of history. Kazin suggests that we find in Pound "the
sense of history as a problem inviting a solution,"[84] which is exactly right—and

Pound is sure that he knows what the solution is.

Let me return briefly to the Sienese Cantos, 42–44. Teresa Winterhalter describes them as "riddled with errors," but like many of Pound's defenders, she argues that "factual representation is not the controlling logic in these pieces." Appealing to the "ripples and spirals" of Pound's vorticist historiography, she suggests that these Cantos "connect the Medician Dukes to Jefferson" and "the formation and continuation of the Monte with the thinking that backed the revolution for American independence," and that they demonstrate the crucial importance of "the governance of a visionary ruler" like the reform-minded eighteenth-century Duke Leopold of Tuscany.[85] In Pound's mind, the Duke rhymes equally well with Jefferson or Mussolini, as Hugh Kenner reminds us: "To know clear simple principles in a time of confusion, this is a great resource; to know that statecraft has principles not beyond grasping, that action can be taken and men (Mussolini) found capable of taking it, that history affords paradigm after paradigm."[86] To know such things might well afford the solution to the problem of history, but *how* does one know such things? We are back to Pound as prosecuting attorney or shaman, amanuensis to the mind of Europe—these are roles that a poet may play well, but when the poet enters the arena of contemporary politics, such roles become very dangerous.

Kenner is Pound's most articulate defender on this point. He writes,

> If we believe that good things have been and will return we can manage to live with bad things. If we believe that the human will is efficacious, we shall want to expedite the bad things' passing away. And the ground for such beliefs was what poets sought in history, writing 'poems including history,' attentive to that ecology of events in which any detail may be symptomatic of everything else that is happening, and avid to characterize truly massive happenings. . . . A poem *about* history, taking note of recurrences, could go on endlessly, like wallpaper. . . . A poem *including* history will contain not only elements and recurrences but a perceiving and uniting mind that can hope one day for a transfiguring vision of order it only glimpses now, and that in carrying simple themes to a massive simultaneous orchestration will achieve the poem's end in discovering its own richest powers.[87]

This is beautifully put, but where does it lead Pound? The visionary poet seeks out the visionary leader: for Pound, history is made by individuals, by "great men," not by the impersonal, implacable forces (economic, social, or natural) that the Annalistes and others named as its driving forces. Leon Surette writes,

> *The Cantos* is not based on the assumption that historical events are caused by some immanent or transcendent power, nor that they instantiate some overarching historical pattern. On the contrary it is grounded on the assumption that history is determined by individuals, and that individual behavior is rational. Hence the way to have some impact on the course of events is to persuade individuals of the truth and disabuse them of error and falsehood. . . Alas, Pound put his 'truth' and 'good ideas' at the service of Mussolini and Hitler.[88]

And therein lies the tragedy or the scandal, depending on one's point of view, of Ezra Pound.

Pound's defenders point out that support for Mussolini in the West, especially in the 1920s, was fairly common. But how do we explain Pound's continued support, even after the invasion of Ethiopia, and the Spanish Civil War, and the alliance with Hitler? How could Pound fail to see what was going on around him? Part of the answer lay in his self-imposed isolation in Rapallo, and part perhaps in mental illness, but another part is simply that hubristic overconfidence that marks so many of his literary, economic, and political judgments. In literature, that confidence helped to launch the careers of Joyce, Eliot, Frost, and others, and it played a large role in the creation of what we call Modernism, but Pound was also convinced that he knew the truth about history, politics, and economics more fully than the historians, political scientists, and economists. He knew, or thought that he knew, that fascism would restore the kind of just social and economic order that he imagined had once existed, and that could exist again. As late as July 6, 1942, he still believed: "There is so much that the United States does not know. This war is proof of such vast incomprehension."[89] But always the incomprehension lay with someone else; he never doubted himself. With apparent seriousness he claimed, "I could have avoided the war with Japan if anyone had the unlikely idea of sending me out there with any thought of official powers."[90] Such remarks would be laughable, but for a man of letters of Pound's stature, tears are the more appropriate response. As Kazin writes, *The Cantos* are "finally a work of such obscene hatred as to make one weep over the manic flaw in Pound, his overbearing illusion that through his innate tie to poetry he could instruct a disordered world."[91]

Pound seems never to have grasped the fundamental truths of fascism and Nazism, and in the post-war Cantos the only errors he ascribes to himself or to Mussolini are errors of degree, not kind. In fact, we find tremendous sympathy for Mussolini and his cause, and as Morrison writes, "The Pisan Cantos confesses to nothing, or nothing more damning than 'the diffidence that faltered.'"[92] On the other hand, on many occasions Pound remarked that his work had been a failure and that he himself had been wrong; for example, he told Allen Ginsberg in 1967 that his writing was "stupidity and ignorance all the way through" and that "the worst mistake I made was that stupid, suburban prejudice of anti-Semitism. All along, that spoiled everything."[93] Similarly, in his 1972 Foreword to *Selected Prose 1909–1965*, he wrote, "re usury: I was out of focus, taking a symptom for a cause. The cause is avarice." But if the cause is really avarice, avarice is a part of the human condition, the kind of vice that we will have with us always, and the problem of history may be mitigated, but it will never be solved. Pound's comment to Ginsberg is heartening, yet we know that he accepted as truth and recommended to others the *Protocols of the Elders of Zion*,[94] and he had nothing to say about the Final Solution.

For all of the rebarbative sophistication of his High Modernism, Pound held a very simple vision of history: strong leaders like Adams or Mussolini, men who embody the Confucian virtues, can create civilizations in which the vices to which we are prone are kept suppressed. This is the populist history of good guys and bad guys, with interest rates and control of credit as its key pieces of evidence. We can understand why Gertrude Stein in *The Autobiography of Alice B. Toklas* called Pound "a village explainer." In *The Sense of an Ending*, Frank Kermode describes historiography, as well as fiction, as "a maker of concords" and "a provider of significance to mere chronicity." We turn to history and to fiction because we want concord or consonance, and our experience of the real world seems so often dissonant or discordant. Effective history or fiction, however, must exhibit a compliance with reality; if it is "too fully explanatory, too consoling,"[95] it induces skepticism and dismissal. Pound identifies the sources of virtue and vice in history so precisely, and offers such a clear solution to the problem of history, that skepticism must be most readers' primary response. Simple accounts of history are attractive because they offer explanations that anyone can grasp, and they often tell comfortable stories that center on what Kenner calls the efficacious will—we want to believe that the problem of history can be solved by strong-willed individuals. But simple accounts of history flounder when, as Jeffrey Walker suggests, readers begin to measure those accounts against their own knowledge and to interpret history's meaning differently: "History, after all, is an independent entity: it contains the limited bard, and it cannot be known in its totality."[96] An epic may be a poem containing history, but in a larger sense, history contains the poem, and the poem's readers' knowledge and experience of history shape the way they read it.[97]

Notes

1. James Joyce, *Ulysses* (New York: Random House, 1961), 33, 34.
2. Quoted in C. David Heymann, *Ezra Pound: The Last Rower* (New York: Seaver Books, 1976), 107, 114, 116. For the transcripts of Pound's radio broadcasts, see *"Ezra Pound Speaking": Radio Speeches of World War II*, ed. Leonard W. Doob (Westport, CT: Greenwood, 1978). Bruce Comens argues that "the Rome radio broadcasts . . . should also be seen as a continuation of the Cantos by other means." See *Apocalypse and After: Modern Strategy and Postmodern Tactics in Pound, Williams, and Zukofsky* (Tuscaloosa: University of Alabama Press, 1995), 71.
3. Archibald MacLeish, "The Venetian Grave," in *Riders on the Earth* (Boston: Houghton Mifflin, 1978), 118–19.
4. Lawrence Rainey, "A Poem Including History: *The Cantos* of Ezra Pound," *Paideuma* 21, nos. 1–2 (1992): 199.
5. Alfred Kazin, "Language as History: Ezra Pound's Search for the Authority of History," in *The Problem of Authority in America*, ed. John P. Diggins and Mark E. Kann (Philadelphia: Temple University Press, 1981), 115.
6. For a thorough discussion of Pound's politics, see Robert Casillo, *The Genealogy of Demons: Anti-Semitism, Fascism, and the Myths of Ezra Pound* (Evanston: Northwest-

ern University Press, 1988); Tim Redman, *Ezra Pound and Italian Fascism* (New York: Cambridge University Press, 1991); and Paul Morrison, *The Poetics of Fascism: Ezra Pound, T. S. Eliot, Paul de Man* (New York: Oxford University Press, 1996).

7. Allen Tate, *Essays of Four Decades* (Chicago: Swallow Press, 1968), 369.

8. Tate, *Essays*, 510.

9. Kazin, "Language as History," 120, 123.

10. Hugh Kenner, *The Pound Era* (Berkeley: University of California Press, 1971), 377.

11. Mary Ellis Gibson, *Epic Reinvented: Ezra Pound and the Victorians* (Ithaca: Cornell University Press, 1995), 6, 45.

12. Ezra Pound, *Personae: Collected Shorter Poems* (New York: New Directions, 1971), 28.

13. Pound, *Personae*, 151.

14. Pound, *Personae*, 152.

15. Pound, *Personae*, 152.

16. Pound, *Personae*, 152, 153.

17. Pound, *Personae*, 154.

18. Pound, *Personae*, 155.

19. Pound, *Personae*, 155, 156, 157.

20. James Longenbach, *Modernist Poetics*, 86, 91, 92.

21. Longenbach, *Modernist*, 91.

22. A. David Moody, *Ezra Pound: Poet, A Portrait of the Man and His Work, Volume I: The Young Genius, 1885–1920* (New York: Oxford University Press, 2007), 306.

23. Kenner, *Pound Era*, 359.

24. Gibson, *Epic Reinvented*, 10.

25. Michael F. Harper, "Truth and Calliope: Ezra Pound's Malatesta," *PMLA* 96, no. 1 (January 1981): 88.

26. Harper, "Truth and Calliope," 91, 94, 99.

27. Peter Makin, *Pound's Cantos* (Baltimore: Johns Hopkins University Press, 1985), 103.

28. Makin, *Pound's Cantos*, 104.

29. Longenbach, *Modernist*, 130.

30. Longenbach, *Modernist*, 141.

31. Longenbach, *Modernist*, 148.

32. Ezra Pound, *The Selected Letters of Ezra Pound to John Quinn, 1915–1924*, ed. Timothy Materer (Durham: Duke University Press, 1991), 217.

33. Rainey, "A Poem Including History," 205.

34. Quoted in Heymann, *Ezra Pound*, 264–65.

35. Ezra Pound, *Guide to Kulchur* (New York: New Directions, 1970), 30–31.

36. Pound, *Kulchur*, 115.

37. Ezra Pound, *The Spirit of Romance* 1910 (New York: New Directions, 2005), 7.

38. Pound, *Kulchur*, 60.

39. Moody, *Ezra Pound*, 214.

40. Quoted in Moody, *Ezra Pound*, 401.

41. Kenner, *Pound Era*, 377.

42. Makin, *Pound's Cantos*, 107.

43. Maud Ellmann, "Ezra Pound: The Erasure of History," in *Post-Structuralism*

and the Question of History, ed. Derek Attridge, Robert Young, and Geoff Bennington (New York: Cambridge University Press, 1987), 245.

44. Jeffrey Walker, *Bardic Ethos*, 105, 106.

45. Kazin, "Language as History," 117, 118.

46. Pound, *Kulchur*, 26–27.

47. Ezra Pound, *Gaudier-Brzeska: A Memoir* (1916; repr., New York: New Directions, 1970), 113–14.

48. Ezra Pound, *Selected Prose*, 21.

49. Pound, *Prose*, 22, 23. Pound's idea of the "luminous detail" is similar to the anthropologist Leo Frobenius's *Kulturmorphologie*, according to which a small number of artifacts can enable a skilled investigator to induce the central characteristics of a culture.

50. Kenner, *Pound Era*, 360, 366.

51. Kenner, *Pound Era*, 423.

52. Pound, *Prose*, 313. In 1944 he continues the historical-event-as-chapter metaphor, describing World War II as "a chapter in the long and bloody tragedy which began with the foundation of the Bank of England in far-away 1694" (*Prose*, 343).

53. Michael Bernstein, *The Tale of the Tribe*, 112.

54. Kenner, *Pound Era*, 433, 434.

55. Mutlu Konuk Blasing, "Designs on History: Ezra Pound, the Puritans, and Self-Fulfilling Prophecies," in *The Calvinist Roots of the Modern Era*, ed. Aliki Barnstone, Michael Tomasek Manson, and Carol J. Singley (Hanover, NH: University Press of New England, 1997), 16.

56. Michael Heller, "Ezra Pound's Gothic Designs on History," *New England Review* 26, no. 3 (2005): 105.

57. Pound, *Kulchur*, 265.

58. Pound, *Prose*, 306.

59. Pound, *Kulchur*, 30–31.

60. Alec Marsh, "Counterfeit Kulchur: Deep Politics, the Great Bass and Secret History in Ezra Pound," *European Journal of English Studies* 12, no. 3 (December 2008): 265.

61. Ezra Pound, *The Cantos* (New York: New Directions, 1970), 258. See Leon Surette's *A Light from Eleusis* (Oxford: Clarendon, 1979) and Michael Bernstein's *The Tale of the Tribe* for good discussions of Pound's sense of the mythic. Bernstein argues that Pound's inability to resolve the tension between his understanding of the mythic and his understanding of history results in "one of the major dilemmas in *The Cantos*" (24), and that Pound finally recognizes this tension "as both the poem's and the world's tragedy" (107).

62. Pound, *Kulchur*, 263.

63. Pound, *Prose*, 150.

64. Kenner, *Pound Era*, 377.

65. Quoted in Heymann, *Ezra Pound*, 106.

66. Wyndham Lewis, *Time and Western Man* (1927; repr., Boston: Beacon Hill Press, 1957), 38.

67. Pound, *Prose*, 300.

68. Pound, *Prose*, 267. Cf. "I don't see that anyone save a sap-head can now think he knows any history until he understands economics." See Ezra Pound, *Literary Essays* (New York: New Directions, 1968), 86. What he means is that nobody can know history

who doesn't understand economics as Pound does.

69. Leon Surette, *Pound in Purgatory: From Economic Radicalism to Anti-Semitism* (Urbana: University of Illinois Press, 1999), 167.

70. Pound, *Prose*, 157.

71. Pound, *Kulchur*, 27.

72. Pound, *Prose*, 147.

73. See Norman Cohn, *The Pursuit of the Millennium, Revolutionary Millenarians and Mystical Anarchists of the Middle Ages* (London: Maurice Temple Smith: 1970). Lynn Hinojosa notes that the art historians Burckhardt and Vasari devise similar three-part models (ancient, medieval, and modern), and that such models are dangerous because they tend to exclude Jews or "the other" from history: "Pound's inheritance and reworking of this historiographic practice, then, can be identified as one source of his anti-Semitism." See "The Modern Artist as Historian, Courtier, and Saint: Typology and Art History from Vasari to Pound," *Clio* 35, no. 2 (2006): 207.

74. Reed Way Dasenbrock, "Constructing a Larger *Iliad*: Ezra Pound and the Vicissitudes of Epic," in *Epic and Epoch: Essays on the Interpretation and History of a Genre*, ed. Steven M. Oberhelm, Van Kelly, and Richard J. Golsan (Lubbock: Texas Tech University Press, 1994), 253–63.

75. George Kearns, *Ezra Pound: The Cantos* (New York: Cambridge University Press, 1989), 21.

76. Alec Marsh, "Counterfeit," 269.

77. Alec Marsh, "John Quincy Adams and/or Martin Van Buren: Cantos 34 and 37," *Paideuma* 34, no. 1 (2005): 71. Bernstein makes a similar point, and adds that J. Q. Adams called Thomas Hart Benton, the hero of Cantos 88-89, "a notorious liar" (*Tale of the Tribe*, 41–42).

78. Peter Makin, "Americanus Natione non Moribus," in *Ezra Pound in America*, ed. Jacqueline Kay (New York: Palgrave Macmillan, 1992), 70.

79. Kazin, "Language as History," 123. Kazin continues: "As Professor Peter Shaw has shown in a devastating examination of what Pound did to *The Works of John Adams* (*Partisan Review*, #1, 1977), Pound transcribed so mechanically that he reproduced even the misprints . . . Just how dotty Pound could get when the word 'Adams' swam into view is suggested by the following: '[Eliot] has renounced America ever since the time of his first departure, but if he would consider the dynasty of the Adamses he would see that it was precisely because it lacked the Confucian law that this family lost the Celestial Decree.'"

80. Pound, *Prose*, 308.

81. Such things are relative: Alec Marsh notes that even in Cantos 88–89, "Pound's telegraphic redactions can lead to obscurities and misprisions" ("Counterfeit," 273).

82. Marsh, "Counterfeit," 263.

83. See Alec Marsh's *Money and Modernity: Pound, Williams, and the Spirit of Jefferson* (Tuscaloosa: University of Alabama Press, 1998) for a thorough discussion of this topic.

84. Kazin, "Language as History," 123.

85. Teresa Winterhalter, "Eyeless in Siena, or Ezra Pound's Vision through History," *Paideuma* 21, no. 3 (1992): 110, 115–17.

86. Kenner, *Pound Era*, 434.

87. Kenner, *Pound Era*, 362, 376.

88. Leon Surette, *Pound in Purgatory*, 166–67.
89. Quoted in Heymann, Ezra Pound, 119.
90. Quoted in Heymann, Ezra Pound, 113.
91. Kazin, "Language as History," 120.
92. Paul Morrison, *Poetics of Fascism*, 43.
93. Quoted in Heymann, *Ezra Pound*, 297, 298.
    94. Robert Casillo, *The Genealogy of Demons: Anti-Semitism, Fascism, and the Myths of Ezra Pound* (Evanston: Northwestern University Press, 1988), 71.
    95. Frank Kermode, *The Sense of an Ending: Studies in the Theory of Fiction* (New York: Oxford University Press, 1967), 56, 161.
    96. Walker, *Bardic Ethos*, 108.
    97. Kazin writes that "Pound the would-be epic writer has a driving sense of history but is really without history" ("Language as History," 123), i.e., his understanding of what Hitler and Mussolini did, and of what World War II signified, is seriously flawed and fundamentally different from that of most of his readers.

Chapter 9
Getting the News from Poems:
William Carlos Williams's
In the American Grain and *Paterson*

It is difficult
to get the news from poems
yet men die miserably every day
for lack
of what is found there.
—*Asphodel, That Greeny Flower*

The truth is that news offers the precise incentive to epic poetry, the poetry of events; and now is precisely the time for it since never by any chance is the character of a single fact ever truthfully represented today.[1]

In my preface, I noted Howard Nemerov's claim that the central "theme" of the work of Yeats, Pound, and Eliot is "the confrontation with the wonder and terror of history."[2] That claim may seem exaggerated, but history is clearly *one* of the themes of these major contemporaries of Williams. Williams was also aware that Stephen Vincent Benét had won the Pulitzer Prize in 1929 for *John Brown's Body*, and that Archibald MacLeish had won the Pulitzer in 1932 for *Conquistador*—in fact, Williams had written on Cortés's conquest of Tenochtitlán in *In the American Grain* several years earlier. In the first half of the twentieth century, one way for poets to demonstrate high seriousness was to take history as their subject, and Williams clearly sees this, but his attitude toward history stands in sharp contrast to Pound's and Eliot's, and to those Pulitzer Prize-winners'.

Williams's primary concern is the aesthetic imagination, which he argues is grounded in the quality of one's attention to sensory perception, the phenomenological here and now of the immediate present. He writes in *Spring and All*, "To refine, to clarify, to intensify that eternal moment in which we alone live there is but a single force—the imagination,"[3] and his entire oeuvre can be read as an exercise in the aesthetics of the perception of that "eternal moment." For Williams, the basic task for each of us is to learn, or perhaps to re-learn, how to see, hear, touch, smell, i.e., how to experience the world freshly: "imagine the New World that rises to our windows from the sea on Mondays and on Saturdays—and on every other day of the week also. Imagine it in all its prismatic color-ings."[4] But this is precisely what most of us cannot do, because "[t]here is a constant barrier between the reader and his consciousness of immediate contact with the world."[5] This "constant barrier" will be a central theme of *In the American Grain* and *Paterson*, the two books in which Williams most fully considers history.

There is no evidence that Williams ever read Nietzsche's *The Use and Abuse of History*, but the parallels between his thinking about history and Nie-tzsche's are strong. In *Kora in Hell* Williams writes, "Of course history is an attempt to make the past seem stable and of course it's all a lie."[6] Williams here is objecting to the kind of master narrative that forecloses variant interpretations of the past, precisely the kind of Hegelian history that Nietzsche attacks in his essay. Unlike Hegel, Nietzsche does not believe that as history progresses, the meaning of human existence will become increasingly clear. For Nietzsche, pro-gress is an illusion; the past and the present are one and the same, made up of eternally present "types," and I will argue that Williams treats history in just this way in both *In the American Grain* and *Paterson*.

In important ways, *In the American Grain* is an example of what Nietzsche calls "monumental" history, i.e., a history that provides inspiring examples of "the man of action," the man who fully embraces life. Nietzsche grants that this is a legitimate use of history, but he warns that this kind of history can force the unique qualities of the past into a misleading general formula. And if history's purpose is to inspire us in the present, then telling the truth about history be-comes problematic:

> As long as the soul of historiography is found in the great incentives a pow-erful man receives from it, as long as the past must be described as some-thing worthy of imitation, something that can be imitated and is possible a second time, so long, at least, is the past in danger of being somewhat dis-torted, of being reinterpreted according to aesthetic criteria and so brought closer to fiction; there are even ages which are quite incapable of distin-guishing between a monumental past and a mythical fiction: for precisely the same incentives can be given by the one world as by the other.[7]

I will argue that Williams comes close to "mythical fiction" in his depictions of such figures as Daniel Boone, Sebastian Rasles, and Aaron Burr.

The "lie" of a stable past that Williams protests in *Kora in Hell* is the sub-ject of Van Wyck Brooks's influential 1918 essay, "On Creating a Usable Past." Like Williams, Brooks finds that "our professors continue to pour out a stream of historical works repeating the same points of view to such an astonishing de-gree that they have placed a sort of Talmudic seal upon the American tradition," with the result that "the interpreters of that past experience have put a gloss upon it that renders it sterile for the living mind."[8] Can we imagine an alternative history that would nourish the present? Brooks writes,

> [T]he past that survives in the common mind of the present is a past without living value. But is this the only possible past? If we need another past so badly, is it inconceivable that we might discover one, that we might even invent one? Discover, invent a usable past we certainly can, and that is what a vital criticism always does.[9]

In *In the American Grain*, Williams invents a *usable* American history, and he uses that history to illustrate his thinking about the centrality of the aesthetic imagination in sensory contact with the surrounding world. Williams develops this same theme in an unfinished book in which he describes

> the way in which human consciousness came in contact with its world. Each child was a Columbus of sorts [. . .] floating across the uncharted ocean of the mother's womb to find itself in a beautiful but alien *Nuevo Mundo*. But [. . .] from the start the new consciousness was subjected to the shock of misinformation, lies [. . . .] His foray into epistemology was—in effect—another version of the Adamic myth. The importance of naming things correctly, of seeing what was there and of possessing one's birthright with as little interference as possible from the special interest groups—the law, the church, the school, the economic structures: that was what he was, finally, after.[10]

In his preface to *In the American Grain*, Williams places himself in the role of Adam, claiming that his goal is "to re-name the things seen, now lost in chaos of borrowed titles, many of them inappropriate, under which the true character lies hid."[11] In other words, Williams is asserting for himself the kind of "consciousness of contact" that he ascribes to the historical figures he most admires in *In the American Grain*. Williams repeatedly stresses the sensory in his praise of these figures. For example, he describes Pére Rasles as "full of taste, a tongue, a laugh, enduring, self-forgetful in beneficence—a new spirit in the New World," living in Maine "with his beloved savages, drawing their sweet like honey, TOUCHING them every day." Without the "dogmatic bitterness" of the English Puritans, Rasles "with a fresh mind could open eyes and heart to the New World," and like Adam, Rasles makes immediate contact with the New World: "For everything his fine sense, blossoming, thriving, opening, reviving—not shutting out—was tuned." Williams is equally insistent on the sensory in his description of Aaron Burr, who "knew what a democracy must liberate. . . . Men intact—with all their senses waking. He had, raised to a different level, the directness of 'common people' . . . to touch, to hear, to see, to smell, to taste."[12]

The opposite of the consciousness Williams praises in Rasles and Burr is a consciousness that withdraws from immediate contact with the surrounding world, closing off direct sensory perceptions and thus choking off the aesthetic imagination, and instead imposing its own will on that world. Such a consciousness may wrap itself, Puritan-like, in layers of theological abstraction, or it may give all its attention and energy to the accumulation of wealth. Williams uses American history to argue that this consciousness of mastery has come to dominate American life. Again emphasizing the sensory, Williams writes, "The characteristic of American life is that it holds off from embraces, from impacts, gaining, by fear, safety and time in which to fortify its prolific carcass—while the spirit, with tongue hanging out, bites at its bars—its object just out of reach." He continues, "Here, through terror, there is no direct touch," for our technology is "a mechanism to increase the gap between touch and thing, *not* to have a contact" and "NEVER to allow touch." Finally, "Our life drives us apart and forces us upon science and invention—away from touch."[13]

Both Beck[14] and Breslin[15] find a Freudian influence on the two types of consciousness Williams depicts in *In the American Grain*: the Puritans embody the willful repression of the instincts and the dominance of the superego, while the Indians represent the liberation of id energies, flowering in a culture rooted in its own earth. But Williams's two types of consciousness are not simply Freudian; they represent two distinct modes of knowing and experiencing the world, two fundamentally different forms of perception that carry profound ethical implications. For Williams,

> The Puritan, finding one thing like another in a world destined for blossom only in "Eternity," all soul, all "emptiness" then here, was precluded from SEEING the Indian. They never realized the Indian in the least save as an unformed PURITAN. The *immorality* of such a concept, the inhumanity, the brutalizing effect upon their own minds, on their SPIRITS—they never suspected.[16]

This binary opposition repeats itself throughout the book: representing the consciousness of mastery and the imposition of the alien and abstract on the local are Eric the Red (more particularly his daughter Freydis), Cortés, Ponce de Leon, the Plymouth pilgrims, Cotton Mather, Benjamin Franklin, and Alexander Hamilton. Those who embody the consciousness of contact with the new and the local include Columbus (especially on his first voyage), De Soto, Raleigh, Champlain, Thomas Morton, Sebastian Rasles, Daniel Boone, Aaron Burr, Sam Houston, and Edgar Allan Poe.

Bremen argues forcefully against this binary reading, criticizing Hillis Miller for "reduc[ing] Williams's idea of American culture into a battle of Puritans against Indians," and arguing that Breslin, Guimond, Kutzinski, Tapscott, Rapp, Weaver, and Whitaker all misread *In the American Grain* "as a simple opposition of political or psychological forces," but his alternative reading of the book as a valorization of violence is too narrow.[17] Breslin argues persuasively that, for Williams, an "agonizing split in the American consciousness" is played out in American history in terms of a "tension between the dominant thrust toward mastery and marginal efforts at contact."[18]

However, Williams's use of history raises a number of questions. Because *In the American Grain* is fundamentally a series of psychological biographies, *exempla* of the two contrasting modes of consciousness described above, historical narrative loses its significance: it hardly matters, for example, whether De Soto preceded or followed de Leon in his explorations, and though the book's chapters generally unfold in chronological order, the fact that the first slaves arrived in Virginia in 1619, while Williams's chapter "The Advent of the Slaves" follows his chapter on Aaron Burr, in no way disrupts Williams's discourse. This means that when readers discuss the importance of "origins" in *In the American Grain*, a confusion between historical origins and psychological origins often occurs. For example, Beck suggests that Williams is searching for the roots of the blockages that prevent contact, "the initial fracturing of unity between self and place,"[19] and that *In the American Grain* is a kind of jeremiad recounting the community's fall from grace. Breslin uses a similar rhetoric: "by tracing the forces acting on us to their origins and by defining precisely their qualities, we can begin to heal this split. *In the American Grain* enacts historically Williams's central quest, the descent to origins for renewal."[20] But the "origins" of the two modes of consciousness are not to be found in early American history; there is no state of "grace" in history from which the community falls, no historical point of origin to which we can descend for "renewal." These modes exist prior to the discovery and settling of North America, and to find their historical origin is beyond the scope of *In the American Grain*. All that Williams can do is to describe the "split" as it manifests itself in different historical figures, or even in the same figure, as in the Columbus of the first voyage compared with the Columbus of the fourth voyage.

Just as the origin of these two modes of consciousness is not to be found in the beginnings of American history, neither does Williams's recounting of that history afford a model for political transformation in the present. Beck argues that Williams is attempting "to grasp the latent revolutionary valence of America's past," and that for Williams, "[t]he idea of contact develops into much more than an aesthetic ideal; it evolves [. . .] into a theoretical critical framework that we might call the political economy of contact, concerned with problems of individualism, capitalism, American identity and historical development."[21] For Beck, Rasles's isolated life with the Abnaki Indians becomes "an alternative to the abstract money economy of the dominant American tradition," an economy of contact in which "part of the self is given over to the community to which it belongs, to the land it inhabits," unlike the Puritan model "where value is converted into money terms [. . .] and used to justify exploitation through an abstract economy of accumulation."[22] The problem with Beck's reading is that Rasles does *not* offer such a model: his is an idiosyncratic life, like Boone's, that depends for its fulfillment on the individual's withdrawal from the political and economic systems of the time, and offers no systemic alternative to those systems. While it is true that the French in Canada generally lived in closer proximity to the Indians than did the English in New England, the French were certainly as interested in the "abstract" money economy as were the English, and just as quick to convert the "value" of North America into "money terms." Rasles might be compared to the Puritans John Eliot and Roger Williams, men who saw the Indians as men, as equals, and while we may wish that such men had been in the colonial majority and that their attitude had been more widespread, it is naïve and simplistic to hold out their examples as affording a practical model for systemic political and economic transformation in the present. D. H. Lawrence makes an error similar to Beck's in his famous review of *In the American Grain*: far from "a sensuous record of the Americanization of the white men in America,"[23] Williams's book is closer to a lamentation for the failure of such Americanization to have occurred more widely.

In the American Grain is a great book not because of what it has to say about history, but because of what it has to say about the aesthetic imagination and the ethical implications of living in contact with one's senses. Williams works hard not only to erase the difference between past and present, but to subsume history within his own imagination. Beck writes that Williams "fuses past and present, compressing time into the figure of the present author, or, more accurately, the present text."[24] Breslin makes a similar point: "for Williams all history is present, at least potentially, in the 'subject,' the perceiver, and the act of historical understanding is identified with an act of self-understanding."[25]

The intensely subjective significance of American history for Williams is made clear in a letter to Horace Gregory written in 1939:

> Of mixed ancestry, I felt from earliest childhood that America was the only home I could ever possibly call my own. I felt that it was expressly founded for me, personally, and that it must be my first business in life to possess it; that only by making it my own from the beginning to my own day, in detail, should I ever have a basis for knowing where I stood. I must have a basis for orienting myself formally in the beliefs which activated me from day to day. Nothing in the school histories interested me, so I decided as far as possible to go to whatever source material I could get at and start my own valuations there: to establish myself from my own reading, in my own way, in the locality which by birthright had become my own.[26]

In the above excerpt, some form of the first-person singular pronoun occurs twenty-one times, grammatical evidence of the essential subjectivity of Williams's engagement with the past. Van Wyck Brooks argues that the historian's crucial question is *"What is important for us?"* and that the question must be answered "personally,"[27] and Williams does precisely that.

In depicting American history as the product of the tension between the consciousness of mastery and the consciousness of contact, Williams flattens history into a kind of eternal present in which these two forces struggle interminably. Breslin reads the chapter on Rasles, which begins with Williams's recounting his conversation with the French historian Valery Larbaud, in terms of

Williams's drawing an explicit parallel between himself and Larbaud, on the one hand, and the Indians and Rasles on the other. In other words, claims Breslin, "the contemporary scene re-enacts an historical one; history moves as a pattern of eternal recurrence." And this is true not only of this particular scene, but of history in general for Williams. The characters in *In the American Grain* are "mythical and eternal," claims Breslin; "Williams looked at history not as a linear progression of events but as as pattern of eternal recurrence."[28]

"Eternal recurrence" is of course Nietzsche's phrase, and Nietzsche's warning about the dangers of "monumental history" is relevant here. Williams identifies strongly with these historical figures: for example, he writes of Aaron Burr, "He's in myself and so I dig through lies to resurrect him."[29] *In the American Grain* is full of Williams's speculating on the psychic lives of early Americans, speculating that sometimes takes the form of a kind of wish-fulfillment fantasizing, as in the chapter on Daniel Boone, "a great voluptuary born to the American settlements against the niggardliness of the damming puritanical tradition." The three months that Boone spent alone in the wilderness of Kentucky, Williams insists, must have been "the great ecstatic moment of his life's affirmation." Boone's life remains "loaded with power," writes Williams, "because of a descent to the ground of his desire." He continues, "And among all the colonists . . . the ecstasy of complete possession was his alone."[30] Such rhetoric helps us to understand the historical Daniel Boone less than it helps us to understand what Williams means by the more intense possibilities of the consciousness of contact.

When Kenneth Burke reviews *In the American Grain*, he writes, "Williams's method . . . tends toward a maximum of 'interpretation' and a minimum of research," and suggests that Williams's "purpose is poetry, not history."[31] Williams is upset by his friend's review, and defends the objectivity of his approach: "I thought I had salted the original matter with enough historic material to have escaped the bald statement 'Subjective History.'"[32] In another letter, he writes, "where possible, I copied and used the original writings [. . .] to prove the truth of the book."[33]

These letters evince a surprising naiveté on Williams's part, as if direct quotation from primary sources were sufficient guarantee against a writer's biases, or against what Breslin calls his "hortatory" tone.[34] He reveals an equal naiveté when he writes, "The plan was to try to get inside the heads of some of the American founders or 'heroes,' if you will, by examining their original records. I wanted nothing to get between me and what they themselves had recorded."[35] In other words, Williams wants to come into immediate contact with historical texts just as he does in his sensory perceptions of the physical world, but such a project is problematic for a number of reasons.

First, Williams clearly has a thesis in mind—that American history embodies the tension between the consciousness of mastery and the consciousness of contact—and that thesis, which is psychological and ethical rather than historical, not only colors his reading but also leads him to ignore much of what we typically think of as "history." We find in *In the American Grain* no mention of political or economic development, nothing on the evolution of American social organization, no narrative account of the course of American history. Instead, we get a series of discrete biographies of "great men," as if history were nothing more than biography writ large. For Williams, American history is entirely the function of two competing modes of consciousness, two attitudes toward the New World that persist, unchanged, from Red Eric and Columbus down to the present.

Bremen argues that "these simple notions of opposition . . . are not what Williams's 'concept of history' is about. For Williams, history *should be* a 'conversation' composed of as many voices as there are in a country." And *In the American Grain*, Bremen writes, includes "the voices of blacks, Indians, Puritans, women, writers, and politicians."[36] But Bremen is wrong: we do *not* hear any black voices in *In the American Grain*. Williams's chapter "The Advent of the Slaves" is wildly reductive: "these [slaves] were just men of a certain mettle who came to America in ships, like the rest. The minor differences of condition were of no importance—the mere condition of their coming is of no importance." Williams can be patronizing: "For purity of religious devotion, in the simplicity of their manoeuvres, they exceed our greatest application." He can also be crudely racist, as when he describes the slaves' "long gorilla arms."[37] But he does not give black Americans a voice. Only one chapter's title names a woman, "Jacataqua," but she is fictional,[38] less than half the chapter is devoted to her, and one of her chief functions is to be sexually attracted to Aaron Burr. Besides Jacataqua, the only other Indian who speaks, briefly, is Montezuma. This is hardly equal participation in the "conversation" that history should be.

A second problem is Williams's tendency to grossly oversimplify his subjects in order to make them better conform to his thesis. For example, "Mather defends the witchcraft persecutions."[39] Mather believed that witchcraft existed and that the Devil wanted to destroy the Puritan settlements in Massachusetts Bay, and he defended the judges against some of their critics, but he was also skeptical of much of the evidence introduced at the trials, and he expressed his skepticism to the judges. Williams's account of King Philip's War in the Rasles chapter is equally oversimplified: the English settlers are depicted as instigating the war and indulging in atrocitites, while the Indians fight "fairly," and only because of the "perfidy" of the English,[40] when in fact the war's origins are far more complex, both sides committed heinous atrocities, and the English were able to win only because so many Indians fought alongside them against Philip, who was finally tracked and killed not by the English, but by their Indian allies.

Occasionally Williams concedes that his generalizations are not ironclad, as when he admits, after blanket condemnation of the Puritans and praise of the French Jesuits in North America, that "[John] Eliot was a good man" and "much the Puritans complained of in the Jesuits was justified," but these isolated sentences are never developed further. Far more typically Williams indulges in exaggerations that go beyond the merely provocative, as when he claims that to know George Washington is to know "practically all there is to understand about the beginnings of the American Republic."[41]

In his chapter on Aaron Burr, Williams is at his most extreme: "if there is agreement on one point in history, be sure there's interest there to have it so and that's not truth [. . . .] if a verdict be unanimous, it is sure to be a wrong one, a crude rush of the herd."[42] Any reasonable historian would agree that skepticism and an openness to new data and interpretations are crucial to the discipline, but Williams goes far beyond such openness. On the basis of listening to his wife's account of a single book she read on Burr,[43] Williams declares that historians' standard depiction of him is completely false, and he minimizes Burr's scheme to separate, with British naval and financial assistance, the trans-Appalachian states from the rest of the Union and to create an empire in the West and South, including Mexico, for which scheme he was indicted for treason. Burr's rival Alexander Hamilton is lumped together with Thomas Jefferson and the rest of the "Virginia Junto,"[44] as if opposition to Burr made Hamilton and Jefferson politically equivalent.

This polemical oversimplification of history is precisely what Nietzsche cautions against, and is the natural result of Williams's constructing "a usable past"—usable in its illustration of his thinking about the aesthetic imagination and its dependence on one's openness to direct contact with sensory experience. It is exciting and provocative, but as historiography it has serious flaws, and I would argue that Williams, as much as he loved the book, implicitly concedes those flaws in his essay "The American Background" (1934). He retains his basic thesis regarding the two modes of consciousness, or "two cultural elements," but here his attitude toward the consciousness that resists the new and "look[s] toward Europe" is less condemnatory, more sympathetic: "It was an inability of the mind to function in the face of overwhelming odds, a retreat to safety, an immediate defensive organization [. . .] against the wilderness." In Plymouth, "It was a harsh world the first men had to face [. . .] The land was from the first antagonistic."[45]

Thomas Jefferson, who in *In the American Grain* is merely an opponent of Burr, is here "a man of delicate and curiously balanced mentality" who "stands out as the sole individual who seems to have had a clear understanding of what was taking place." Similarly Benjamin Franklin, who is depicted as a kind of secular Puritan in *In the American Grain*, is here "a man of unusual sagacity [. . .] the most persistent and successful exponent of the project to take into native hands and to deal directly [. . .] with the world of their time," and his technical talent allows Franklin an indirect success at promoting a local culture.[46] Williams also recants what Nietzsche would call the "mythical romance" of much of *In the American Grain*. "It is not hard to fabricate a melodramatic part" for such figures as Boone and Houston, he writes, and then concedes that "Boone . . . was not a romantic," as we recall the great ecstatic "voluptuary" of *In the American Grain*.[47]

At the end of "The American Background," Williams offers a definition of a genuine culture that I read as a model for his great poem *Paterson*, which represents the final stage in his thinking about history:

> [A culture] has to be where it arises, or everything related to the life there ceases [. . . .] It is the realization of the qualities of a place in relation to the life which occupies it; embracing everything involved, climate, geographic position, relative size, history, other cultures—as well as the character of its sands, flowers, minerals and the condition of knowledge within its borders. It is the act of lifting these things into an ordered and utilized whole which is culture.[48]

In *Paterson*, Williams approaches history differently from the way he approaches it in *In the American Grain*. Whereas *In the American Grain* gives us a kind of epic struggle between the consciousness of contact embodied by such figures as Rasles, Boone, and Burr and the consciousness of mastery embodied by the New England Puritans, *Paterson* gives us isolated fragments about such obscure figures as Cornelius Doremus or John Dalzell. Alexander Hamilton appears in *Paterson*, but there is no Aaron Burr to stand against him. Instead of focusing on particular individuals in North American history and moving in roughly chronological fashion from Red Eric to Edgar Allan Poe, Williams focuses on the flotsam and jetsam of Paterson's history—instead of the city's more famous citizens, such as gun manufacturer Samuel Colt or submarine designer John Holland, we read about a corpse found in a wheelhouse or local policemen shooting at what they think is a mink.

Several readers have tried to justify Williams's insertions of such curious historical material. Breslin claims that "they are there simply because they are historical truth. We are assured that the poem does not just emanate from the poet's visionary imagination."[49] And Mariani suggests that Williams needed "historical material to broaden the base of his poem,"[50] but these are extremely vague justifications, and each implies that Williams could have used *any* "historical material." Williams claims that he specifically chose Paterson, "with its rich colonial history," as his subject because it was "associated with many of the ideas upon which our fiscal colonial policy shaped us through Alexander Hamilton."[51] But Bernstein argues that Williams idealizes Paterson's historical significance, and points out that "the political, historical, and economic reality of Paterson [. . .] is curiously missing" from the poem.[52]

Bernstein is right. More importantly, the naïve epistemological self-confidence of *In the American Grain* is gone, along with the polemical tone. In *Paterson* Williams foregrounds the question of methodology. In his preface, he suggests his initial strategy: "To make a start, / out of particulars," but immediately he acknowledges that he has only "defective means" at his disposal, and he compares himself to a three-legged dog sniffing around for "a musty bone." Perhaps the poem's most famous line is "no ideas but in things,"[53] which seems to endorse the empirical, inductive method suggested by "making a start out of particulars." Later in Book One, however, Williams is clearer about the difficulty of the historian's (and the epic poet's) task: "a mass of detail / to interrelate on a new ground, difficultly; / an assonance, a homologue / [. . .] / pulling the disparate together to clarify / and compress." In asserting assonances and homologues among the disparate details of history, however, the poet's compressing is almost inevitably Procrustean. Ezra Pound defines an epic as a poem containing history, but Williams writes of "The vague accuracies of events dancing two / and two with language which they / forever surpass," conceding that the events of history always exceed the language that attempts to contain them.[54]

In *In the American Grain*, Williams reads and writes history for the insight it offers into two modes of consciousness, and in "The American Background" he suggests that one of those modes, the consciousness of mastery, has grown increasingly dominant over the course of American history. *Paterson* develops that argument, but suggests that mastery has always been the dominant mode. Many of the prose passages in the poem illustrate the ubiquity of Americans' tendency to exploit and commodify their natural environment as well as their fellow human beings. In Book One, for example, a poor shoemaker finds pearls in the mussels he collects to feed his large family. Some of these are quite valuable, and in the ensuing "excitement" millions of mussels are destroyed, "often with little or no result." In a similar episode, a lake is drained, and "millions of fish" and eels are exposed and killed. A passage on Cornelius Doremus (1714–1803) consists almost entirely of a list of his possessions and the monetary value of each, as if the meaning of the man lay entirely in the value of his possessions.[55]

This tendency to exploit and commodify is greatly magnified as we move from the level of the individual to the level of the institution, at which powerful ideologies can transform people into abstractions based upon race, class, or gender, and alienation (or "divorce," as Williams calls it) becomes our common condition. In *Paterson*, the avatar of this tendency is Alexander Hamilton, and what he "saw when he looked (at the falls!)": "His fertile imagination envisioned a great manufacturing center, a great Federal City, to supply the needs of the country. Here was water-power to turn the mill wheels and the navigable river to carry manufactured goods to the market centers: a national manufactory."[56] Hamilton is the enemy of the local: in the earliest days of the American republic, his is among the loudest voices in favor of a strong central government with "authority over the States." He is no democrat, either, and refers to the people as "a great beast"[57] that must be tamed and kept in its place.

As chief architect of the plan by which the federal government would assume the debt incurred by the individual states during the Revolutionary War, and the powers of taxation necessary to pay off such debt, Hamilton establishes the ground for an economic system that generates tremendous wealth but concentrates the bulk of that wealth in the hands of a small elite. Hamilton sees that only the establishment of an industrial economy can generate the income necessary to pay the nation's debt and establish its credit, ensuring its future economic growth, but for Williams such an economy is fatally flawed because of its grounding in usury. Williams's thinking about economics, especially his embrace of Social Credit theory, is strongly influenced by Ezra Pound, although Williams is never as didactic or pedantic as Pound can be. Like Pound, Williams zig-zags through America's economic history, leaping from the eighteenth-century Hamilton to the twentieth-century Federal Reserve System[58] as if the one were unquestionably the child of the other, when in fact private banking interests vigorously opposed the establishment of such a system. And like Pound, Williams can be enigmatic, even opaque: he cites *"les idées Wilsoniennes nous / gâtent,"*[59] which Weaver glosses as Wilson's opposition to the dangerously centralized control of credit.[60] But Wilson was no Social Credit disciple; in fact, he was an early advocate of a federal reserve system, though he was unsatisfied with the system that was finally created. Williams prints parts of three Social Credit pamphlets[61] attacking the federal reserve system and the tax burden it imposes on U.S. citizens, but the author of the final pamphlet, August Walters, disagrees with Social Credit leaders such as Gorham Munson,[62] and unlike Pound, Williams never claims to have the solution to Paterson's economic problems.

For Williams, America's economic history is symptomatic of the dominance of the consciousness of mastery, especially as it plays itself out in terms of race-, class-, and gender-based exploitation. One prose passage in Book One describes the Tuscarora Indians who, driven from Tennessee by white settlers in the late eighteenth century, attempt to walk to upstate New York to join the Iroquois confederation. Some of the Tuscarora women and "stragglers" get no farther than the Suffern, New Jersey, area, "where they were joined by Hessian deserters from the British Army, a number of albinos among them, escaped negro slaves and a lot of women and their brats released in New York City after the British had been forced to leave." These women had been brought to New York to provide sex for British soldiers stationed there, and then been abandoned. Their story is linked to that of "some thousands of Irish women and children" who were purportedly shipped by Cromwell in the seventeenth century to the West Indies to be sold as slaves: "Forced by their owners to mate with the others these unfortunates were succeeded by a few generations of Irish-speaking negroes and mulattos."[63]

These stories of displaced, abused groups might be dismissed as extreme, isolated cases, but in *Paterson* they are tesserae of a larger mosaic. The consciousness of mastery dominates American history not because it manifests itself in particular individuals such as Hamilton or Cromwell, but because it creates extremely powerful institutions that shape or control large areas of individual people's lives, sharply diminishing the possibility of the consciousness of contact. In Book Two one voice complains that "guilty bastards" in the Senate are trying to blind average Americans by crying "Communist!" as they block David Lilienthal's nomination as chair of the Atomic Energy Commission and attempt to place control of atomic weapons in the hands of "a few industrialists." And the "bastards" do blind most Americans, as is evident in Book Four when Cory-

don, replying to Phyllis's remark that she trained as a nurse in Paterson, says, "[.
. .] They / used to have silk mills there . / until the unions ruined them."[64]

For Williams, the political and economic institutions responsible for "the
economic distress occasioned by human greed and blindness" are "aided, as
always, by the church, all churches in the broadest sense of that designation."[65]
The Christian church in its several denominations presents itself to the exploited,
working-class citizens of Paterson as the spiritual solution to the problem of
their difficult, diminished material lives, but it proves as inimical to the consciousness of contact as was the Puritan church in *In the American Grain*. An
evangelist's sermon is interspersed throughout Book Two's discussion of Hamilton and the federal reserve, but the evangelist's solution to the problem of poverty is to accept it and turn one's entire attention to spiritual salvation. The
church thus serves the interests of Wall Street, a point Williams reiterates in
Book Four when he describes the evangelist Billy Sunday's visit to Paterson, "as
paid for / by the United Factory Owners' Ass'n . / . to 'break' the strike / and put
those S.O.Bs in their places, be / Geezus, by calling them to God! / —getting his
27 Grand in the hotel room / after the last supper (at the *Hamilton*)."[66]

Throughout Paterson's history, the American economic system has encouraged its citizens to commodify and exploit the world around them, alienating
them from direct contact with that world. This alienation is made clear in people's tendency, evident throughout Paterson's history, to see the world as a *spectacle*, as something remote from their own experience. The viewer stands apart
from the spectacle, cut off and isolated, untouched—precisely the posture that
most inhibits the consciousness of contact. And as we shall see, for Williams
most historiography casts its readers in the role of spectator. For example, in
Book Two's "Sunday in the Park" on Garrett Mountain, small boys climb onto
rocks and spy on a pair of lovers, "where she lies sweating at his side." In their
childish voyeurism the boys "stare down, / from history!" writes Williams,[67]
suggesting that much of what history records, and much of what interests us, is
mere spectacle. In Book One, some of the spectacles take the form of the monstrous: in the eighteenth century "a monster in human form," a young man
whose head is as long as the rest of his body, and whose "limbs are small and
much deformed," is a "natural curiosity" who draws many visitors, including
George Washington. In 1817, a 126-pound sturgeon is "pelted with stones by
boys" and then brought to shore, the incident described in a local newspaper
under the headline "The Monster Taken."[68]

Violent death, or at least the display of corpses that have suffered violent
death, is another common form of spectacle in the history recounted in *Paterson*.
In 1812 Sarah Cumming, the new bride of a local minister, falls or leaps from a
ledge overlooking the Great Falls of the Passaic River, and her body is recovered a day later, deep beneath the river's surface. In 1828–29 Sam Patch makes
a spectacle of himself by diving from great heights into the Passaic, the Niagara,
and other rivers, drawing large crowds. Patch is killed attempting a 125-foot
dive into the Genesee River, and his body recovered the following spring, "fro-

zen in an ice-cake." In 1875 a corpse is discovered "lodged between two logs" in the chasm near the wheelhouse of the waterworks at the Falls. "The news of its finding attracted a very large number of visitors all that day."[69]

Murder is perhaps the most common of the violent spectacles presented in *Paterson*. In 1880 on Garrett Mountain, William Dalzell shoots John Joseph Van Houten for trespassing, and a violent mob attempts to seize Dalzell, who is saved only by the intervention of the police and a local clergyman. In 1779, Jonathan Hopper is shot in the abdomen by a group of men who break into his house at night and deliver "nineteen or twenty cruel bayonette thrusts," killing him in front of his wife and two infant children. In 1850, John Johnson murders John Van Winkle and his wife in their bedroom at night with a knife and hatchet. Johnson is convicted and hanged "in full view of thousands who had gathered on Garrett Mountain and adjacent house tops to witness the *spectacle*" (my italics). And in 1950 Fred Goodell murders his six-month-old daughter "by twice snapping the wooden tray of a high chair into the baby's face . . . when her crying annoyed him" and fracturing her skull. Goodell buries his daughter's corpse on Garrett Mountain.[70]

But spectacle is not limited to voyeurism or violence. Perhaps more insidious because of its apparent benignity is the spectacle afforded by nostalgia for a misremembered, or selectively remembered, past. Williams presents just such a nostalgic spectacle in Book Four, quoting extensively from Charles Longwell's 1901 *A Little Story of Old Paterson as Told by an Old Man*. "In a deep-set valley between hills, almost hid / by dense foliage lay the little village," it begins, and continues with "the quiet of those colonial days" and the "hearty old / Dutch stock" that settled Paterson. Little girls strew flowers in the great Lafayette's path when he visits in 1824, and the circus comes to town and presents its "weird but dazzling *spectacle*" (my italics).[71] This falsely idyllic account of Paterson's history is punctured, however, by Williams's insertion of prose accounts of the Goodell and Van Winkle murders.

What emerges from Williams's digging about in the "particulars" and "things" of Paterson, then, is a tissue of spectacle—the monstrous, the violent, the nostalgic—as well as the repeated, institutionalized exploitation and commodification of people and the natural environment. For some readers, history in *Paterson* points toward political action. Beck, for example, argues that Williams seeks "to demonstrate and embody the promise of the nation's origins" and that "Williams's belief in the potential for constructive change and growth that lies latent but undisclosed in the American continent, language, and political system, is articulated through a grammar of radical liberalism."[72] Bremen finds in *Paterson* "a political model" and argues that Williams contrasts "what history *is*" with "what history *should be*": eliminating economic exploitation, giving voice to women and other silenced minorities, and supporting "antithetical" forces like Lilienthal and Altgeld.[73]

But Williams does not engage in such optative history. Bernstein argues persuasively that Williams presents no "historically grounded alternatives" to

Paterson's economic despoliation, and that

> the solutions Williams proposes for his town's dilemma are so abstract and
> general ("invention," "credit," respect for nature, etc.) that he unwittingly suc-
> ceeds in making the terrible waste seem historically both inevitable and irre-
> versible, grounded in human weakness rather than in specific and changeable
> social circumstances. History itself [. . .] thus becomes largely [. . .] a numbing
> repetition of archetypal disasters from which no really useful instigations can
> arise.[74]

Williams does not do this "unwittingly," but Bernstein is right if by "useful instigations" he means the kind of political model that Beck and Bremen claim to find in the poem. Rather than drawing political conclusions from his sniffing, scratching, and digging into Paterson's historical record, Williams presents history as just the kind of "numbing repetition" that Bernstein describes, i.e., the kind of "eternal recurrence" that Breslin sees in *In the American Grain*. In other words, in both *In the American Grain* and *Paterson*, history dissolves into myth. In Book One, for example, Williams describes a *National Geographic* photograph of the nine wives of an African chief, and he focuses on the oldest, "the first wife," whom Williams links to "a first beauty" which he describes as a flower "whose history" laughs at and escapes from the names with which writers attempt to trap it.[75] This is a history fundamentally different from the catalog of exploitation and spectacle we find in the rest of the poem; this is a history of "first" or primary experience, history as experienced in the consciousness of contact. As such it cannot be trapped by names; it evades all historiography. But it can be pointed at, signified, by poetry, and it can be imagined in the genre of myth.

When Williams writes of "The giant in whose apertures we / cohabit, una-ware," the giant is not simply figurative. At certain moments of contact, we may "sens[e] a little / the rushing impact of the giants' / violent torrent rolling over us," and amid our conversation we may be dimly aware that the silence grounding our conversation "speaks of the giants / who have died in the past and have / returned to those scenes unsatisfied."[76] In other words, *Paterson* presents history in terms similar to what Mircea Eliade calls "chronos," the secular time of calendars and conventional history, as well as "kairos," the sacred time that lies outside chronos, but to which we still may have access. Williams does not use the vocabulary of religion that Eliade uses, but in Book Five, he suggests that to "WALK in the world," in contact, can open up "a secret world, / a sphere, a snake with its tail in / its mouth / rolls backward into the past." Later Williams repeats and clarifies this image: "the serpent / its tail in its mouth" and "the serpent / has its tail in its mouth / AGAIN! / the all-wise serpent," with the result that "time has been washed finally under."[77] Weaver suggests that this is Ouroboros, the serpent of Gnosticism,[78] and the image confirms that for Williams the linear, progressive, teleological movement of most historiography is false. In *In the American Grain,* two modes of consciousness manifest themselves repeatedly in different historical figures, but the modes themselves remain unaffected by history, outside its grip, archetypal. Such archetypal forces are figured in the image of the giants of Book One, and their eternal return is represented by the serpent with its tail in its mouth.

If archetypal forms such as the two modes of consciousness underlie all of American history, then the study of history might offer *exempla* of those forms, but apart from that, history cannot have much significance, and paying too much attention to history is like paying too much attention to spectacles of violence or nostalgia, spectacles which distract and distance us from contact with primary experience. This point is the subject of Book Three, "The Library."

Early in Book Three, the speaker seeks to escape "a hot afternoon" amid the "cool of books" in the library, telling himself three times that he does this in order "to lead the mind away." "Books will give rest," he tells himself, promising respite from the heat of immediate experience, respite from the "heavy cost" of loving "the locust tree / in bloom." "The Library / is sanctuary to our fears," and in that sanctuary, as the speaker reads the violent spectacle that is one aspect of Paterson's history—"a child burned in a field" and "Two others, / boy and girl, clasped in each other's arms / . . . Drowned / wordless in the canal"—he separates himself from the violence, intoning "So be it" after each event or item, as if sealing it off from himself.[79]

Similarly, he separates himself from the city's economic violence. Reading that Catholine Lambert's "Castle," i.e., his mansion Belle Vista, is to be razed, he murmurs "So be it," and then recalls that Lambert, "the poor English boy, / the immigrant, who built it / was the first / to oppose the unions." Lambert, one of Paterson's wealthiest industrialists, is quoted: "This is MY shop. I reserve the right (and he did) / to walk down the row (between his looms) and / fire any son-of-a-bitch I choose without excuse / or reason more than that I don't like his face." But both Lambert's attempt to break the unions and the excerpt from a letter to Williams from trade unionist Bob Brown, mentioning the 1913 Madison Square Garden "Pagent" for striking workers in Paterson, are tangential or parenthetical to the "history" the speaker is reading, the narrow focus of which is merely Lambert's "castle."[80]

The library's promise of rest and sanctuary, however, proves deceptive. Soon the speaker is overwhelmed by the library: "a roar of books / from the wadded library oppresses him," and he realizes, "The Library is desolation, it has a smell of its own / of stagnation and death." To read the history of Paterson is to give oneself over to the spectacular: an account of European settlers brutally torturing Indians who have been falsely accused of killing livestock, or an account of tightrope daredevilry above the Great Falls. And giving oneself over to historical spectacle is, in effect, "loaning blood / to the past," i.e., refusing to live in contact with the present.[81] Nietzsche makes this same point, arguing that we are flooded with an indigestible excess of history, "an enormous number of concepts which are drawn from the highly mediate knowledge of past ages and peoples, not from the immediate perception of life."[82]

In the middle of Book Three, the library begins to burn, as the Danforth Free Public Library actually burned in the great Paterson fire of 1902, and the fire is not merely destructive but also purgative—relieving the "consuming historical fever"[83] that Nietzsche claims is caused by too much attention to historical texts—and its purgation creates a space for the possibility of contact. So the library "must go down" because, insists Williams, "it / contains nothing of you."[84] History perpetually postpones its promise of knowledge, of truth: "Texts mount and complicate them- / selves, lead to further texts and those / to synopses, digests and emendations."[85] History and its scholarship demand that we continue reading, like Ezra Pound with his pedantic lists, but Williams recognizes that Pound's reading list is just another library.

Amid references to Eliot ("Who is it spoke of April? Some / insane engineer") and Hart Crane ("build no more / bridges"), who like Pound take history seriously in their poetry, Williams announces, "The past is dead." And near the end of Book Three he concludes, "the roar of the present [. . .] / is, of necessity, my sole concern." His interest is in "Neither the past nor the future," he insists; "I cannot stay here / to spend my life looking into the past: / the future's no answer."[86] And we recall his injunction in *Spring and All* about clarifying and intensifying our present experience, "that eternal moment in which we alone live."

Williams's stance toward history is not, however, merely an anti-historicist know-nothingism. If he rejects the polemical dogmatism of Pound—whom we hear one last time in the poem, claiming that what he is "offering" is simply "history" and calling Roosevelt "an ambulating dunghill"[87]—and his own earlier polemicism in *In the American Grain*, he also writes, "Equally laughable / is to assume to know nothing."[88] Williams knows that the past is an image of the present, and that in its voices and stories we can recognize our common condition.

Paterson is Williams's "image large enough to embody the whole knowable world about me,"[89] and the image includes "the news" of that world's history, in all its problematic forms. However, the most important "news" in *Paterson* is not the spectacular stories of Sam Patch or Mrs. Cumming, nor is it the unspectacular but insidious stories of Alexander Hamilton and the control of American credit. The important "news," what Pound called "news that stays news," is the story of the radiant gist, the story of Beautiful Thing, the story of the unicorn tapestries in the Cloisters, the story of the beckoning descent—it is the news that amid the wreckage of Paterson, the consciousness of contact persists. Nietzsche writes that "only, perhaps, if history suffers transformation into a pure work of art, can it preserve instincts or arouse them." However, he admits that such a poetic history "would thoroughly contradict the analytical and inartistic trend of our time[;] it would even be perceived as falsification,"[90] which is what happens with *In the American Grain*. In my introductory chapter I quoted Walter Benjamin's distinction between news (information) and stories, a distinction that illuminates the greater accomplishment of *Paterson*:

Every morning brings us the news of the globe, and yet we are poor in noteworthy stories. This is because no event any longer comes to us without already being shot through with explanation. In other words, by now almost nothing that happens benefits storytelling; almost everything benefits information. Actually, it is half the art of storytelling to keep a story free from explanation as one reproduces it. [. . .] The most extraordinary things, marvelous things, are related with the greatest accuracy, but the psychological connection of the events is not forced upon the reader. It is left up to him to interpret things the way he understands them, and thus the narrative achieves an amplitude that information lacks.[91]

In *Paterson*, Williams lifts history into a whole that is an image of the knowable world, and in so doing achieves an amplitude that few American poems can match.

Notes

1. Quoted in Mike Weaver, *William Carlos Williams: The American Background* (New York: Cambridge University Press, 1971), 120.

2. Nemerov, *Reflexions*, 52.

3. William Carlos Williams, *Imaginations*, ed. Webster Schott (New York: New Directions, 1970), 89.

4. Williams, *Imaginations*, 90.

5. Williams, *Imaginations*, 88.

6. Williams, *Imaginations*, 41.

7. Nietzsche, *Advantage and Disadvantage*, 17.

8. Van Wyck Brooks, "On Creating a Usable Past," in *Van Wyck Brooks: The Early Years*, ed. Claire Sprague (Boston: Northeastern University Press, 1993), 219, 220.

9. Brooks, "Usable Past," 223.

10. Paul Mariani, *William Carlos Williams: A New World Naked* (New York: Norton, 1981), 283.

11. William Carlos Williams, *In the American Grain* (1925; repr., New York: New Directions, 1956), v.

12. Williams, *Grain*, 120, 121, 206.

13. Williams, *Grain*, 175, 176, 177, 178, 179.

14. John Beck, *Writing the Radical Center: William Carlos Williams, John Dewey, and American Cultural Politics* (Albany: SUNY Press, 2001), 97.

15. James E. B. Breslin, *William Carlos Williams: An American Artist* (Chicago: University of Chicago Press, 1970), 88.

16. Williams, *Grain*, 113.

17. Brian A. Bremen, *William Carlos Williams and the Diagnostics of Culture* (New York: Oxford University Press, 1993), 5, 6, 202.

18. Breslin, *American Artist*, 87, 104.

19. Beck, *Radical Center*, 97.

20. Breslin, *American Artist*, 87.

21. Beck, *Radical Center*, 69, 79–80.

22. Beck, *Radical Center*, 104, 105.

23. in Charles Doyle, ed., *William Carlos Williams: The Critical Heritage* (Boston: Routledge, 1980), 90.

24. Beck, *Radical Center*, 99.

25. Breslin, *American Artist*, 91.

26. William Carlos Williams, *Selected Letters*, ed. John Thirlwall (New York: McDowell, Oblensky, 1957), 185.

27. Brooks, "Usable Past," 225.

28. Breslin, *American Artist*, 91, 89.

29. Williams, *Grain* 197.

30. Williams, *Grain* 130, 136, 137.

31. In Doyle, *Critical Heritage*, 87, 88.

32. Mariani, *New World Naked*, 252.

33. Williams, *Letters*, 187.

34. Breslin, *American Artist*, 88.

35. William Carlos Williams, *The Autobiography* (1951; repr., New York: New Directions, 1967), 178.

36. Bremen, *Diagnostics*, 140, 141.

37. Williams, *Grain*, 208, 211, 209.

38. Bryce Conrad, *Refiguring America: A Study of William Carlos Williams'* In the American Grain (Urbana: University of Illinois Press, 1990), 132, 150.

39. Williams, *Grain*, 80.

40. Williams, *Grain*, 117.

41. Williams, *Grain*, 127, 140.

42. Williams, *Grain*, 188, 190.

43. Williams, *Letters*, 186–87.

44. Williams, *Grain*, 202.

45. William Carlos Williams, *Selected Essays* (1954; repr., New York: New Directions, 1969), 135, 134–35, 136–37.

46. Williams, *Essays*, 138.

47. Williams, *Essays*, 140.

48. Williams, *Essays*, 157.

49. Breslin, *American Artist*, 174.

50. Mariani, *New World Naked*, 465.

51. *Autobiography*, 391.

52. Bernstein, *Tale*, 202.

53. William Carlos Williams, *Paterson*, rev. ed., (New York: New Directions, 1992), 6, repeated on 9, slightly altered on 27: "No ideas but / in the facts."

54. Williams, *Paterson*, 19, 23.

55. Williams, *Paterson*, 9, 34–35, 33.

56. Williams, *Paterson*, 10, 70.

57. Williams, *Paterson* 67; Williams uses the phrase "a great beast" ironically on 46, 54, and 80.

58. Williams, *Paterson*, 73–74.

59. Williams, *Paterson*, 179.

60. Weaver, *Williams*, 214.

61. Williams, *Paterson*, 73, 74, 180.

62. Weaver, *Williams*, 215.

63. Williams, *Paterson*, 12, 13.

64. Williams, *Paterson*, 62, 151.

65. Williams, *Letters*, 259.

66. Williams, *Paterson*, 172.

67. Williams, *Paterson*, 58, 59.

68. Williams, *Paterson*, 10, 11.

69. Williams, *Paterson*, 14, 16, 35.

70. Williams, *Paterson*, 46, 186-87, 197, 202, 194–95.

71. Williams, *Paterson*, 192, 196.

72. Beck, *Radical Center*, 136, 137.

73. Bremen, *Williams*, 11, 162–64.

74. Bernstein, *Tale*, 210.

75. Williams, *Paterson*, 20, 21, 22.

76. Williams, *Paterson*, 23, 24.

77. Williams, *Paterson*, 211–12, 229, 230.

78. Weaver, *Williams*, 149.

79. Williams, *Paterson*, 95–98.

80. Williams, *Paterson*, 99.

81. Williams, *Paterson*, 100–04.

82. Nietzsche, *Advantage*, 60.

83. Nietzsche, *Advantage*, 8.

84. Williams, *Paterson*, 123, twice.

85. Williams, *Paterson*, 130.

86. Williams, *Paterson*, 142, 144–45.

87. Williams, *Paterson*, 216.

88. Williams, *Paterson*, 235.

89. Williams, *Autobiography*, 391.

90. Nietzsche, *Advantage*, 39.

91. Walter Benjamin, *Illuminations*, ed. Hannah Arendt, trans. Harry Zohn (New York: Schocken, 1969), 89.

Chapter 10
Charles Olson's *Maximus*: Looking for Oneself, Looking for the Evidence

I would be an historian as Herodotus was, looking
for oneself for the evidence of
what is said
—"Letter 23," *The Maximus Poems*

At the Vancouver Poetry Conference in 1963, Charles Olson took part in a panel with Robert Creeley, Robert Duncan, Allen Ginsberg, and Philip Whalen where, in response to Creeley's question "what is, 'history'?" Olson read his text "Place; & Names." When he finished, Ginsberg responded, "I don't understand what you're saying,"[1] a remark that speaks for many readers for whom Olson's work seems difficult, obscure, even opaque. Guy Davenport, for example, writes, "His poetry is inarticulate. His lectures achieved depths of incoherence. His long poem *Maximus* was left unfinished, like most of his projects and practically all of his sentences."[2] On the other hand, Charles Altieri calls Olson "the central figure of postmodern poetics,"[3] and his influence on younger poets such as Ed Dorn, Susan Howe, Sharon Doubiago, and even Amy Clampitt, whose poetry seems so very different from Olson's, yet who read Olson carefully and quotes from him in some of her strongest poems, is clear.

Olson's idea of history unfolds first in his prose of the late 1940s and early 1950s, and then more fully in *The Maximus Poems*, begun in the early 1950s and still in process at the time of his death in 1970.[4] In *Call Me Ishmael* (1947), his study of Herman Melville, Olson suggests that Western history has been profoundly marked by two distinct kinds of human will, each of which is dominant in different historical periods: "To Melville it was not the will to be free but the will to overwhelm nature that lies at the bottom of us as individuals and a people."[5] This will is exemplified by two literary characters who mark the beginning and the end of what Olson calls Western humanism, Homer's Ulysses and Melville's Ahab:[6]

Homer was an end of the myth world from which the Mediterranean began. But in Ulysses he projected the archetype of the West to follow . . . Homer's world was locked tight in River Ocean which circled it, in Anaximander's map, like a serpent with tail in mouth. But in the Odyssey Ulysses is already pushing against the limits, seeking a way out. Homer gave his hero the central quality of the men to come: search, the individual responsible to himself.[7]

Ulysses is the archetypal Western hero, the man who seeks to master the world around him, and his odyssey within the Mediterranean marks the first major impulse of the humanist will. Dante's Ulysses, like Columbus, moves from the Mediterranean out into the Atlantic in the second "great shift" of Western man, and the "third and final odyssey was Ahab's." Ahab is the apotheosis of the Western humanist hero, who has moved from the Mediterranean into the Atlantic and then into the Pacific: "The Pacific is the end of the UNKNOWN which Homer's and Dante's Ulysses opened men's eyes to. END of individual responsible only to himself. Ahab is full stop."[8] In the culmination of Ahab's odyssey, Melville depicts "a collapse of a hero through solipsism which brings down a world,"[9] the world of the humanist imagination and its will to overwhelm nature. The survivor is Ishmael, afloat in a coffin, whose escape marks the possibility of a restoration of the mythic world of man's immersion in and full awareness of his environment, and the re-emergence of the will that preceded that of humanism.

This is speculative, intuitive history similar to that found in D. H. Lawrence's foreword to *Fantasia of the Unconscious*, which Olson cites in his *Mayan Letters* to Creeley. Lawrence speculates that a great pagan world must have existed before the melting of the glaciers (the Great Flood that drowns Atlantis and Mu, the lost continent of the Pacific), and that this pagan world had established a "vast science" that was carried all over the globe. The Flood destroyed this civilization, although half-remembered fragments of it persisted among the ancient Greeks, Egyptians, Druids, Etruscans, Chaldeans, and Chinese, especially in the symbolic form of myth and ritual.[10] Olson is strongly attracted to the idea of an antediluvian or prelapsarian civilization of people living in harmony with the natural world and with each other, embodying a disposition or stance toward the world directly opposite that of the humanist will.

What that pre-humanist will may have looked like is the subject of "The Gate and the Center"[11] (1951), in which Olson speculates that the earlier will was evident in Sumeria—the "ONE CENTER" of civilization—around 3378 BC, when "a city was a coherence which, for the first time since the ice, gave man the chance to join knowledge to culture and, with this weapon, shape dignities of economics and value sufficient to make daily life itself a dignity and a sufficiency." This older consciousness was driven by what Olson calls "a will to cohere," and it flourished until "just about 1200 BC," when "something broke . . . a bowl went smash, and . . . as a consequence, this artificial business of the 'East' and the 'West' came into its most false being." Returning to the idea of humanism developed in *Call Me Ishmael*, Olson suggests that the will to cohere was displaced by a conception of "heroism solely in terms of man's capacity to overthrow or dominate external reality." Such heroism is "the inevitable consequence of a contrary will to that of Sumer, a will which overcame the old will approximately 2500 BC and succeeded in making itself boss approximately 1200 BC. It is the long reach of this second will of man which we have known, the dead of which we are witnesses." In other words, we have "known" this "second will" throughout Western history, right down to "the dead" of Auschwitz and Hiroshima, still fresh in Olson's memory. The first will was displaced in the second millennium BC, but Olson believes that things have come full circle: Melville signals the eclipse of the second will, and Olson declares that "now, only, once again, and only a second time, is the FIRST WILL back in business."[12]

Olson's two "wills" are roughly analogous to the two types of consciousness that Williams illustrates in *In the American Grain*, except that Olson extends their reach around the world and into prehistory. It may be tempting to trace Olson's and Williams's thinking back to Yeats's primary and antithetical gyres, but Yeats's gyres wax and wane in predictable cycles, while Olson and Williams suggest that while one "type" or "will" may be more evident in certain historical periods or places, each represents an aspect of the human psyche that is potentially always available. In other words, even during the period of Western humanism's dominance, some individuals continue to manifest that earlier will, as Olson will make clear in the first volume of the *Maximus*.

Call Me Ishmael and "The Gate and the Center" are quintessential Olson: audacious, provocative, excited, wide-ranging texts that approach their topics from unusual angles. Olson reads *Moby-Dick* through the lens of Shakespeare (as a Harvard graduate student, he discovered Melville's heavily annotated copies of Shakespeare), Freud's *Moses and Monotheism*, and the economics of the nineteenth-century whaling industry. His sources for "The Gate and the Center" and other essays and letters from around this time include established scholars like Carl Sauer, the Cambridge classicist Jane Ellen Harrison, Samuel Noah Kramer, Hans Güterbock, and Cyrus Gordon, as well as more controversial figures such as Leo Frobenius, Brooks Adams, Victor Berárd, and L. A. Waddell.[13] Olson is always interested in the marginal or overlooked, and often skeptical of the mainstream position. In his *Mayan Letters* to Robert Creeley, he writes, "the substances of history now useful lie outside, under, right here [i.e., in the Yucatan, where he is living at the time], anywhere but in the direct continuum of society as we have had it (of the State, same, of the Economy, same, of the Politicks."[14] A "useful" approach to history, for Olson, has nothing to do with linear notions of progress or evolution, and it does not imagine history in terms of static abstractions such as "State," "Economy," or "Politicks"; in fact, it does not conceive the past itself in terms of a static "thing," an unchanging "object" that we can know as we know the objects of the natural world. Olson writes to Creeley in 1951 that the central problem facing any poet who wants to contain history in his poems is "getting rid of nomination," i.e., getting rid of the idea of history as a nominative, a noun, a thing that can be "known" by means of generalization and classification. Pound tried to solve this problem in *The Cantos*, Olson suggests, by driving through historical time with "the beak of his ego," replacing the time-line sense of history with what Olson calls "a space-field," the "extensions and comprehensions" of which are bounded simply by Pound's ego. Williams tried to solve it in *Paterson* "by making his substance historical of one city," but in doing so, "Bill completely licks himself, lets time roll him under as Ez does not." So for Olson, *The Cantos* and *Paterson* "are HALVES, that is, I take it (1) that the EGO AS BEAK is bent and busted but (2) whatever it is that we can call its replacement (Bill very much a little of it) HAS, SO FAR, not been able to bring any time so abreast of us that we are in this present air, going straight out, of our selves, into it."[15]

Pound and Williams offer partial solutions to the problem of "nominalized" history, but neither fully grasps the depth of the problem. In his essay "Human Universe" (1951), Olson traces the problem to its root in Socrates, Plato, and Aristotle and their enclosing of all speculation within a "universe of discourse," i.e., their enclosing of serious thought within the confines of logic, classification, and generalization. The Greeks define what it means to think for the next two and a half thousand years in the West—they give us "discursive reason"—but for Olson this mode of thinking, which has become so habitual as to seem almost unavoidable, in fact "intermit[s] our participation in our experience." We filter or interpret our direct phenomenal experience through a medium of classification and generalization because "the rational mind," writes Olson, "hates the familiar, and has to make it ordinary by explaining it, in order not to experience it."[16] Olson quotes Heraclitus on the result: "man is estranged from that with which he is most familiar."[17] In the place of "familiar" experience, Plato erects the *episteme*, an edifice of genuine or "philosophical" knowledge, which Olson calls "one of the most dangerous inventions in the world"[18] because it so thoroughly estranges us from our familiar experience of ourselves and the world.

This estrangement applies to the writing of history as well, and it results in the problem of nominalization:

> What makes most acts—of living and of writing—unsatisfactory, is that the person and/or the writer satisfy themselves that they can only make a form (what they say or do, or a story, a poem, whatever) by selecting from the full content some face of it, or plane, some part. And at just this point, by just this act, they fall back on the dodges of discourse, and immediately, they lose me, I am no longer engaged, this is not what I know is the going-on (and of which going-on I, as well as they, want some illumination, and so, some pleasure). It comes out a demonstration, a separating out, an act of classification, and so, a stopping, and all that I know is, it is not there, it has turned false. For any of us, at any instant, are juxtaposed to any experience, even an overwhelming single one, on several more planes than the arbitrary and discursive which we inherit can declare.[19]

In February 1952, Olson refines this point in an essay titled "History" that he sends to Creeley:

> The law would seem to be: it is impossible to slide out any plane from a sphere

and have anything more than a plane, ever have a sphere from it. Yet this is what all divisions of reality and investigations of same divisions attempt. An event, for example, one of your own or those of some others which, collected together, make history—how can a presentation of the bearing—of the sphere of it—be accomplished so that the presentation shall be as the bearing, as round and as multiple in its planes?[20]

In both of these passages, Olson uses the image of selecting or sliding a "plane" out of a sphere to illustrate the problem: the event itself, in all its manifold planes or facets, is "stopp[ed]" or frozen, and then analyzed or "divi[ded]" into a reductive "form," a static nominative, that purports to be an accurate representation of the event, but in fact presents only one plane or aspect as the whole truth about that event.

But how does one restore the familiar and step outside the universe of discourse? How does one write history without nominalization? These questions animate Olson's *Maximus Poems*, the first of which he drafts in 1950. Conceived of first as "letters" to the citizens of Gloucester from the persona "Maximus," so that many of the poems bear titles such as "Maximus to Gloucester, Letter 15," both the epistolary conceit and the Maximus persona will fade as the sequence continues. By 1953, Olson begins to incorporate material from the history of colonial Massachusetts into the sequence, and as he thinks about how to use that material, how to "do" history, he is lecturing on J. A. K. Thomson's *The Art of the Logos* (1935) at Black Mountain College's Institute on the New Sciences of Man. Thomson explains that the words *muthos* and *logos* were at one time essentially synonyms: each meant something like "what is said." As Olson summarizes Thomson, "Story was once all *logos*, the art of the logos . . . Herodotus calls Aesop a Logopoies, and is himself called by Aristotle . . . 'the *Muthologos*,' . . . [and] the first words of [Herodotus's] book—*oi logoi*—are 'those skilled in the logoi.'"[21] These aren't the very first words, but they're close, and they're usually translated "those who have knowledge of history." Olson's point is that "history" is fundamentally "story," as *muthos* or *logos*. Thomson states that both *logos* and *muthos* could mean "a traditional narrative," irrespective of fictional status, but that Pindar separates the two, linking *muthos* with false stories or myths, and *logos* with true stories. Pindar's assertion that *mythos* is false, while *logos* is true, may be taken as a metonym for that larger project in which the rational displaces the mythological, and the poets are exiled from the ideal Republic.[22] In a similar sense, Plato's *episteme* restricts itself to *logos*, that which is true at all times and in all places, that which is necessarily true as opposed to contingent, that which involves knowledge of the eternal Forms. Outside the *episteme* lies *muthos*, or the kind of knowledge Plato terms *doxa*, usually translated into English as "opinion," but referring more precisely to knowledge of things that change, that come into being and then pass away (*gignomena*), the merely contingent as opposed to the universal and eternal.

History is concerned with things that come into being and then pass away, which would seem to align it with *doxa* and not *episteme*, but isn't it equally concerned to distinguish *logos* from *muthos*, or true stories from false? We might think that Olson would embrace Aristotle's claim in the *Poetics* that poets are closer to philosophers than historians are, because poets deal with "what might be" instead of with "what has been," or in other words with universals rather than particulars—Aristotle might seem to be revoking the poets' expulsion from the Republic that Plato had prescribed. But Olson sees Aristotle's distinction as a false dichotomy: "We inherit an either-or, from the split of science and fiction," but in fact "[b]oth are necessary." In one sense the historian has to imagine the past, or "make it up" (this is the "existential historicism" of Collingwood and Dilthey), but in an equally important sense she or he has to "try to find out. . . . .'*istorin* [the Greek root of the English "history," often translated as "inquiry" or "to inquire into"] appears to mean 'finding out for oneself.'" And he continues, "I cannot begin to indicate what history is if the dimension of fact as the place of the cluster of belief isn't understood to be the heart of it."[23]

In *The Maximus Poems*, Olson writes history as both *muthos* and *logos*. He pays careful attention to the archival record, to primary sources, to the "facts," but he pays equally careful attention to history as "story" in the broadest sense of that term: "stories" are told by historians, diarists, letter writers, fishermen, philosophers, poets, collecters of myths, and many others, and Olson himself is the *muthologos* or storyteller of the *Maximus*. Most readers stress either the *muthos* (mythic) or the *logos* (history or politics) of the *Maximus*, and favor those sections of the poems that emphasize one or the other. Robert von Hallberg, for example, prefers volume one, in which Olson's concerns are chiefly political, while Paul Christensen offers his highest praise for volume two, which treats myth more extensively. In fact, Christensen finds myth, infused with terms from Whitehead's metaphysics, at the core of Olson's vision of history:

> Maximus the persona confronts a city in the twentieth century [Gloucester] which, with only accidental differences, the earlier Maximus [of Tyre] experienced nearly two thousand years before. Rise and dissolution of civilizations occur as permanent forms of events—even though the details that are swept into these forms may greatly vary. The historic and mythic elements are cited to show the presence of the eternal among the scattered objects of the present time. Gloucester is itself rooted in the eternal: it grows out of an earth that has no past or future, only forms of events that recur whenever eternal objects come to reside in them.[24]

History imagined as the recurrence of "permanent forms of events" would seem to be merely a repetition of archetypal patterns that we are fated to re-enact indefinitely. Michael Bernstein takes the opposite position, suggesting that "Olson's ideal historical poem would, in effect, demythologize history itself so that it might again become what is most familiar: the expression of our own activity in the world." He argues that for Olson history is not the reiteration of archetypal forms of events, but rather "a series of choices adopted by living men in particular circumstances," and that Olson shows us that we can either "continue earlier patterns or . . . change our emphasis and create new ones in their place."[25]

Both Christensen and Bernstein are correct, but they are correct in the sense that the six blind men in the Indian folktale are correct about the elephant: each blind man grasps one part of the elephant—the tail, or an ear, or a leg, for instance— and announces "an elephant is like a rope" or like a fan, or like a tree trunk. And each is right, but also wrong.

Good readers like Christensen and Bernstein fall into these partial readings for the same reason that other readers find Olson difficult or obscure: Olson is trying to write and to think outside "the universe of discourse," from a place where *muthos* and *logos* are not mutually exclusive. Describing his associative, metonymic style of thinking, Olson writes, "I do go in circles, in fact believe that only if one does does one finally suck up the vertu in anything."[26] And in "Letter 15" we read, "He sd, 'You go all around the subject.' And I sd, 'I didn't know it was a sub- / ject.' He sd, 'You twist' and I sd, 'I do.'"[27]

So how does this work? Facts, says Olson, are at "the heart" of history, but the historian also has to "make it up." In what follows I will look closely at two *Maximus* poems that illustrate how Olson "does history" in the Maximus sequence. One of the best known of the early *Maximus Poems* is "Letter 23," which Olson drafts in 1953 at Black Mountain College. The poem is about the first English settlement of Cape Ann, Massachusetts, and it begins plainly: "The facts are: / 1st season 1623/4 one ship, the *Fellowship* 35 tons / with Edward Cribbe as master (?—cf. / below 3rd season) / left 14 men Cape Ann." These "facts" mark the first attempt of the Dorchester Company to establish a fishing station at Cape Ann in 1623 (Olson's "1623/4" refers to the Old and New Style calendars in use in the early seventeenth century). The Company had been established by the Reverend John White of Dorchester, England, and a group of merchant "adventurers" who invested in fishing expeditions to the Western Atlantic. The merchants were interested in a return on their investment, but White was a socially active clergyman seeking funds for various charitable activities, and perhaps a potential emigration site for non-Separatist Puritans (the Plymouth colony, settled in 1620, was predominantly Separatist). One hundred nineteen investors bought stock in the Company, which purchased the 35-ton *Fellowship* and sent it to Cape Ann in 1623. The Company held a patent enabling it to establish a settlement there, so the *Fellowship* "left 14 men" to winter at Cape Ann and await the return of the *Fellowship* and another Company boat the next spring, with instructions in the meantime for "John Tilly to oversee the fishing" and "Thomas Gardner the 'planting.'"

That seems clear enough, and Olson is scrupulous enough to let us know that the "fact" that Cribbe was the ship's master is inferred from the fact that he was the ship's master during the third season, or 1625. His "(?—cf. / below 3rd season)" refers to his source, Frances Rose-Troup's little-known *John White, the Patriarch of Dorchester and the Founder of Massachusetts*,[28] which states explicitly that Cribbe was master of the *Fellowship* during the third season, but only indirectly that he was master during the first. But "the facts" may also be placed at the service of very different narratives; the standard histories of colonial New England, such as Samuel Eliot Morison's *Builders of the Bay Colony* or James Truslow Adams's *The Founding of New England*, pay scant attention to Cape Ann. They begin with the Puritan settlements at Plymouth (1620) and Boston (1630), and the struggle between Puritanism and the Church of England forms a central strand in their narratives. In "Letter 23," Olson will point to a very different struggle that he sees as far more significant in the history of New England.

"Letter 23" continues with an account of a fight in 1625 between a group of "Dorchester fishermen" and a group of "Plymouth men" for the control of a fishing stage that the Plymouth men had erected the year before on Cape Ann. Heavily in debt from their trans-Atlantic migration, the Plymouth settlers had secured a patent in 1624 entitling them to erect a wooden stage for drying and salting codfish on Cape Ann, which they expected would turn a considerable profit (in fact their fishing proved unprofitable, and they abandoned it). They intended to use the stage only during the fishing season, and not to establish a permanent settlement in competition with the Dorchester Company's, and the Dorchester Company's patent pre-dated Plymouth's, so Plymouth's was in fact invalid. However, in the spring of 1625, when a group of Dorchester fishermen led by a Captain Hewes arrived on the Massachusetts coast and found the stage unoccupied, they began to use it. When the Plymouth men arrived, they asserted their claim, but Hewes refused to give up the stage, so the Plymouth men called in Miles Standish, their military leader, and threatened to take it back by force. Hewes and the Dorchester men armed themselves and barricaded the stage with hogsheads, and Standish prepared to storm it but was dissuaded by Roger Conant, a clergyman who had recently moved from Plymouth to Cape Ann and had become the settlement's leader. Conant was able to achieve a peaceful arbitration of the dispute, and after economic difficulties led to the Dorchester Company's dissolution in 1626, he led the settlers who wished to remain in New England down the coast to Naumkeag, which would become Salem.[29]

For most historians, the fight for the fishing stage is a very minor footnote in the history of colonial New England; the real history happens in Plymouth and Boston. But for Olson, both the fight itself and historians' dismissal of its significance are extremely important. He writes,

> What we have here—and literally in my own front yard, as I sd to Merk,
> asking him what delving, into 'fishermans ffield' recent historians . . .
> not telling him it was a poem I was interested in, aware I'd scare him
> off, *muthologos* has lost such ground since Pindar.[30]

Fishermans Field is the contemporary name of that part of West Gloucester where the fishing stage had been erected in 1624 (it's called Stage Fort Park today), and it's Olson's "front yard" because his family had rented a summer cottage there throughout his childhood. "Merk" is the Harvard history professor with whom Olson did Ph.D. work in American Civilization, and to whom he writes in the early 1950s from Black Mountain College, asking for guidance on contemporary historians' work on colonial Massachusetts.[31] But he won't tell

Merk that he wants the information for a poem because like most academics, Merk has presumably fallen under the baleful influence of men like Pindar, whom Olson quotes as follows: "Poesy / steals away men's judgment / by her *muthoi.*" Olson takes the Pindar quotation from Thomson's *Art of the Logos,* and he adds that Plato "agree[d] / that *muthos* / is false. *Logos* / isn't—was facts. Thus / Thucydides."[32]

But if fact is so central to history for Olson— after all, the poem begins "The facts are," and in a 1968 interview Olson describes "Letter 23" as "an attempt to be completely careful about the facts of the first use of this harbor, Gloucester Harbor"[33]—then what's wrong with Thucydides? In 1955, Olson reviews the new Penguin paperback translations of Thucydides and Herodotus, and he begins his review with a story:

> It is like that Bulldog Drummond mystery, of leaving the room in your hotel to come back and find that there is no such room, the manager shows you, there is no such number, no door, nothing as you had had it, no recognition of you, no belongings, the registry doesn't show that you ever put up there, you were never here, you know the face, the place, you were here, but all is bland, the smiles are proper, the shaking of the known heads over your bewilderment—only, no help, you don't exist as far as anyone here lets on. And you are thus anonymous, you are without a face, a name, clothes, set down in the midst of the city a no-face. And not even treated badly, simply treated blandly, as they are bland.
>
> It is crazy, where one history has left us. You damn well know Thucydides. It is any day. It is as it has been. It is commodity. But the door has been erased. The shrewdness which ran the house, the curiosity which led you out into the street, the business—you come back and all is changed. They don't want your money. They don't want you!
>
> And the other, Herodotus? It is as though Thucydides wanted to be sure, like the manager of what was just now your hotel, that all your nonsense about having lived here, that this was where your belongings at least were—"where are my things," you shout, "where's my baggage, you bastard"—that all your protestations are just what he says any other history is, not the equal of his eyewitness. That evidence. That you see the door ain't there. It was. But it ain't. You can see for yourself. Listen to the hotel keeper:
>
> I do not think that one will be far wrong in accepting the conclusions I have reached from the evidence which I have put forward. It is better evidence than that of the poets, who exaggerate the importance of their themes, or of the prose chroniclers, who are less interested in telling the truth than in catching the attention of their public, whose authorities cannot be checked, and whose subject matter, owing to the passage of time, is mostly lost in the unreliable streams of mythology.[34]

Thucydides, whom Olson is quoting in that last paragraph, is the objective historian who asserts that if a participant in the event being described should protest that the narrative doesn't reflect *his* experience of that event, then his experience gets dismissed: "It was. But it ain't." Just as Plato's universe of discourse intervenes between the individual and his/her experience, filtering that experience and discarding anything that cannot be articulated in the terms of the universe of discourse and its episteme, so Thucydides reduces the "sphere" of the Peloponnesian War to a "plane," i.e., he demonstrates that the War unfolds as it does as a result of certain universal laws of human nature, and these laws enable him to establish the *logos* operant in all history, of which the War is merely one example. By nominalizing the War, he can reduce the manifold aspects of the sphere to a single, coherent plane in which events fit neatly together in a cause-and-effect nexus rooted in those universal laws. Such a reduction of history is what Olson has in mind when he reviews *The Saga of Billy the Kid* in 1954 and writes, "if you have ever cut behind any American event or any presentation of them, to the primary documents, you will know the diminishment I am here asserting."[35] Herodotus never slides a plane out of a sphere; he never asserts that only one true version of the past exists: his. Instead, he reports whatever information he uncovers from various informants, some of whom, like Olson's hotel guest, may insist that the door once *was* there, although it isn't there now. Some tales may contradict those of other informants, and sometimes Herodotus tells us which he finds more persuasive, but at other times he leaves the decision up to his reader.

If Thucydides is correct, then we *know* history in the same way that we know other objects of the natural world, and once we have his text of *The Peloponnesian War*, we need look no further for the truth about that event. But Olson valorizes another kind of history: "I would be an historian as Herodotus was, looking / for oneself for the evidence of / what is said."[36] To do history in that way requires that one not simply take Morison's or Adams's word for it, that one not imagine the English settling of Massachusetts simply in terms of Separatist and Non-Separatist Puritans, but that one consider as well the ways in which the settling of Gloucester and other sites in New England never fit the pattern found at Plymouth and Boston. So Olson reads less-well-known historians, such as Babson and Rose-Troup, and he scours the archives of Salem's Essex Institute and all of the primary sources he can put his hands on. At the 1963 Vancouver Poetry Conference, he says, "in the first chapter if not the first paragraph of Herodotus . . . he says 'I'm using this as a verb *'istorin*, which means to find out for yourself."[37] Olson takes that definition from Thomson, who writes that *'istorin* "appears to mean 'finding out for oneself,' instead of depending on hearsay. The word had already been used by the philosophers. But while these are looking for the truth, Herodotus is looking for the evidence."[38] In "Letter 2," Olson concludes a set of tales of heroic Gloucester mariners with "Bowditch brought the Eppie Sawyer / spot to her wharf a Christmas morning,"[39] i.e., Nathaniel Bowditch sailed the boat through a terrible northeast snowstorm safely into Gloucester Harbor on Christmas morning, 1803, to the amazement of the ship's owners. But "Letter 15" begins, "It goes to show you. It was not the 'Eppie Sawyer,'" and goes on to correct the name of the ship, the severity of the storm (a "gale" that "had blown itself out by the 23rd"), and the harbor Bowditch entered (Salem, not Gloucester). What "it goes to show you" is the activity of *'istorin*, the act of inquiry, the unending process of finding out for oneself, as distinct from history as blocks of inert, unchanging fact, history as "noun," related by an omniscient narrator. In "Letter 23," after finding out for himself everything that he can about the fight for the fishing stage, Olson concludes his poem:

> What we have in this field in these scraps among these fishermen,
> and the Plymouth men, is more than the fight of one colony with
> another, it is the whole engagement against (1) mercantilism
> (cf. the Westcountry men and Sir Edward Coke against the Crown,
> in Commons, these same years—against Gorges); and (2) against
> nascent capitalism except as it stays the individual adventurer
> and the worker on share—against all sliding statism, ownership
> getting in to, the community as, Chamber of Commerce, or theocracy;
> or City Manager[40]

The fight, in other words, is a metonym within a larger struggle: Coke led the fight in Parliament against the mercantilist thinking that resulted in the granting of monopolistic royal patents such as Sir Ferdinando Gorges's, which granted him control of all North American territory between the 40th and 48th parallels, i.e., roughly between Newfoundland and New Jersey. "Westcountry men" were from places like John White's Dorchester, or from the ports of Weymouth or Bristol, where the tradition of "individual adventurers" investing in the voyages of particular fishing boats, and "the worker[s]" of each boat receiving a "share" of its profits, developed, and if Gorges's patent had been upheld, it would have shut them out from fishing. Olson develops an idea of "community" or "polis" in the early *Maximus Poems* that depends heavily on people's connection with their environment; the real community is not embodied in groups like the Chamber of Commerce, is not led by a "City Manager," and is not measured by "ownership." A genuine polis is not to be confused with the institutions of a state.

Olson's didacticism can tempt even good readers into narrow interpretations. Paul Christensen, for example, is persuasive when he reads "Letter 23" as "pivotal" and writes, "The Dorchestermen who came to fish are emblematic of the struggle and defeat of others who wished to remain free and independent in the new colony." But he misinterprets the stage fight when he claims that the Plymouth settlers, "instead of welcoming or accommodating these new citizens into their community . . . routed the fishermen by military means." As noted above, Conant mediated the conflict, the two groups shared the stage that year, and Plymouth abandoned its Cape Ann operation soon afterwards. He is on even shakier ground when he asserts that the outcome of the stage fight signals "the inexorable transformation of Gloucester fishermen from self-employed independent seafarers to corporate drudges."[41] Olson deplores the rise of profit-obsessed corporate capitalism and its indifference to local conditions, but "the whole engagement" that he describes at the end of the poem has not been won by the bad guys; it is still being fought out. "Letter 2," for example, celebrates contemporary Gloucester fishermen who are as independent and as far from "corporate drudges" as one can imagine. Nothing about Gloucester's history has been "inexorable."

As Olson studies the history of colonial New England he is especially interested in what men saw when they first came to New England: what kind of life did they imagine it would be possible to build there? What kind of relationship with the land and the sea did they imagine establishing? What kind of community did they imagine building? In "Letter 6," he writes, "polis is / eyes," i.e., belonging to a place or a community is a function of "attention" and "care," and he notes that in contemporary Gloucester, "so few / have the polis / in their eye." But he concludes, "So few need to, / to make the many / share (to have it, / too)," and finally: "There are no hierarchies, no infinite, no such many as mass, there are only / eyes in all heads, / to be looked out of."[42]

Much of the colonial history in the first *Maximus* volume concerns individuals who looked at New England with care and attention, such as John Smith, whom Olson praises for his excellent mapmaking, or Christopher Levett, who establishes a settlement in what is now Maine at around the time of the Dorchester Company's Cape Ann settlement. Such people, along with leaders like John White and Roger Conant, "have the polis / in their eye," but they are opposed by others who see New England only as a site on which to impose their dreams of rigid, intolerant "theocracy," like the Plymouth colonists, or by those who see only raw materials to be exploited for profit, men like the slave traders John and Richard Hawkins of "Letter 14." In that poem, Olson imagines colonial America in terms of a "moral struggle" between men like the Basque fishermen who were among the first to fish "the Banks," and men like the Hawkinses, whose family crest depicts an African in chains. In "Letter 16," Olson cites Nathaniel Bowditch, a New England merchant and insurance executive, as

> representative of "that movement of NE monies
> away from primary production [such as fishing] & trade
> to the several cankers of profit-making
> which have, like Agyasta [sic], made America great.[43]

George Butterick explains that in Hindu myth, Agastya attempts to defeat a group of sea-dwelling demons by swallowing the entire ocean. He gets rid of the demons, but without the sea, all life is threatened, and order is restored only by the descent from heaven of the sacred river Ganges.[44] Small-scale profit-making is of course one of the motives behind "primary production & trade" activities such as the Dorchester Company's, but when it takes the extreme forms of mercantilism or finance capitalism, and the state's prosperity and security are used to justify war, slavery, or colonialism, then like Agastya, we destroy what sustains us, and polis is displaced by what Olson calls "pejorocracy,"[45] the rule of the worst.

Olson's approach to history in *The Maximus Poems* will grow more complicated in the second and third volumes, as he extends his inquiry to the ancient history of the Eastern Mediterranean and begins to draw more heavily on the myths of that region. He reads Alfred North Whitehead's *Process and Reality* in the spring of 1955, again in 1956, and yet again in 1957, and Whitehead, whom Olson calls "my great master and the companion of my poems,"[46] deepens Olson's conception of history. This may seem odd, for Whitehead is a great systematizer, a cosmologist whose notion of "eternal events" seems to many readers very close to Plato's ideal "forms," and we know what Olson thought of Plato. So why does Olson find Whitehead so useful?

Olson's differentiation of Whitehead from Plato is clarified in "A Later Note on Letter #15," where Olson contrasts Whitehead with Descartes, whom Olson sees in direct descent from Socrates and Plato. "Descartes was the value," writes Olson, "until Whitehead, who cleared out the gunk / by getting the universe in."[47] Like Platonism, Cartesianism gunks up our experience because it imagines the world as static, as composed of "substances" or "nouns" that can do things to what we might call "predicates." In other words, discrete "things" perform discrete "actions," and these discrete things and actions can be objectively known, as in science or Thucydidean history. The Cartesian *cogito*, or what Olson calls "man alone," isolated from the "universe," establishes as its ideal "the objective (example, Thucidides [sic], or / the latest finest tape-recorder, or any form of record on the spot / —live television or what," all of which is simply "a lie,"[48] or another way of sliding a plane out of a sphere and declaring that knowing the plane is equivalent to knowing the sphere. Olson finds Whitehead so important to his understanding of history because for Whitehead the fundamental elements of reality are not discrete "things" that perform "actions," but organic "events" that unfold over time.

In *Science and the Modern World* Whitehead writes, "The Ionian philosophers asked, What is nature made of? The answer is couched in terms of stuff, or matter . . . which has the property of *simple location* in space and time." This manner of thinking persisted into the Enlightenment: "The answer . . . which the seventeenth century gave to the ancient question of the Ionian thinkers, 'What is the world made of?' was that the world is a succession of instantaneous configurations of matter . . . this is the famous mechanistic theory of nature, which has reigned supreme ever since the seventeenth century."[49] Whitehead dismisses the concept of "simple location" and the mechanistic theory of nature as simply unworkable in twentieth-century physics, and he replaces the notion of a thing existing at a particular *here* and enduring through a succession of *now*-points with his concept of the *event*. An *event* is the organic unification of several elements into a discernible pattern or structure that unfolds over time. These elements may include particular details unique to that event, as well as what Whitehead calls "eternal objects," which are abstract qualities common to many different events. Eternal objects remind many readers of Platonic forms, but Whitehead posits no transcendent realm of eternal objects, nor does he suggest that eternal objects are somehow more "real" than the particular events with which they intersect. An event occurs both synchronically and diachronically, so the past retains a "presence" in the unfolding of any event, and any event is best understood in terms of the process of its temporal unfolding. In addition, events may overlap with one another, and smaller events may nest within larger events, so that the entire world may be understood as a swirling field of unfolding events.

Understood in terms of Whiteheadian events, history looks very different. The "edges" of a historical event may seem fluid and porous, and "eternal objects" may function archetypally to connect events that seem quite remote in terms of chronology or geography. For example, as *The Maximus Poems* continue, the Puritan Governor of the Massachusetts Bay colony, John Winthrop, will be labeled a Mycenaean *wanax*, or high king, and credited with "Vedic / senses."[50] Episodes from history will be presented alongside stories from Native American, Norse, Greek, Egyptian, and Hittite myth, functioning as parts of a larger whole. Colonial New England history will remain a central theme, but aspects of that history will be juxtaposed with such topics as Pytheas the Navigator, ancient Phoenician history, and the Parian Chronicle.

As a result of his immersion in Whitehead, Olson offers a seminar at Black Mountain College in 1956 called "The Special View of History,"[51] in which he leavens his reading of Whitehead with John Keats's idea of negative capability: Olson connects traditional, Thucydidean history with Keats's description of the "man of power," who is characterized by his "Irritable reaching after fact and reason," his inability to be comfortable not knowing; this is the mindset, writes Olson, that creates logic in Classical Greece and the experimental method in Enlightenment Europe.[52] Keats contrasts the Man of Power with the Man of Achievement, who is "capable of being in uncertainties, Mysteries, doubts, without any irritable reaching after fact and reason." For Olson the Man of Power is Cartesian or Platonic; the Man of Achievement is Whiteheadian or Keatsian. Heraclitus's fragment "Man is estranged from that with which he is most familiar" summarizes the "will to disperse" and to master nature that characterizes Humanism, but Keats is one of the signs that the older "will to cohere" is re-emerging. "Negative Capability is the readmission of the familiar," writes Olson, and "Negative capability is Keats' way of talking about staying in process, instead of trying to know by stopping."[53] "Stopping" would mean seeing the world in terms of static things and mechanistic cause-and-effect; it is Thucydides's history.

One of the clearest early examples of Whitehead's impact on Olson's thinking about history is "Letter, May 2, 1959," one of the last poems in the first volume of *Maximus*. Like "Letter 23," this poem begins with facts, but here the "facts" are Olson's pacing off seventeenth-century property lines: "125 paces Grove Street / fr E end of Oak Grove cemetery / to major turn NW of / road," and so on. At the bottom of the poem's first page, fragments such as "old stonewall" or "—between Bruen and Eveleth?" are typed on a slant, so that the poem itself looks almost like a typographical map. The poem ends with a kind of map as well, or rather a chart, of the depths of the shipping channel in Gloucester Harbor, from Eastern Point to Rocky Neck, which Olson indicates by typing numbers (for depths) and names such as "Ten Pound Island" or "Rocky Neck" at different points on the page.

So the poem is framed by geography, by maps and the kinds of "facts" that such things yield, but comparing seventeenth-century descriptions of property lines with the contemporary topography of Gloucester, or Samuel de Champlain's 1606 map of Gloucester Harbor with the contemporary harbor, emphasizes the shifting, "processual" nature of reality. Has Olson found the "old stonewall" that once stood "between" Bruen's and Eveleth's property? He cannot be certain, and in this poem the reader stands on difficult terrain. The seven pages framed by the "maps" that open and close the poem present a kaleidoscopic mish-mash of history and current events that can make Olson's description of the poem as "a big congested . . . dirty poem, dirty in the sense of just messing everything up,"[54] seem quite accurate. But the poem begins to seem less congested, less of a dirty mess, if we think of it as representing the "event" that occurs on May 2, 1959, when Charles Olson is tramping around what used to be the Meeting House Hill section of Gloucester, trying to "read" old property deeds against the topography of present-day Gloucester, and as he does so, thinking about seventeenth-century Gloucester. As he does this, Olson's thinking unfolds in a metonymic web ranging from the public works project that brought the Route 128 highway over the Annisquam River and connected Gloucester to the mainland in 1950, to the great Second Millennium BC battle between Ramses II of Egypt and the Hittites on the Orontes River.

Sometimes the metonymic chains of the web are easy to follow, as when Olson thinks about the early settlers carrying marsh grass in flatboats they called "gundalows," after Venetian "gondolas," and the reference to Venice reminds him of Stefansson's "proposition" in *The Northward Course of Empire* (1922) that, historically, centers of "commerce" moved in a northwestern direction from ancient Sumeria to Phoenicia, to the Aegean, to Rome, to Venice, to London, and to New York. Olson points out that the line leads to "the dead end" of the Arctic "ice," and implies that such linear thinking about history is always a dead end.

Olson draws a more audacious metonymic link when he uses the orations delivered at the 1892 celebration of Gloucester's 1642 incorporation by the Reverend Daniel Wilson, who told his audience, "we must reckon / with the great sea the influences / of it," and compared Gloucester to Zebulon, who in Genesis 49:13 "dwell[s] at the haven of the sea; and he shall be for a haven of ships," and the Reverend John Trask, from whom Olson borrows the phrase "these times, of combustion." He then leaps to a much earlier time of combustion, the second millennium BC in the eastern Mediterranean, when a much earlier group of "sea people," the so-called "Peoples of the Sea," went to war with the Egyptian pharaoh Ramses II and his son Meneptha. These migrating, Late Bronze Age "sea peoples" are juxtaposed against the Englishmen who migrated to Gloucester in the 1600s, and the question of knowing history is focused as Olson asks about one of those Englishmen, "what was Bruen doing," repeating his earlier question, "What did Bruen want? He had already shifted from Piscataqua / to Plymouth, then to Gloucester and now to New London and / would go from New London to found Newark, N.J." This is Obadiah Bruen, Gloucester's first town clerk, who left Gloucester for New London, Connecticut, in 1650. Knowing what Bruen wanted is as difficult to establish as the identity of the Sea Peoples, which has long been a source of controversy and speculation.[55] Don Byrd, one of Olson's most careful readers, uncharacteristically slips when he writes that Olson "realizes that the evidence demonstrates clearly that Bruen was one of those restless, unsettled souls who are responsible for the destruction which the city has suffered."[56] In fact, the poem suggests quite the opposite. After asking what Bruen wanted, Olson writes, "I am not here to / have to do with Englishmen," which sounds as if Olson is speculating on Bruen's motivation. If so, then he is aligning Bruen with those "maverick" settlers of early New England whom he mentions in his letter to Merk, such as Samuel Maverick and William Blackstone, who were living around Massachusetts Bay before Winthrop and the Puritans arrived. They were uncomfortable with what Olson called the Puritan "theocracy," and they eventually moved on, like Bruen. In terms of "polis," or community, they were looking for something different. For any historian, it must be tempting to claim to know who the Sea Peoples were, or what Bruen wanted, but Olson, like Herodotus, resists that temptation.

Another metonym links the causeway that Alexander the Great built to gain access to and conquer the Phoenician seaport of Tyre (home of Maximus of Tyre, the second century Greek philosopher who is one of the sources of Olson's persona, Maximus), to the bridge that brought the Route 128 highway over the Annisquam River and into Gloucester in 1950. When he reads this poem at Goddard College, Olson calls this a poem "about a bridge over a river, a very huge highway bridge," and then links the bridge to Alexander's conquest of Tyre: "the only thing in the world that confronted the universalization that Alexander proposed, which I think is the great complement to the present, was Tyre. It so refused to be knocked down by this Macedonian athlete that it was the sole place in the world which bucked him. And it took Alexander, I can always be corrected, but was it three or four years to reduce Tyre?"[57] Like Tyre, Gloucester is cut off from the mainland and retains a local culture that to some extent resists the larger, universalizing culture. And like Tyre, Gloucester cannot resist the advance of that universalizing culture. As Olson paces off old property lines, he recalls a bulldozer that took "the top off / Meeting House Hill" in preparation for the extension of Route 128 and the arrival of more of "the rubbish / of white man."

Sherman Paul reads this as a poem of "complaint" and "despair,"[58] but while the poem registers those emotions, it also recognizes that Alexander's empire was short-lived, and that the edges of historical events are never final. Olson remembers that in geological time, Meeting House Hill was once a mere sand dune, and that ice once rolled over "this stuck-out / 10 miles Europe-pointing / cape." It is true that "The Diesels / shake the sky" as they rumble over the new bridge, but Olson also recognizes that the past persists in the present: "I take my air / where Eveleth [a seventeenth-century settler] walked," and "From / then to now nothing / new, in the meaning / that that wall walked / today, happened." Sherman Paul takes the phrase "nothing /new" simply as the answer to the question "what did Bruen want?" i.e., Bruen "wanted what everyone since has wanted . . . despoilers all, come to possess and exploit."[59] This is accurate to a point, for many Europeans came to North America "to possess and exploit" whatever they could. On the other hand such a claim is simplistic and reductive, for even as Olson gives vent to his anger over contemporary Gloucester—"the present / is worse give nothing now your credence / start all over . . ."—he also knows that Gloucester is a place "where polis / still thrives."[60]

Near the end of the poem, Olson refers in three cyptic, highly condensed lines to the Orontes River, which flows into the Mediterranean not far from Tyre, and to Typhon, the chthonic monster whom Zeus finally defeats and confines in Tartarus. The Orontes is not far from Mount Casius, which according to some sources was the site of the Zeus/Typhon battle, and both the river and Typhon will recur in later *Maximus* poems, but in this poem they echo the earlier references to the second millennium Battle of Kadesh, and to the Sea Peoples' attacks on Egypt and other nations. As I read the poem, these fragmentary allusions are simply Olson's means of recording his lively stream of consciousness on one particular day, May 2, 1959, spent trying to trace seventeenth-century property lines in what was once the Meeting House Hill section of Gloucester. Other readers, however, have found in these lines, and in Olson's references to geography and geology, evidence of what Sherman Paul calls "the exhaustion of historiographical impulse."[61] Von Hallberg agrees: "The history of the recent European migration to America leads forward only to war and destruction of the land. . . . Maximus dismisses European history as the old war business and turns toward geography, which he finds more interesting." In this poem, "History is a dead-end."[62]

Von Hallberg is quoting from the end of the poem, when Olson is discussing the map of Gloucester Harbor drawn by Samuel de Champlain on his 1606 visit. On that visit, Champlain was attacked by Indians, "in ambush at the head of Rocky Neck, old European business as seven or / eight arquebusiers," writes Olson, and then "the depths of the channel more interesting," and he produces a rough version of Champlain's chart of the harbor. But Olson does not mean that he now finds geography "more interesting" than history; indeed, if this poem is about anything, it is about the inextricable entanglement of geography and history. Far from signaling Olson's "exhaustion" with or "dismiss[ing]" of history, "Letter, May 2, 1959" signals an expansion of Olson's conception of history. The didactic tone ("What we have here . . .") of "Letter, 23," in which Olson looks for himself at a narrow range of historical evidence, and articulates a thesis that challenges the Puritan-driven narratives of other prominent historians, has given way to the enacting of a Whiteheadian event. Over the course of this seven-page poem, we follow Olson's imagination as it *apprehends*, in Whitehead's sense, a variety of metonymically linked aspects of the destruction of the old Meeting House Hill section of Gloucester, where at the poem's beginning Olson is trying to pace out seventeenth-century property lines. That destruction, which was necessary for the construction of the Route 128 bridge, is one aspect of a palimpsest-like event-in-process, other aspects of which include the retreat of the glaciers that formed Cape Ann's topography, the Algonquin "wigwams at Harbor Cove" depicted on Champlain's 1606 map, and the complete absence of Native Americans when the Dorchester Company arrived in 1623 (due most likely to smallpox), the failure of the Dorchester Company settlement in 1626, the resettlement of Gloucester in the 1630s and its incorporation in 1642, and its persistence as a community of "sea people," living at the edge of a much larger republic, and echoing various other "sea peoples" on other seacoasts who also struggled against a variety of "universalizing" forces. Clearly the building of the bridge is an unhappy occurrence for Olson, signaling the continuing pernicious, Agastya-like activity of what Keats called "Men / of Power."[63] However, the bridge does not mark the end of this historical event, for as we have seen, the edges of a Whiteheadian "event" always resist simple definition, in the root sense of *de finire*, to set limits or boundaries around something. In this poem, Olson gives rein to his frustration and anger, but he gives equal rein to the tremendous intellectual and aesthetic excitement that he finds in the openness of this kind of history.

This kind of history cannot tell him, finally, what Bruen wanted, or what he was doing at Piscataqua, nor can it show him how to stop the construction of future bridges, as Thucydides suggested that his *History* might be used as a template to prevent the kinds of errors that marked the Peloponnesian War. For Olson history is rooted in Herodotus's inquiries, or questions, and he asks them throughout this poem and throughout the *Maximus* sequence. Unlike Pound, who has far more answers than questions, or Williams, who worries that historical questions will divorce us from contact with the present, Olson finds that such questions deepen and enrich his contact with the present. To experience, with both depth and intensity, the world around him and the community in which he lives, to know that world and that community with familiarity, requires the dimension of history. Following Whitehead's lead, he can imagine Gloucester as an event-in-process, intersected at multiple points by other events, so that finally Gloucester is not only another late-industrial wreck of a city in inexorable decline, but a place where it is possible to "start all over." When Olson finally completed the financial and legal business involved in closing Black Mountain College in 1957 (he was its final Rector), he moved back to Gloucester and wrote to his friend, the poet Vincent Ferrini, describing conversations with fishermen who tell him how tough things are, or others who worry that the future will hold only "[t]ourists" and that the harbor will become "one big marina—for . . . the outboard motor cowboys." Such fears are real, but they are only one "plane" or aspect of the "sphere" that is Gloucester, and Olson ends his letter by telling Ferrini of his desire "to go to England very soon to get the information to show how this city was in the mind of John White even without his knowing what she was, as a place to go fishing from. She is still a place to go fishing from. She is still le beauport [Champlain's name for Gloucester Harbor]. She is a form of mind."[64] To see this side of Gloucester requires only that one look, for oneself, that one engage in the activity of history.

Notes

1. Charles Olson, "On History," in Ralph Maud, ed., *Muthologos: Lectures and Interviews*, revised second ed. (Vancouver: Talonbooks, 2010), 46–47.
2. Guy Davenport, "In Gloom on Watch-House Point," *Parnassus* 4, no. 2 (1976): 251–52.
3. Charles Altieri, *Enlarging the Temple* (Lewisburg: Bucknell University Press, 1979), 102.
4. *The Maximus Poems*, numbering more than three hundred poems, appeared in *The Maximus Poems / 1–10* (Jargon, 1953), *The Maximus Poems / 11–22* (Jargon, 1956), *The Maximus Poems* (Jargon/Corinth, 1960—this volume includes the two earlier volumes, as well as additional poems, and is commonly referred to as "volume one"), *Maximus Poems IV, V, VI* (Cape Goliard/Grossman, 1968—commonly referred to as "volume two"), and *The Maximus Poems: Volume Three* (edited by Charles Boer and George Butterick, and posthumously published by Grossman, 1975). In 1983, the three volumes were collected into a single volume, edited by George Butterick with a slightly revised and expanded volume three, and published by the University of California Press. All quotations are from the California edition. Butterick's magisterial *A Guide to The Maximus Poems of Charles Olson* (University of California Press, 1978) is indispensable to any informed reading of the poems.
5. Olson, *Call Me Ishmael*, 1947, reprinted in *Charles Olson: Collected Prose*, ed. Donald Allen and Benjamin Friedlander (Berkeley: University of California Press, 1997), 17.
6. In a letter to Robert Creeley, Olson writes, "humanism is (homer) coming in, and (melville) going out." Charles Olson, *Selected Writings*, ed. Robert Creeley (New York: New Directions, 1966), 112.
7. Olson, *Ishmael*, 104.
8. Olson, *Ishmael*, 105.
9. Olson, *Ishmael*, 66.
10. D. H. Lawrence, *Fantasia of the Unconscious*. 1922 (New York: Viking, 1960), 54–55.
11. The essay opens in a typically excited rush of questions: "what is the story of man, the FACTS, where did he come from, when did he invent a city, what did a plateau have to do with it, or a river valley? What foods were necessary (I am thinking here of Steffanson on diets, Carl Sauer on starch crops and how, where they could be domesticated)? Were the people on the edge of the retreating ice, marauders, or were they (as Sauer so beautifully argues) fisher-folk?" (Olson, *Prose*, 168).
12. Olson, *Prose*, 170, 171
13. Carl Sauer was for many years chair of the Geography Department at the University of California at Berkeley. Samuel Noah Kramer was then the world's leading authority on Sumerian history. Hans Güterbock was an expert on Hittite civilization, and Cyrus Gordon was a specialist on ancient Near Eastern languages. Vilhjálmur Stefánsson was an Arctic explorer who believed that the Chinese reached North America in the fifth century. Leo Frobenius, well known for his idea of *paideuma*, believed he had discovered proof that Atlantis existed. Victor Berárd believed that the characters and events of the *Odyssey* were based on actual place-names in the Mediterranean. L. A. Waddell, author of *The Makers of Civilization in Race and History* and Olson's source for most of the dates in "The Gate and the Center," based much of his speculative ancient history on

bizarre etymologies. He believed that King Brutus of Troy founded London, and that the Old Icelandic *Poetic Edda* was actually an ancient British (not Celtic) text recounting the story of King Thor, or Arthur, who ruled in the fourth millennium BC. Olson concedes that Waddell is "too crazy," but he calls him "one of the most exciting men I have ever read" (*Charles Olson and Frances Boldereff: A Modern Correspondence*, ed. Ralph Maud and Sharon Thesen (Hanover, NH: University Press of New England, 1999), 432, 433).

14. Olson, *Selected Writings*, 84.

15. Olson, *Selected Writings*, 81–83.

16. Charles Olson, *The Special View of History*, ed. Ann Charters (Berkeley: Oyez, 1970), 31.

17. Olson, *Special View*, 14.

18. Olson, "Under the Mushroom," in *Muthologos*, 85.

19. Olson, "Human Universe," in *Collected Prose*, 157.

20. Charles Olson and Robert Creeley, *The Complete Correspondence*, vol. 9, ed. Richard Blevins (Santa Rosa, CA: Black Sparrow, 1990), 102.

21. Olson, *Special View*, 20. Herodotus calls Aesop a Logopoies at Book II, line 134, of his *Histories*, and Aristotle calls Herodotus "the Muthologos" or storyteller in *de generatione animalium*, Book 3, Part 5.

22. At around this time, thinkers such as Hecataeus of Miletus and Xenophanes of Colophon were attacking Homer, Hesiod, and Greek myth in general as irrational, while Protagoras of Abdera was proclaiming man the measure of all things—humanism in a nutshell.

23. Olson, *Special View*, 20, 21.

24. Paul Christensen, *Charles Olson: Call Him Ishmael* (Austin: University of Texas Press, 1979), 143.

25. Michael Bernstein, *The Tale of the Tribe*, 135, 235.

26. Olson, *Special View*, 35.

27. Olson, *Maximus*, 72.

28. Frances Rose-Troup, who figures in both of the poems that I focus on in this chapter, is a model historian for Olson, not only because of her careful attention to little-known archival records, but because her thesis on the earliest English settlements in Massachusetts so challenges the conventional wisdom.

29. In an earlier poem, "Maximus to Gloucester, Letter 11," Olson suggests that if the fight had continued, the Dorchester men would have prevailed: "And the Short Chimney [Miles Standish] / wld have died right there, been plugged by a fisherman if / Conant had not ordered Capt Hewes to lower his gun, to listen / to what the little man from Plymouth had to squawk about" (*Maximus*, 52). By the time he comes to write "History is the Memory of Time," however, he has done more research and concludes, "Hewes had reason / to give way: 3 Plymouth vessels / on station" (*Maximus*, 116–17), including the 300-ton *White Angel* and the 100-ton *Charity*. Hewes was heavily outmanned and outgunned.

30. Olson, *Maximus*, 104.

31. For Olson's letter to Merk, see his *Selected Letters*, ed. Ralph Maud (Berkeley: University of California Press, 2000), 202–6.

32. Olson, *Maximus*, 104.

33. Olson, *Muthologos*, 296.

34. "It Was. But It Ain't." 1955; repr. in *Collected Prose*, 342-43.

35. Olson, *Collected Prose*, 311.

36. Olson, *Maximus*, 104–5.

37. "On History," in *Muthologos*, 47.

38. J. A. K. Thomson, *The Art of the Logos* (London: Allen & Unwin, 1935), 237.

39. Olson, *Maximus*, 11.

40. Olson, *Maximus*, 105.

41. Christensen, *Olson*, 131.

42. Olson, *Maximus*, 30, 32, 33.

43. Olson, *Maximus*, 76.

44. Butterick, *Guide*, 109–10.

45. Olson, *Maximus*, 75.

46. Olson, *Muthologos*, 216.

47. Olson, *Maximus*, 249.

48. Olson, *Maximus* 249.

49. Alfred North Whitehead, *Science and the Modern World* (1926; repr., New York: Cambridge University Press, 2011), 61–62.

50. Olson, *Maximus*, 305, 408.

51. Olson offers a similar seminar at the Poetry Center in San Francisco in 1957. Ann Charters edited Olson's notes and typescripts for the Black Mountain seminar in *The Special View of History* (Berkeley: Oyez, 1970).

52. Olson, *Special View*, 41.

53. Olson, *Special View*, 42.

54. "At Goddard College, April 1962," in *Muthologos*, 17.

55. Robert Von Hallberg, in *Charles Olson: The Scholar's Art* (Cambridge: Harvard University Press, 1978) mistakenly identifies the "Peoples of the Sea" as Hittites (108), but that is almost certainly untrue. In a 1962 essay, Olson writes that "the so-called 'Sea Peoples' (the Philistines of the Bible) sweep over the Eastern Mediterranean between 1225 & 1175, devastating the Hittite Empire and destroying Tyre and Phoenician power" (*Collected Prose*, 198).

56. Don Byrd, *Charles Olson's Maximus* (Urbana: University of Illinois Press, 1980), 107.

57. *Muthologos* 17. "I can always be corrected" recalls the opening of "Letter 15," where Olson corrects the story that he tells in "Letter 2" about a Gloucester sea captain bringing his ship safely home to port amid a great storm: "It goes to show you. It was not the 'Eppie Sawyer'. It was the ship 'Putnam'. It wasn't Christmas morning, it was Christmas night, after dark" (*Maximus*, 71), and so on.

58. Sherman Paul, *Olson's Push: Origin, Black Mountain, and Recent American Poetry* (Baton Rouge: Louisiana State University Press, 1978), 185, 186.

59. Paul, *Olson's Push*, 173.

60. Olson, *Maximus*, 26. Olson maintained a lover's quarrel with Gloucester for his entire adult life. See, for example, his letters to *The Gloucester Daily Times*, collected in *Charles Olson: Maximus to Gloucester*, ed. Peter Anastas (Gloucester: Ten Pound Island Book Co., 1992).

61. Paul, *Olson's Push*, 185.

62. Von Hallberg, *Olson*, 110, 131.

63. Olson, *Maximus*, 533. This is from Olson's long poem "The usefulness," from volume three of the *Maximus*, in which he once again contrasts Whitehead with Descartes and Plato, and considers Perry Miller's argument in *Orthodoxy in Massachusetts* on the circumstances surrounding the founding of Boston.

64. Olson, *Selected Letters*, 251, 252.

Bibliography

Adams, Hazard, ed. *Critical Theory Since Plato*. New York: Harcourt Brace, 1971.

Adams, Henry. *The Education of Henry Adams*. Boston: Houghton Mifflin, 1973.

————. "The Tendency of History." In *Annual Report of the American Historical Association for the Year 1894*, 17–24. Washington DC: Government Printing Office, 1895.

Adorno, Theodor. "Cultural Criticism and Society." In *Prisms*. Translated by Weber, Samuel, and Shierry Weber. 17–34. Cambridge: The MIT Press, 1981.

Altieri, Charles. *Enlarging the Temple*. Lewisburg: Bucknell University Press, 1979.

Appleby, Joyce, Lynn Hunt, and Margaret Jacob. *Telling the Truth about History*. New York: Norton, 1994.

Aristotle. "De Poetica (Poetics)." In *Introduction to Aristotle*. Translated by Bywater, Ingram, edited by McKeon, Richard. 624–67. New York: Random House, Modern Library, 1947.

Arvin, Newton. "A Minor Epic." *New York Herald Tribune Books*, August 12, 1928, 1–2.

Asher, Kenneth. *T. S. Eliot and Ideology*. New York: Cambridge University Press, 1995.

Barthes, Roland. "The Discourse of History." *Comparative Criticism* 3, (1981): 7–20.

Beard, Charles. "That Noble Dream." *American Historical Review* 41, (1935): 74–87.

Beck, John. *Writing the Radical Center: William Carlos Williams, John Dewey, and American Cultural Politics*. Albany: SUNY Press, 2001.

Becker, Carl. "Detachment and the Writing of History." *Atlantic Monthly*, October 1910, 526–28

Bedient, Calvin. *He Do the Police in Different Voices: The Waste Land and Its Protagonist*. Chicago: University of Chicago Press, 1986.

————. "Postlyrically Yours." *The Threepenny Review*, Summer 1994, 18–20.

Benét, Stephen Vincent. "High Achievement." *The Saturday Review of Literature*, April 2, 1932, 629–30.

————. *John Brown's Body*. Chicago: Ivan R. Dee, 1990.

Benjamin, Walter. "The Storyteller." In *Illuminations*. Translated by Zohn, Harry, edited by Arendt, Hannah, 83–110. New York: Schocken, 1969.

Bernstein, Michael. *The Tale of the Tribe: Ezra Pound and the Modern Verse Epic*. Princeton: Princeton University Press, 1980.

Blackmur, R. P. "Mr. MacLeish's Predicament." *The American Mercury*, April 1934, 507–8.

Blasing, Mutlu Konuk. "Designs on History: Ezra Pound, the Puritans, and Self-Fulfilling Prophecies." In *The Calvinist Roots of the Modern Era*, edited by Barnstone, Aliki,

Michael Tomasek Manson and Carol J. Singley, 3–19. Hanover, NH: University Press of New England, 1997.

Bloom, Harold, ed. *Robert Penn Warren*. New York: Chelsea House, 1986.

Breisach, Ernst. *On the Future of History: The Postmodernist Challenge and Its Aftermath*. Chicago: University of Chicago Press, 2003.

Bremen, Brian A. *William Carlos Williams and the Diagnostics of Culture*. New York: Oxford University Press, 1993.

Bremner, Robert, ed. *Essays on History and Literature*. Columbus: Ohio State University Press, 1966.

Breslin, James E. B. *William Carlos Williams: An American Artist*. Chicago: University of Chicago Press, 1970.

Brooks, Cleanth. *Modern Poetry and the Tradition*. Chapel Hill: University of North Carolina Press, 1939.

Brooks, Van Wyck. "On Creating a Usable Past." In *Van Wyck Brooks: The Early Years*, edited by Sprague, Claire, 219–28. Boston: Northeastern University Press, 1993.

Brunner, Edward. *Splendid Failure: Hart Crane and the Making of "The Bridge"*. Urbana: University of Illinois Press, 1985.

Buber, Martin. *I and Thou*. Translated by Kaufmann, Walter. New York: Scribner's, 1970.

Burrow, John. *A History of Histories: Epics, Chronicles, Romances, and Inquiries from Herodotus and Thucydides to the Twentieth Century*. New York: Random House, 2009.

Burt, John. *Robert Penn Warren and American Idealism*. New Haven: Yale University Press, 1988.

Butterick, George. *A Guide to The Maximus Poems of Charles Olson*. Berkeley: University of California Press, 1978.

Byrd, Don. *Charles Olson's Maximus*. Urbana: University of Illinois Press, 1980.

Calhoun, John C. "Selection from *A Disquisition on Government* (c. late 1840s)." In *The American Intellectual Tradition*, edited by Hollinger, David A. and Charles Capper. 6th ed. Vol 1, 458–66. New York: Oxford University Press, 2011.

Canary, Robert, and Henry Kozicki, eds. *The Writing of History: Literary Form and Historical Understanding*. Madison: University of Wisconsin Press, 1978.

Canby, Henry Seidel. "Stephen Vincent Benét." *Saturday Review of Literature*, March 27, 1943, 14.

Carruth, Hayden. "Homage to A. MacLeish." *Virginia Quarterly Review* 53, no. 1 (1977): 146–54.

Casillo, Robert. *The Genealogy of Demons: Anti-Semitism, Fascism, and the Myths of Ezra Pound*. Evanston: Northwestern University Press, 1988.

Cavanagh, Michael. "The Problems of Modern Epic: MacLeish's *Conquistador*." *Papers on Language and Literature* 17, no. 3 (1981): 292–306.

Christensen, Paul. *Charles Olson: Call Him Ishmael*. Austin: University of Texas Press, 1979.

Clark, William Bedford. "'Canaan's Grander Counterfeit': Jefferson and America in *Brother to Dragons*." In *Robert Penn Warren's "Brother to Dragons": A Discussion*, edited by Grimshaw, James, Jr., 144–52. Baton Rouge: Louisiana State University Press, 1983.

———, ed. *Critical Essays on Robert Penn Warren*. Boston: G. K. Hall, 1981.

Collingwood, R. G. *The Idea of History*. New York: Oxford University Press, 1994.

Conrad, Bryce. *Refiguring America: A Study of William Carlos Williams' "In the American Grain."* Urbana: University of Illinois Press, 1990.

Corrigan, Lesa Carnes. *Poems of Pure Imagination: Robert Penn Warren and the Romantic Tradition.* Baton Rouge: Louisiana State University Press, 1999.

Crane, Hart. *Complete Poems and Selected Letters.*, edited by Hammer, Langdon. New York: The Library of America, 2006.

Dasenbrock, Reed Way. "Constructing a Larger *Iliad*: Ezra Pound and the Vicissitudes of Epic." In *Epic and Epoch: Essays on the Interpretation and History of a Genre*, edited by Oberhelm, Steven M., Van Kelly and Richard J. Golsan, 248–65. Lubbock: Texas Tech University Press, 1994.

Davenport, Guy. "In Gloom on Watch-House Point." *Parnassus* 4, no. 2 (1976): 251–59.

Davie, Donald. *Ezra Pound: Poet as Sculptor.* New York: Oxford University Press, 1964.

Dembo, L. S. *Hart Crane's Sanskrit Charge: A Study of "The Bridge."* Ithaca: Cornell University Press, 1960.

Derrida, Jacques. *Of Grammatology.* Translated by Spivak, Gayatri. Baltimore: Johns Hopkins University Press, 1974.

———. *Writing and Difference.* Translated by Bass, Alan. Chicago: University of Chicago Press, 1978.

Diamond, Jared. *Guns, Germs, and Steel: The Fates of Human Societies.* New York: Norton, 1998.

Dillard, Annie. "For the Time Being." In *The Best American Essays, 1999*, edited by Hoagland, Edward, 74–89. Boston: Houghton Mifflin, 1999,

Donaldson, Scott. *Archibald MacLeish: An American Life.* Boston: Houghton Mifflin, 1992.

Doyle, Charles, ed. *William Carlos Williams: The Critical Heritage.* Boston: Routledge, 1980.

Eastman, Max. "America Attempts an Epic." *The Bookman* 68, no. 3 (1928): 362–63.

Ehrenpreis, Irvin. *Poetries of America: Essays on the Relation of Character to Style.* Charlottesville: University Press of Virginia, 1989.

Eliade, Mircea. *Cosmos and History: The Myth of the Eternal Return.* Translated by Trask, Willard. New York: Harper & Row, 1954.

Eliot, T. S. *Christianity and Culture.* New York: Harcourt Brace, 1967.

———. *Collected Poems 1909–1962.* New York: Harcourt Brace, 1970.

———. *On Poetry and Poets.* New York: Farrar, Straus & Giroux–Noonday Press, 1961.

———. *Selected Essays.* New York: Harcourt Brace, 1960.

———. *Selected Prose.* Edited by Kermode, Frank. New York: Harcourt Brace, 1975.

Ellmann, Maud. "Ezra Pound: The Erasure of History." In *Post-Structuralism and the Question of History*, edited by Attridge, Derek, Robert Young and Geoff Bennington, 244–62. New York: Cambridge University Press, 1987.

Emerson, Ralph Waldo. *Selected Writings*, edited by McQuade, Donald. New York: Modern Library, 1981.

Falk, Signi Lena. *Archibald MacLeish.* New York: Twayne, 1965.

Fenton, Charles A. *Stephen Vincent Benét: The Life and Times of an American Man of Letters.* New Haven: Yale University Press, 1958.

Fink, Thomas. "*A Different Sense of Power": Problems of Community in Late Twentieth-Century U.S. Poetry.* Madison, NJ: Fairleigh Dickinson University Press, 2001.

Fisher, Clive. *Hart Crane: A Life.* New Haven: Yale University Press, 2002.

Forché, Carolyn. *The Angel of History.* New York: Harper Collins, 1994.

———. *Blue Hour*. New York: Harper Collins, 2003.

———. *The Country Between Us*. New York: Harper & Row, 1981.

———. "H.D. after H.D." In *H.D. and Poets After*, edited by Hollenberg, Donna Krolik, 255–65. Iowa City: University of Iowa Press, 2000.

Foucault, Michel. *The Archeology of Knowledge*. Translated by Smith, A. M. Sheridan. New York: Harper & Row, 1972.

Frye, Northrop. *Anatomy of Criticism*. Princeton: Princeton University Press, 1957.

Gadamer, Hans-Georg. *Truth and Method*. New York: Crossroad, 1982.

Gardner, Jared. "Our Native Clay: Racial and Sexual Identity and the Making of Americans in *The Bridge*." *American Quarterly* 44, no. 1 (1992): 24–50.

Geertz, Clifford. *Local Knowledge: Further Essays in Interpretive Anthropology*. New York: Basic Books, 1983.

Gibson, Mary Ellis. *Epic Reinvented: Ezra Pound and the Victorians*. Ithaca: Cornell University Press, 1995.

Gioia, Dana. *Can Poetry Matter?* Minneapolis: Graywolf, 2002.

Gish, Nancy. *Time in the Poetry of T. S. Eliot*. Totowa, NJ: Barnes & Noble, 1981.

Gomme, A. W. *The Greek Attitude to Poetry and History*. Berkeley: University of California Press, 1954.

Gregory, Eileen. "Poetry and Survival: H.D. and Carolyn Forché." In *H.D. and Poets After*, edited by Hollenberg, Donna Krolik, 266–81. Iowa City: University of Iowa Press, 2000.

Griffith, John. "Narrative Technique and the Meaning of History in Benét and MacLeish." *The Journal of Narrative Technique* 3, no. 1 (1973): 3–19.

Grimshaw, James Jr., ed. *Robert Penn Warren's "Brother to Dragons": A Discussion*. Baton Rouge: Louisiana State University Press, 1983.

Hall, Donald. *Remembering Poets: Reminiscences and Opinions*. New York: Harper Colophon, 1979.

Harper, Margaret Mills. "Versions of History in *Brother to Dragons*." In *Robert Penn Warren's "Brother to Dragons": A Discussion*, edited by Grimshaw, James Jr., 226–43. Baton Rouge: Louisiana State University Press, 1983.

Harper, Michael F. "Truth and Calliope: Ezra Pound's Malatesta." *PMLA* 96, no. 1 (1981): 86–103.

Hegel, G. W. F. *Lectures on the Philosophy of World History*. Translated by H. B. Nisbet. New York: Cambridge University Press, 1975.

Helle, Anita. "Elegy as History: Three Women Poets 'By the Century's Deathbed'." *South Atlantic Review* 61, no. 2 (1996): 51–68.

Heller, Michael. "Ezra Pound's Gothic Designs on History." *New England Review* 26, no. 3 (2005): 99–108.

Herodotus. *The Histories*. Translated by Blanco, Walter. New York: Norton, 1992.

Heymann, C. David. *Ezra Pound: The Last Rower*. New York: Seaver Books, 1976.

Hollinger, David A. and Charles Capper, eds. *The American Intellectual Tradition*, 6th ed. Vol. I. New York: Oxford University Press, 2011.

Holman, C. Hugh. "Original Sin on the Dark and Bloody Ground." In *Robert Penn Warren's "Brother to Dragons": A Discussion*, edited by Grimshaw, James Jr., 193–99. Baton Rouge: Louisiana State University Press, 1983.

Holton, Robert. *Jarring Witnesses: Modern Fiction and the Representation of History*. New York: Harvester Wheatsheaf, 1994.

Homer. *Odyssey*. Translated by Fitzgerald, Robert. Garden City, NY: Doubleday Anchor, 1963.

Jackson, Frederick H. "Stephen Vincent Benét and American History." *The Historian* 17, (1954): 67–75.

Jarrell, Randall. "On the Underside of the Stone." In *Critical Essays on Robert Penn Warren*, edited by Clark, William Bedford, 43–44. Boston: G. K. Hall, 1981.

Jefferson, Thomas. "Notes on the State of Virginia." In *Writings*, edited by Peterson, Merrill D., 123–325. New York: The Library of America, 1984.

Jones, Frank. "Bon Voyage, S.V.B." *The Nation*, September 12, 1942, 217–18.

Joyce, James. *Ulysses*. New York: Random House, 1961.

Justus, James. *The Achievement of Robert Penn Warren*. Baton Rouge: Louisiana State University Press, 1981.

Kazin, Alfred. "Language as History: Ezra Pound's Search for the Authority of History." In *The Problem of Authority in America*, edited by Diggins, John P. and Mark E. Kann, 13–25. Philadelphia: Temple University Press, 1981.

Kearns, George. *Ezra Pound: The Cantos*. New York: Cambridge University Press, 1989.

Kenner, Hugh. *The Pound Era*. Berkeley: University of California Press, 1971.

Kermode, Frank. *The Sense of an Ending: Studies in the Theory of Fiction*. New York: Oxford University Press, 1967.

Kronick, Joseph. *American Poetics of History: From Emerson to the Moderns*. Baton Rouge: Louisiana State University Press, 1984.

Law, Richard G. "*Brother to Dragons*: The Fact of Violence vs. the Possibility of Love." In *Critical Essays on Robert Penn Warren*, edited by Clark, William Bedford, 193–209. Boston: G. K. Hall, 1981.

———. "Notes on the Revised Version of *Brother to Dragons*." In *Critical Essays on Robert Penn Warren*, edited by Clark, William Bedford, 210–215. Boston: G. K. Hall, 1981.

Lawrence, D. H. *Fantasia of the Unconscious*. 1922. New York: Viking, 1960.

Levi-Strauss, Claude. *The Savage Mind*. Chicago: University of Chicago Press, 1966.

Lewis R. W. B. *The Poetry of Hart Crane: A Critical Study*. Princeton: Princeton University Press, 1967.

Lewis, Wyndham. *Time and Western Man*. Boston: Beacon Hill Press, 1957.

Longenbach, James. *Modernist Poetics of History: Pound, Eliot, and the Sense of the Past*. Princeton: Princeton University Press, 1987.

Lurie, Peter. "Querying the Modernist Canon: Historical Consciousness and the Sexuality of Suffering in Faulkner and Hart Crane." *The Faulkner Journal* 20, no. 1–2, (2005): 149–76.

MacLeish, Archibald. *Collected Poems, 1917–1982*. Boston: Houghton Mifflin, 1985.

———. *Letters of Archibald MacLeish, 1907–1982*, edited by Winnick, R. H. Boston: Houghton Mifflin, 1983.

———. *Reflections*, edited by Drabeck, Bernard A. and Helen E. Ellis. Amherst: University of Massachusetts Press, 1986.

———. *Riders on the Earth: Essays and Recollections*. Boston: Houghton Mifflin, 1978.

Mailer, Norman. *The Armies of the Night*. New York: New American Library, 1968.

Peter Makin, "Americanus Natione non Moribus." In *Ezra Pound in America*, edited by Kay, Jacqueline, 55–78. New York: Palgrave Macmillan, 1992.

———. *Pound's Cantos*. Baltimore: Johns Hopkins University Press, 1985.

Mariani, Paul. *William Carlos Williams: A New World Naked*. New York: Norton, 1981.

Marsh, Alec. "Counterfeit Kulchur: Deep Politics, the Great Bass and Secret History in Ezra Pound." *European Journal of English Studies* 12, no. 3 (2008): 261–76.

———. "John Quincy Adams and/or Martin Van Buren: Cantos 34 and 37." *Paideuma* 34, no. 1 (2005): 59–88.

Marx, Karl and Frederick Engels. *The German Ideology*, edited by Arthur, C. J. New York: International Publishers, 1970.

McPherson, James M. *Battle Cry of Freedom: The Civil War Era*. New York: Random House Ballantine, 1988.

McWilliams, John. "The Epic in the Nineteenth Century." In *The Columbia History of American Poetry*, edited by Parini, Jay, and Brett C. Miller, 33–63. New York: Columbia University Press, 1993.

Merrill, Boynton, Jr. *Jefferson's Nephews: A Frontier Tragedy*. Princeton: Princeton University Press, 1976.

———. "The Murder." In *Robert Penn Warren's "Brother to Dragons": A Discussion*, edited by Grimshaw, James Jr., 283–93. Baton Rouge: Louisiana State University Press, 1983.

Miller, James. *The American Quest for a Supreme Fiction: Whitman's Legacy in the Personal Epic*. Chicago: University of Chicago Press, 1979.

Momigliano, Arnaldo. "The Introduction of History as an Academic Subject and Its Implications." In *The Golden and the Brazen World: Papers in Literature and History, 1650–1800*, edited by Wallace, John M. 187–204. Berkeley: University of California Press, 1985.

Monroe, Harriet. "A Cinema Epic." *Poetry* 33, (1928): 91–96.

———. "The Conqueror." *Poetry* 40, (1932): 216–22.

Moody, A. David. *Ezra Pound: Poet, A Portrait of the Man and His Work, Volume I: The Young Genius, 1885–1920*. New York: Oxford University Press, 2007.

Morrison, Paul. *The Poetics of Fascism: Ezra Pound, T. S. Eliot, Paul de Man*. New York: Oxford University Press, 1996

Nakadate, Neil, ed. *Robert Penn Warren: Critical Perspectives*. Lexington: University Press of Kentucky, 1981.

Neff, Emery. *The Poetry of History*. New York: Columbia University Press, 1947.

Nemerov, Howard. *Reflexions on Poetry and Poetics*. New Brunswick: Rutgers University Press, 1972.

Nietzsche, Friedrich. *On the Advantage and Disadvantage of History for Life*. Translated by Preuss, Peter. Indianapolis: Hackett, 1980.

———. *The Portable Nietzsche*, edited by Kaufmann, Walter. New York: Penguin, 1977.

Nilsen, Helge. *Hart Crane's Divided Vision: An Analysis of "The Bridge."* Oslo: Universitetsforlaget, 1980.

Oakeshott, Michael. "The Activity of Being an Historian." In *Rationalism in Politics and Other Essays*, 151–83. Indianapolis: Liberty Press, 1991.

Olson, Charles. *Call Me Ishmael*. In *Charles Olson: Collected Prose*, edited by Allen, Donald and Benjamin Friedlander, 1–106. Berkeley: University of California Press, 1997.

———. *Charles Olson and Robert Creeley: The Complete Correspondence*, edited by Blevins, Richard. Vol. 9. Santa Rosa, CA: Black Sparrow, 1990.

———. *Charles Olson: Collected Prose*, edited by Allen, Donald and Benjamin Friedlander. Berkeley: University of California Press, 1997.

———. *The Maximus Poems*, edited by Butterick, George. Berkeley: University of California Press, 1983.

———. "On History." In *Muthologos: Lectures and Interviews*, edited by Maud, Ralph. Revised, 2nd ed., 45–61. Vancouver: Talonbooks, 2010.

———. *Selected Writings*, edited by Creeley, Robert. New York: New Directions, 1966.

———. *The Special View of History*, edited by Charters, Ann. Berkeley: Oyez, 1970.

Orr, Linda. "The Revenge of Literature." In *Studies in Historical Change*, edited by Cohen, Ralph, 84–108. Charlottesville: University of Virginia Press, 1992.

Oser, Lee. *T. S. Eliot and American Poetry*. Columbia: University of Missouri Press, 1998.

Partner, Nancy. "Historicity in an Age of Reality-Fictions." In *A New Philosophy of History*, edited by Ankersmit, Frank and Hans Kellner, 21–39. Chicago: University of Chicago Press, 1995.

Paul, Sherman. *Olson's Push: Origin, Black Mountain, and Recent American Poetry*. Baton Rouge: Louisiana State University Press, 1978.

Perkins, David, ed. *English Romantic Writers*. New York: Harcourt Brace, 1967.

———. *A History of Modern Poetry, Volume II: Modernism and After*. Cambridge: Harvard University Press, 1987.

Peterson, Merrill D. *John Brown: The Legend Revisited*. Charlottesville: University of Virginia Press, 2002.

Plato. *The Symposium*. Translated by Hamilton, Walter. New York: Penguin, 1951.

Pound, Ezra. *The Cantos*. New York: New Directions, 1970.

———. *Gaudier-Brzeska: A Memoir*. New York: New Directions, 1970.

———. *Guide to Kulchur*. New York: New Directions, 1970.

———. *Literary Essays*. New York: New Directions, 1968.

———. *Personae: Collected Shorter Poems*. New York: New Directions, 1971.

———. *The Selected Letters of Ezra Pound to John Quinn, 1915–1924*, edited by Materer, Timothy. Durham: Duke University Press, 1991.

———. *Selected Prose, 1909–1965*, edited by Cookson, William. New York: New Directions, 1973.

_____. *The Spirit of Romance*. New York: New Directions, 2005.

Prescott, William. *History of the Conquest of Mexico*, edited by Munro, Wilfred Harold. Vols. I–IV. Philadelphia: J. B. Lippincott, 1904.

Pritchard, William. *Lives of the Modern Poets*. New York: Oxford University Press, 1980.

Purdy, R. R., ed. *Fugitive's Reunion: Conversations at Vanderbilt, May 2–5, 1956*. Nashville: Vanderbilt University Press, 1959.

Rainey, Lawrence. "A Poem Including History: *The Cantos* of Ezra Pound." *Paideuma* 21, no. 1–2 (1992): 190–220.

Rawls, John. "The Idea of an Overlapping Consensus." In *The American Intellectual Tradition*, edited by Hollinger, David, and Charles Capper. 6th ed. Vol. 2. 544–61. New York: Oxford University Press, 2011.

Reed, Brian. *Hart Crane: After His Lights*. Tuscaloosa: University of Alabama Press, 2006.

Riddel, Joseph. "Hart Crane's Poetics of Failure." In *Modern American Poetry: Essays in Criticism*, edited by Mazzaro, Jerome, 272–300. New York: David McKay Co., 1970.

Rowe, John Carlos. "The 'Super-Historical' Sense of Hart Crane's *The Bridge*." *Genre* 11 (1970): 597–625.

Ruppersburg, Hugh. *Robert Penn Warren and the American Imagination*. Athens: University of Georgia Press, 1990.

Russell, Sue. "The Workings of Chance and Memory." *Women's Review of Books*, July 1994, 31.

Sartre, Jean-Paul *Nausea*. Translated by Alexander, Lloyd. New York: New Directions, 1964.

Schwartz, Delmore. "The Dragon of Guilt." In *Critical Essays on Robert Penn Warren*, edited by Clark, William Bedford, 44–46. Boston: G. K. Hall, 1981.

Simpson, Lewis. "The Poet and the Father: Robert Penn Warren and Thomas Jefferson." In *The Legacy of Robert Penn Warren*, edited by Madden, David, 130–54. Baton Rouge: Louisiana State University Press, 2000.

Smith, Grover. "Archibald MacLeish." In *Seven American Poets*, edited by Donoghue, Denis, 16–54. Minneapolis: University of Minnesota Press, 1975.

Sontag, Susan. "In Jerusalem." *The New York Review of Books*, June 21, 2011, 22.

Southgate, Beverley. *History Meets Fiction*. New York: Pearson, 2009.

Stein, Kevin. *Private Poets, Worldly Acts: Public and Private History in Contemporary American Poetry*. Athens: Ohio University Press, 1996.

Stern, Fritz, ed. *The Varieties of History*. 2nd ed. New York: Random House, 1972.

Strachey, Lytton. *Eminent Victorians*. London: Chatto & Windus, 1928.

Strand, Mark, ed. *The Best American Poetry 1991*. New York: Macmillan Collier, 1991.

Strandberg, Victor. *The Poetic Vision of Robert Penn Warren*. Lexington: University Press of Kentucky, 1977.

Stroud, Parry. *Stephen Vincent Benét*. New York: Twayne, 1962.

Strout, Cushing. *The Veracious Imagination*. Middletown, CT: Wesleyan University Press, 1981.

Surette, Leon. *Pound in Purgatory: From Economic Radicalism to Anti-Semitism*. Urbana: University of Illinois Press, 1999.

Tate, Allen. "Hart Crane." In *Essays of Four Decades*, 310–23. Chicago: Swallow Press, 1968.

———. "The Irrepressible Conflict." *The Nation*, September 19, 1928, 274.

———. "Not Fear of God." *The New Republic*, June 1, 1932, 77–78.

Thomson, J. A. K. *The Art of the Logos*. London: Allen & Unwin, 1935.

Thoreau, Henry David. *A Week on the Concord and Merrimack Rivers*. New York: Harper & Row, 1961.

Thucydides. *The Peloponnesian War*. Translated by Warner, Rex. Baltimore: Penguin Classics, 1954.

Trachtenberg, Alan, ed. "Introduction: Hart Crane's Legend." In *Hart Crane: A Collection of Critical Essays*, edited by Trachtenberg, Alan, 1–12. Englewood Cliffs, NJ: Prentice Hall, 1982.

———. "The Shadow of a Myth." In *Brooklyn Bridge: Fact and Symbol*. 2nd ed. Chicago: University of Chicago Press, 1979.

Von Hallberg, Robert. *Charles Olson: The Scholar's Art*. Cambridge: Harvard University Press, 1978.

Walker, Jeffrey. *Bardic Ethos and the American Epic Poem: Whitman, Pound, Crane, Williams, Olson*. Baton Rouge: Louisiana State University Press, 1989.

Warren, Robert Penn. *Brother to Dragons: A Tale in Verse and Voices. A New Version.* Baton Rouge: Louisiana State University Press, 1979.

———. "Foreword to *Brother to Dragons: A Play in Two Acts.*" In *Robert Penn Warren's "Brother to Dragons": A Discussion,* edited by Grimshaw, James Jr., 295–300. Baton Rouge: Louisiana State University Press, 1983.

———. "Edmund Wilson's Civil War." *Commentary,* August 1962, 151–58.

———. "The Use of the Past." In *New and Selected Essays,* 29–53. New York: Random House, 1989.

———. "The Way *Brother to Dragons* Was Written." In *Robert Penn Warren: Critical Perspectives,* edited by Nakadate, Neil, 212–13. Lexington, KY: University Press of Kentucky, 1981.

Weaver, Mike. *William Carlos Williams: The American Background.* New York: Cambridge University Press, 1971.

Westover, Jeffrey. *The Colonial Moment: Discoveries and Settlements in Modern American Poetry.* DeKalb: Northern Illinois University Press, 2004.

White, Hayden. *The Content of the Form: Narrative Discourse and Historical Representation.* Baltimore: Johns Hopkins University Press, 1990.

———. *Figural Realism: Studies in the Mimesis Effect.* Baltimore: Johns Hopkins University Press, 1999.

———. *Metahistory: The Historical Imagination in Nineteenth-Century Europe.* Baltimore: Johns Hopkins University Press, 1973.

———. *Tropics of Discourse.* Baltimore: Johns Hopkins University Press, 1986.

Whitehead, Alfred North. *Science and the Modern World.* New York: Cambridge University Press, 2011.

Wiesel, Elie. *Night.* Translated by Rodway, Stella. New York: Bantam, 1982.

Williams, William Carlos. *The Autobiography.* New York: New Directions, 1967.

———. *Imaginations,* edited by Schott, Webster. New York: New Directions, 1970.

———. *In the American Grain.* New York: New Directions, 1956.

———. *Paterson.* Revised ed. New York: New Directions, 1992.

———. *Selected Essays.* New York: New Directions, 1969.

———. *Selected Letters,* edited by Thirlwall, John. New York: McDowell, Oblensky, 1957.

Wills, Garry. *Lincoln at Gettysburg: The Words That Remade America.* New York: Simon & Schuster, 1992.

Wilson, Edmund. *Patriotic Gore: Studies in the Literature of the American Civil War.* New York: Oxford University Press, 1962.

Winterhalter, Teresa. "Eyeless in Siena, or Ezra Pound's Vision through History." *Paideuma* 21, no. 3 (1992): 109–22.

Wood, Gordon. *Revolutionary Characters: What Made the Founders Different.* New York: Penguin, 2006.

Woodress, James. *A Yankee's Odyssey: The Life of Joel Barlow.* Philadelphia: Lippincott, 1958.

Woodward, C. Vann. *The Burden of Southern History.* Baton Rouge: Louisiana University Press, 1993.

Wright, David. "Assembling Community: A Conversation with Carolyn Forché." University of Illinois at Urbana-Champaign, Accessed July 17, 2005. http://www.english.uiuc.edu/maps/poets/a_f/forche/wrightinterview.htm

Yeats, William Butler. *Mythologies.* New York: Macmillan Collier, 1959.

Index

About the Author

Gary Grieve-Carlson is professor of English and former Director of General Education at Lebanon Valley College in Annville, Pennsylvania, where he has taught for more than twenty years. The recipient of awards for teaching excellence at three colleges, he has been a Fulbright junior lecturer in the Federal Republic of Germany and has lectured at universities in the People's Republic of China and New Zealand. He is the editor of *Olson's Prose* and has published in such journals as *Mosaic*, *Paideuma*, *The New England Quarterly*, *Modern Language Studies*, and *Soundings*.

www.ingramcontent.com/pod-product-compliance
Lightning Source LLC
Chambersburg PA
CBHW030642110726
47901CB00002B/539

9 781498 550451

www.ingramcontent.com/pod-product-compliance
Lightning Source LLC
Chambersburg PA
CBHW030642110726
47901CB00002B/539